African Political, Economic, and Security Issues

Tunisia

Economic, Political and Social Issues

AFRICAN POLITICAL, ECONOMIC, AND SECURITY ISSUES

Additional books in this series can be found on Nova's website under the Series tab.

Additional E-books in this series can be found on Nova's website under the E-book tab.

GLOBAL POLITICAL STUDIES

Additional books in this series can be found on Nova's website under the Series tab.

Additional E-books in this series can be found on Nova's website under the E-book tab.

African Political, Economic, and Security Issues

Tunisia

Economic, Political and Social Issues

Matheux Pusatieri
and
Jihed Cannamela
Editors

Nova Science Publishers, Inc.
New York

For permission to use material from this book please contact us:
Telephone 631-231-7269; Fax 631-231-8175
Web Site: http://www.novapublishers.com

LIBRARY OF CONGRESS CATALOGING-IN-PUBLICATION DATA

Tunisia : economic, political and social issues / editors: Matheux Pusatieri and Jihed Cannamela.
p. cm.
Includes index.
ISBN 978-1-61942-157-8 (hardcover) 1. Tunisia--Economic conditions--1987- 2. Tunisia--Politics and government--1987- 3. Tunisia--Social conditions--1987- 4. Natural resources--Tunisia--Management. I. Pusatieri, Matheux. II. Cannamela, Jihed.
HC820.T86 2011
330.9611--dc23

2011043375

Published by Nova Science Publishers, Inc. † New York

CONTENTS

PREFACE

In early 2011, a rapid and radical transformation started in Tunisia. After the desperate act of self-immolation of a young, unemployed graduate student, a massive wave of protests sparked the country. After several days of violent clashes between government forces and protestors, the broad public opposition managed to break down the government of Ben Ali. While the country may have embarked on a path towards more democracy, uncertainty about Tunisia's future remains and many problems have yet to be solved. This book presents current research in the study of Tunisia's economic, political and social issues.

Chapter 1 – Language and politics have been undeniably mixed. Colonization has been an historical event with economic, political as well as cultural projects. Arab postcolonial regimes have started with the recuperation of cultural identities and followed a policy of Arabization of the economic and educational sectors. The Arab world is living a turning point in its history. Some have called the events which started in Tunisia the "real independence", "the democratic revolution", "the spring of Arabs". It seems that Arab countries are now facing serious challenges. Dictatorships have not allowed free debate over political economic or linguistic projects. They implemented their own projects without democratic consultation of the population. The one party regimes which prevailed in the majority of Arab countries have claimed several ideological orientations: Socialist, Nationalist, Baathist, Jamahyrist and Islamist. However, the real policies have had devastating repercussions in all the domains. The uprising in the Arab countries is the result of the exasperation of excluded population living under the rule of a minority of ruthless gangs who have lost touch with realities and relied on oppression, conspiracy and bribery. The chapter will first present the major linguistic policies since independence in 1956. Then, an assessment of the current linguistic situation in Tunisia will be given. The final section will review linguistic projects of the major parties after January 14th 20011 in an Arab/Muslim/North African which is witnessing for the first time in its history an open debate on the issue of language. It is the first time in the history of postcolonial Tunisia that political groups openly present their economic, cultural projects. The chapter is a reading of these projects and a discussion of the main differences as well as the threats and promises that the linguistic policies may instil.

Chapter 2 – In order to continue its socio-economic development and to solve its probably most pressing problem, the unemployment, Tunisia needs economic growth. Many factors need to be fulfilled for this to happen, most of them are not easy to achieve. One of the most important factors is to make sure that the electricity supply keeps pace with economic activity –without electricity, growth, and consequently job creation, will be slowed down. Tunisia's present power system is almost exclusively based on fossil fuels, which are imported at an ever-increasing, over time possibly unsustainable, level. Hence, two alternative pathways to a continued and increased dependency on fossil fuels for power generation have emerged: nuclear and renewable power. In this chapter, these two alternatives are explored, discussed and compared with respect to their financial, technical and socio-economical impacts and viability. We look in detail at the issues of investment needs and feasibility, the fit of the options with the existing electricity infrastructure system, the effects on local industry and economy, and fulfilment of seawater desalination needs. We conclude that the nuclear option is hardly viable, as it constitutes too large an investment, its techno-economical characteristics do not fit the small Tunisian power system, and the socio-economic benefits of nuclear power are few. The prospects for renewables are better, although many significant challenges remain: as renewables projects are of a more decentralised nature, they are more attractive investments than nuclear power, the expansion plans are embedded in an international investment context, and they fit better with the existing power system. However, renewables are too expensive to be a real alternative to fuel desalinisation plants in the short term. Most importantly, a well-designed policy effort to support renewables holds the potential of significant job creation and the emergence of a new Tunisian industry, with strong positive socio-economic effects.

Chapter 3 – In the face of growing international competitiveness, one of the main challenges for the olive oil sector in traditional olive oil-producing countries such as Tunisia is to open up in non-traditional, emerging markets such as Japan. Many medical and medicinal effects of Tunisian olive oil components on health such as anti-oxidant, anti-aging, anti-allergy and anti-metabolic syndrome have been detected by the multifaced bioassay technique. This chapter investigates olive oil consumption behavior of Japanese consumers and examined their preferences using a sample of 532 consumers living in Tokyo. Six attributes were chosen in the design of the experiment: country of origin, price, olive oil type, taste, color and component. To reflect the components of Tunisian olive oil, a health attribute represented by a high concentration of polyphenol was explicitly included in the product design. By applying the conjoint technique, a rank-ordered logit (ROL) model and a cross effect model were estimated. Results suggested that Japanese consumers prefer extra virgin and virgin olive oil and sweet taste. While the country of origin when indicated as Tunisia has a negative effect, the preference for olive oil increases if the oil contains a high concentration of polyphenol. As a net effect, the WTP (Willingness to Pay) increased at 202.2 yen for the Tunisian product with a high concentration of polyphenol. Female, elder consumers with a higher educational status and those who frequently use olive oil prefer purchasing olive oil with a high concentration of polyphenol. This chapter verifies the significance of emphasising a health attribute to valorize and increase the export of Tunisian olive oil products to the Japanese market, even though products from Italy and Spain still dominate the market.

Chapter 4 – Mediterranean climate forests product several benefits, such as food, pharmaceutical, cosmetics and other non-food goods. In Tunisia, forest and woodlands cover circa 1.1 million hectares which includes Aleppo pine stands (about 300 000 hectares). Aleppo pine seed production is an important food sub-sector in Tunisia, currently restructured due to the increasing needs of population consumption. Furthermore, the forest and woodlands constitute a source of income in the main inland regions, such as Kasserine, Le Kef, Siliana, Kairouan, Beja and Zaghouan where more than 96% of Aleppo pine forests are located. The effects of environmental factors on the Aleppo pine production of these forests were evaluated. Bioclimatic zones, stand characteristics and tree measurements (including height and age) were submitted to simple and multiple regression analyses for explaining their interaction on the average seed and cone mass, in addition to the seed production per cone and per tree. Overall, results under simple regression showed longitude and altitude as the most explanatory variables relating average seed production and cone mass. Average cone length showed highly significant relationship with seed number per cone and the cone mass. Moreover, bioclimatic zones, stand density, basal area, tree size and age were linked to cone number and seed mass per tree. However, under multiple regression analysis, longitude was the most explanatory variable for average seed and cone mass, in addition to the seed mass per cone. The average cone length was influenced by the bioclimatic zone and longitude. Total height and age of the tree were the most explanatory variables for the cone number, but these two variables were added to the crown diameter for explaining their influences on the total seed mass per tree. The results have practical implications for the management of Aleppo pine for seed production and subsequent reforestation planning.

Chapter 5 – Tunisia is among countries that face deep and growing water shortages. The water is mainly used in the agricultural sector and many studies show that it is still inefficiently used and allocated despite the deep reforms and institutional innovations brought during the last three decades. In this period, Tunisia is celebrating a peaceful and democratic revolution expected to bring freedom and democracy to the Tunisian population. Many studies state that democracy and economic growth and development are significantly and positively correlated. By simply introducing democracy into its political and economic system a country can easily gain more growth and wealth. This is a very important statement that should encourage Tunisian people looking forward the economic development of their country through the implementation of new and sustainable democratic political and economic institutions. However, this economic developed will not be realized without higher pressure on natural resources, especially water, which are already suffering from deep shortage and inefficient use. In this paper, we propose to discuss the possible implications of the Tunisian revolution on the water sector management, with a focus on agricultural water management. Our main objective is to provide guidelines on how to evaluate the future management of the irrigation water sector in the country within the new political context of democratic and efficient economic institutions. Main guidelines of the current agricultural water management tools will be described as well as their limits and potentialities. Then, recommendations and perspectives for future improvement of water management and governance in the country will be provided.

Chapter 6 – Tunisia is one of the six countries located in Northern Africa, where most parts are deserts or semi-deserts, and covered by drought resistant shrublands. However, forests exits in the northern regions of Tunisia. These forests produce several natural products offering goods and services that are often undervalued. Wood forest products (WFP) and non-wood forest products (NWFP) represent a real employment and income source for the rural population of these forest areas. Local and national incomes of NWFP in

Tunisia have a crucial role in comparison to WFP. The main WFP is timber for pulpwood, particleboard, fiber-board and cardboard packaging. Similarly, NWFP produced in Tunisia include plant and animal products. The most important NWFP are edible plants, fruits, mushrooms, seeds, oils, cork, fiber, fodder, tannins, resins and gums. Furthermore, animal foodstuffs, is constituted by bush meat, trophy hunting, honey and snails. Important socioeconomic value is also attributed to medicinal and aromatic plants, such as Thymus spp., Laurus nobilis and Rosmarinus officinalis. This review pretends to emphasizes the socioeconomic importance of NWFP produced by these forests. Currently, the WFP are well known and valued while NWFP, even if they are much appreciated, they are undervalued and underestimated.

Chapter 7 – Water quality was investigated at seven Mediterranean freshwater reservoirs. Physico-chemical parameters and chlorophyll *a* were measured at all reservoirs to determine the trophic status. The species composition of zooplankton was also studied estimate the trophic level of the reservoirs. The environmental parameters indicated an oligo-mesotophic and mesotrophic environments. The presence of zooplankton species known to be indicators of eutrophic status reflected the high trophic condition of the Kasseb, Nabhana and Sidi Saâd reservoirs.

Chapter 8 – The fishing of pelagic fish constitutes an important economic activity in the fisheries of Tunisia. Indeed, the production contributes in 2009 to 48% of the national production of the fishery products. It employs approximately 5506 fishermen and utilizes approximately 393 units of fishing whose majority are seiners.

In: Tunisia: Economic, Political and Social Issues ISBN: 978-1-61942-157-8
Eds: M. Pusatieri and J. Cannamela

Chapter 1

ON LINGUISTIC/POLITICAL PROJECTS IN CHANGING TUNISIA

Tahar Labassi
University of Tunis, Tunisia

ABSTRACT

Language and politics have been undeniably mixed. Colonization has been an historical event with economic, political as well as cultural projects. Arab postcolonial regimes have started with the recuperation of cultural identities and followed a policy of Arabization of the economic and educational sectors.

The Arab world is living a turning point in its history. Some have called the events which started in Tunisia the "real independence", "the democratic revolution", "the spring of Arabs". It seems that Arab countries are now facing serious challenges. Dictatorships have not allowed free debate over political economic or linguistic projects. They implemented their own projects without democratic consultation of the population. The one party regimes which prevailed in the majority of Arab countries have claimed several ideological orientations: Socialist, Nationalist, Baathist, Jamahyrist and Islamist.

However, the real policies have had devastating repercussions in all the domains. The uprising in the Arab countries is the result of the exasperation of excluded population living under the rule of a minority of ruthless gangs who have lost touch with realities and relied on oppression, conspiracy and bribery.

The chapter will first present the major linguistic policies since independence in 1956. Then, an assessment of the current linguistic situation in Tunisia will be given. The final section will review linguistic projects of the major parties after January 14th 20011 in an Arab/Muslim/North African which is witnessing for the first time in its history an open debate on the issue of language. It is the first time in the history of postcolonial Tunisia that political groups openly present their economic, cultural projects. The chapter is a reading of these projects and a discussion of the main differences as well as the threats and promises that the linguistic policies may instil.

INTRODUCTION

The chapter focuses on linguistic issues in relation to recent political events in Tunisia. It is on language and politics in Tunisia after January 14th, 2011; the day Ben Ali, former president fled the country and a transitional government took over.

Investing in languages is more than an economic option, it is rather a political enterprise *par excellence*. The overview of the linguistic policies implemented by the former regime brings further evidence to the claim that linguistic choices and priorities might have repercussions on the political situation. Some of the most important events in postcolonial Tunisia may have their explanation in the linguistic policies that the ruling party has implemented over the last fifty years. Linguistic policies require a great deal of anticipation as their repercussions are measured in decades. Nations will inevitably have to deal with the positive or negative outcomes of what they are implementing now. Decision makers usually handle linguistic policies with the necessary care; particularly in countries where there is no consensus on issues of identity, religion, and linguistic models.

The Arab world is living a turning point in its history. Some have given many labels to the events which started in Tunisia: the “real independence”, “the democratic revolution”, or “the spring of Arabs”, to mention but a few. It seems that Arab countries, particularly Tunisia and Egypt, are now facing serious challenges. Dictatorships have not allowed free debate over political economic or linguistic projects, but imposed their own projects without democratic consultation of the population. The one party regimes that have prevailed in the majority of Arab countries have ruled under the banners of several ideologies: Socialism, Nationalism, Baathism, and Islamism. However, the real policies have had devastating repercussions in all the domains.

The uprising in the Arab countries is the result of the exasperation of excluded populations living under the rule of corrupted regimes that have lost touch with realities and relied on oppression, conspiracy and bribery.

The chapter will first present the major linguistic policies in Tunisia; the Arab country where protests started, after Mohamed Bouazizi, a street vendor, who set himself on fire after the confiscation of his wares by officials from the municipality of Sidi Bouzid, a town in the centre of Tunisia, sparked protests in Egypt, Yemen, Libya, and now Syria. Then, an assessment of the current linguistic situation in Tunisia will be given. The final section will review current debate on linguistic projects proposed by the main actors on the tumultuous political scene in Tunisia after January 14th, 20011 (1/14, henceforth).

The case of Arabic, the national language in Tunisia, is particularly significant. All Arab countries have undergone colonization with economic, political as well as cultural repercussions. Recent events in Tunisia are paving the grounds for reforms in several fields; not least among them education and the issue of identity. Language is at the heart of debates over these issues. Recent studies on linguistic policies have shown the close connection between linguistic priorities, economic issues, and political concerns, (Tollefson 2002, Evans 2008). Evans (2008, p. 48), for instance, argues that since the early 1990s applied linguists and English-language specialists have come increasingly to recognise that the policies and practices which determine the content, methods and processes of second language instruction are shaped by social, political and economic forces outside the classroom, and that these forces reflect the power and prestige of dominant groups in society.

It is the first time in the history of postcolonial Tunisia that political groups openly present their economic and cultural projects. The chapter is a reading of these projects and a discussion of the main differences as well as the threats and promises that the linguistic policies may instil.

The chapter examines the positions of the different political groups towards the issue of language(s) in post 1/14 Tunisia. But first, an overview of the linguistic policies, implemented by the unique party which governed Tunisia since its independence in 1956, is presented.

I. LINGUISTIC POLICIES IN POSTCOLONIAL TUNISIA

Tunisia is a North African former French colony (1881-1956), and part of the Arab world. In addition to Arabic, the national language, French has a special status. It is the most widely spoken language among middle-aged educated Tunisians, or the language of the privileged (Jrad, 2004). French was inherited from the country's colonial past, and used as the language of education and administration in the early decades after independence (Daoud, 2000; 2007). The status of French in postcolonial Tunisia has, mostly depended on the political agenda of the ruling *élite*. Recently, attitudes towards the language of the former colonizer have changed, probably because of the loss of prestige and influence of French in the worlds of science, technology and business. The advent of English in Tunisia is relatively recent. It has made the linguistic situation more complicated (Battenburgh, 1996; Walters, 1999; Champagne, 2007; Daoud, 2007, Labassi, 2009a).

I.1. The Historical Weight of Arabic

In addition to Standard Arabic, Tunisians speak a lower variety of the language which results in a diglossic situation. With independence, Arabic gained a higher status, and particularly in education. According to Daoud (2001) Arabization has been considered an essential means to remove the vestiges of colonialism. In fact, a ten-year plan was conducted and initiated an Arabisation campaign. Habib Bourguiba (1903- 2000), one of the leaders of the struggle for independence, and who became the first president of the first Tunisian Republic (1957-1987), declared that "education in the secondary schools will be oriented towards Arabisation and the use of Arabic, so that it can serve to teach all subjects." (Daoud, 2001, p. 25).

In 1987, the army general, and then Prime Minister, Zine El Abidin Ben Ali assumed the Presidency after some physicians declared Bourguiba medically incapacitated. Bourguiba was eighty four when Ben Ali made his bloodless *coup d'état*. He reinforced the Arabisation process, and, as argued by Daoud (2001, p.27) "the discourse and policy of the current leadership, which came into power in 1987, indicate further commitment to Arabisation and a greater sense of independence vis-à-vis the former colonial power".

What is the place of Arabic in today's Tunisia? The status of the official language is more delicate as it relates to issues of sovereignty, as well as cultural and religious identity. The first article in the Tunisian constitution stipulates that Tunisia is a Republic; its language is Arabic, and Islam its religion. The founding fathers mentioned Arabic as the national language, and Islam as the national religion. But the first reform of the educational system in independent Tunisia was the work of Messadi, the first Minister of Education in independent Tunisia. Messadi held an *Aggrégation* in Arabic; the most prestigious French degree, from the prestigious French University *Sorbonne*. The reform started in 1958 and aimed at teaching two languages; Arabic to have *bonne conscience*, and French to have access to science and technology. In this model, French was privileged: 70% of subjects in secondary schools were taught in French (Jrad 2004). At university the same language was used to teach all the subjects including human sciences. In this reform, Arabic had a symbolic status, whereas French was the instrument that would help the country catch up with modernity, and developed countries.

By the mid 1970s, Tunisia engaged in a policy of progressive Arabization, led by the Prime Minister, Mohamed Mzali (1925-2010). Progressive Arabization started with humanities in secondary, then tertiary levels (Philosophy, sociology, history, and geography). Scientific and medical studies had been spared, due to the reluctance that most teachers expressed, at that time (Daoud, 2007). Resistance against the use of Arabic for the teaching of hard sciences was led by a majority of teachers, who either held degrees from French universities, or from Messadi's 1958 Francophone schools.

With the resurgence of Islamism in most Arab countries; by the early 1980s, and as an aftermath of what the 1979 Revolution in Iran, Tunisia engaged in a new linguistic policy; particularly with the project of the Minister of Education, Mohamed Charfi (1936-2008), who inaugurated an era of open confrontation with Arab Nationalists and Islamists. Charfi's mission was the reform of the educational system, and the conduct of a policy that would counter the emergence of Islamism among the younger generations. The main strategy was a new linguistic policy, i.e.; a new status of Arabic and French. It was thought that the promotion of the teaching of foreign languages, particularly French, will stop or, at least reduce the appeal to Arabism, and by way of consequence, Islamism among younger generations. The teaching hours devoted to French increased considerably, and the language was given the status of *"langue étrangére privilégiée"* (Jrad 2004, p. 534) (privileged foreign language: Translation, mine).

The ambivalent strategy of the Tunisian authorities has not resolved the issue of Arabic as a burden. There are perceivable signs of a country that is no longer the exception in the region. The policy of Arabization in post-colonial neighbouring Algeria has had devastating results: a civil war between radical Islamists, speaking one language, and a minority made of Francophones backed up by the army and former colonizers. However, the bilingual option of education in post-colonial Tunisia after independence has given a bilingual, liberal, pro-democratic, anti-fundamentalist, middle class which, to my mind, is the most credible, efficient and legitimate bulwark to fundamental liberties. I believe that this option, among other wise decisions (education, family planning, women rights) has spared the country the fate of its neighbour (Labassi, 2009a). The bilingual, moderate, educated, westernized, urban minority joined the rebellion against Ben Ali's regime, which started in December 2011 in the central regions of the country, and ended in front of the Ministry of the Interior on the main avenue of the capital Tunis on January 14th, 2011.

I.2. French: The Colonial Legacy

How have successive governments dealt with French? What is the place of French in Tunisia today, if education is Arabized and the language of the former colonizer is no longer the language of science, business and technology, has French become another burden? Can Tunisia get rid of the tight-jacket of Francophony? These are some of the urgent questions that a viable future linguistic policy should address.

A close examination of the linguistic situation in Tunisia shows that French is still used as a medium of instruction especially for maths, sciences and technology subjects (Hemissi, 1985; Battenburgh,1996; Labassi, 2009a). French has a firm foothold in the country's administrative and educational system, as well as in general everyday use among middle-aged and educated members of the middle class. It is true that the *élite* that led the fight against the French has been educated in France. Bourguiba and the new leaders did not cut ties with former colonizers, and relied on French instructors to teach in Tunisian schools after independence. French experts remained in the country until the early 1980s after Tunisian universities trained sufficient numbers of professionals; particularly in the domains of education, health, and business (Labassi, 2009a).

Tunisia has opted for a bilingual education after independence. The 1970s witnessed a resurgence of Arabic, but this option has been reconsidered by the end of the 1980s, as mentioned earlier. Thus, French language regained some of its former spaces. It seems that the history of the country is tightly connected to French. The country is bound to keep some sort of connection with the language of its former colonizer. Amazingly, one of the reasons for the success of private primary schools in Tunisia was the decision to Arabize public education. When the state decided to respond to the wishes of the Arabophone community, the Francophone privileged minority found its own way to defend its linguistic wealth. They paid for the education of their children in private schools which started the teaching of French in the first years of training. Underprivileged classes did not have the means to pay for the expensive fees in private schools and sent their children to public Arabized schools (Jrad 2004).

French has not lost most of its appeal for several reasons. Tunisian parents, living in the main cities, have paid for courses in French because they know that, at least in the near future, French would keep a privileged status in the country. Administration is Arabized, but access to higher administrative positions requires some mastery of French. Education is Arabized, but most research is carried out in French. Most parents know that their sons and daughters have to master French if they want, one day, to join prestigious higher institutions such as Faculties of Medicine or some reputed Business Schools where French remains the medium of instruction (Labassi, 2009a). As will be explained in the section on the different linguistic projects after 1/14, this bilingual minority is the social backbone of the political/linguistic project defended by the moderate left, and particularly the *Pole Démocrate Moderniste* (Democratic Modernist Pole. PDM, henceforth).

I believe that French will occupy its privileged position as long as Tunisia has not altered the terms of exchange with France. Exchange does not only concern business; France is still Tunisia's first partner in terms of export and import. 21.4% of the country's imported goods come from France, and 32.2% of the products made in Tunisia are exported to the same country (*La Presse*, April 27, 2008. p. 5). France still recruits Tunisia's top graduates who join France's top schools (*Les Ecoles Préparatoires* and then *Les Grandes Ecoles* such as *Polytechniques* and *L'Ecole Des Mines*). What's more, Tunisian local researchers are offered grants to fund research stays in French universities and research centres.

Most Masters and Ph.Ds in most scientific disciplines in Tunisia are carried out in collaboration with French laboratories, and most visiting professors in Tunisian universities come from France. Most decision makers in the educational sector hold French degrees (Labassi, 2009a). Even if, after democratic elections that may bring to power an Arabist, anti western majority who will engage in a policy of Arabization on a large scale, a powerful bilingual minority will always exist. The members of this French educated minority will always occupy top positions in the administration, and post 1/14 regimes will most probably have to rely on their competence, at least during a transitional period. Those who wish to reconsider the place of French in Tunisia should rely on other allies in order to provide funds for research, and to promote collaboration in other sectors. Some voices, including Arab nationalists and Islamists, are now proposing other options. However, linguistic realities may not be disturbed easily. Indeed, Arabization failed because of the resistance of those who felt that their interests would be threatened. Linguistic policies do depend on political will, but they also require grounded, meticulous and realistic follow up. Change will only occur when those whose role is to implement it, participate in the process of decision making, and are convinced of its benefits (Champagne, 2007; Labassi, 2008).

I.3. English: The Unavoidable Intruder

The promotion of Arabic was accompanied by a policy of teaching foreign languages with a special emphasis on English as the language through which Tunisians will interact with the rest of the world (Daoud, 2000). In this sense, French lost some of its presence as the first non-Arab language in the country. In this respect, Tossa (1995, p.38) testifies that: "an Anglophone breeze seems to be blowing over the Maghreb. One is apt to think that the language of Moliére is losing its place to that of Shakespeare". In addition to this, Arabization was accompanied by promoting the generalising of computer literacy and the teaching of the English language. Labassi (1995) found that a higher number of potential employers in the private sectors (business, industry, tourism) seem to require expertise in English as a condition for recruitment.

The presence of English in Tunisia is relatively recent. It has been introduced in secondary schools in the early 1960s with the modest aid of some American institutions such as US Aid and the Ford Foundation, as well as the British Council (Hemissi 1985). Most teachers of English were British Volunteers for Overseas, Peace Corps Volunteers and Fulbright lecturers. In the 1980s only 54% of higher institutions in Tunisia offered English courses (Hemissi 1985). By the 1990s more than fifty science, business and engineering departments taught English, but the major boost came with the 1998 Reform which generalized the teaching of English at the undergraduate level in all the Faculties (Labassi, 2009a).

English has been gaining grounds over the last few decades. However, here again, the linguistic policy lacks consistency. It seems that English has served as a cover language for French. In other words, the decision to promote the teaching of foreign languages, including English, was taken in order to hide the intended regain of importance of French in the early 1990s, for the reasons explained earlier. Therefore, decision makers did not accompany the generalization of the teaching of English with the necessary measures: training of qualified teachers, design and evaluation of programmes (Labassi, 2009a). In this respect, Nunan (1999) rightly argues that countries which decide to teach English to larger audiences should support their decision with adequate resources, with appropriately trained teachers, and with programs that are sensitive to the context in which they are used. It was not the case in Tunisia.

English has unconvincingly been introduced to justify the official rhetoric of the need to master foreign languages, in order to create an open-minded generation, and to have access to sciences. English has always been second best, because of the historical presence of the first best language: French. It seems that, in Tunisia, English will not occupy the place that the rest of the world, including France, willy-nilly accepts, because of the undiminished prestige of French. It seems that the sheer number among the community of academics of defendants of French as the language of science and technology, is much more considerable in the former colonies than in Metropolitan France. One is tempted to account for this attitude by the claims made by some postcolonial writers that decolonization of the minds takes more time (Labassi, 2009a). Many factors will determine the position of French in relation to Arabic and English in Tunisia. Recent events have overthrown Ben Ali's regime, but constructing a new administrative, economic, and educational system will depend on power relations among the nascent political groups.

Tunisian former educational authorities have not joined the action of promoting the status of English to their word that English is the language of science and technology. In the 1990s there was an overwhelming rhetoric in favour of the promotion of the status of English in the country. But the rhetoric has not been followed by practical measures. One cannot deny the fact that many conferences, seminars, meetings, and even two or three National Days, in the presence of former Ministers in charge to discuss the measures to be taken in order to promote the teaching of foreign languages, have been organized. But this frenzy has not given tangible results on the grounds. It is as if all the events were meant to bury the project by too much talk. Some advocators of the conspiracy theory claim that the failure to pass to action is explained by the conscious and intended attitude of the Francophone lobby in the Ministries in charge of education at all levels to counter the spread of English, or at least work out the conditions for its failure. The rhetoric would then be: we tried our best, but in vain. English does not work in Tunisia and the country is doomed to be Francophone (Labassi, 2009a).

The generalization of English teaching after the application of the 1998 Reform of Tertiary Education in Tunisia has created a critical mass of English instructors. In an unprecedented step, the former Tunisian state decided to generalize the teaching of English to all the undergraduate students in the country. *The Journal Officiel de la République Tunisienne* (The Official Journal of the Tunisian Republic) published the details of the Reform (Daoud, 2000). The text of the law recommended the immediate implementation of the decision which started during the academic year 1998-1999. However, the fundamental condition for the success of language reforms is when the official discourse reflects the discourse of specialists in the matter (Labassi, 2010).

I believe that the fate of English will depend on more sensible, and less inconsistent changes in the linguistic policies. If decision makers perpetuate their inconsistent and shifting policies, the status of English will raise and fall with the political moods of the times. Over the last few years, some indicators which assess the output of the Tunisian educational system are somewhat worrying. The rank of Tunisian pupils in international evaluative tests such as TIMSS (Trends in International Mathematics and Science Study) realized by the American Institute for Educational Sciences, is very low. Tunisia is ranked behind Armenia, Iran and Egypt. Some Fulbright Tunisian applicants did not get the required TOEFL score. A recent job offer to recruit Tunisian teachers of English to work in the United Arab Emirates (*Essabah*, April 24th, 2008), requires IELTS certificate in addition to the Tunisian BA and a two year professional experience. These examples show the degree of erosion of the reputation of Tunisian diplomas. A few years ago Gulf countries competed to recruit Tunisian professional because of their excellent reputation, compared to other teachers from other Arab countries (Labassi, 2009a). It seems that lack of proficiency in English has resulted in the devaluation of the quality of Tunisian graduates and professionals. Over the last few weeks, some Tunisian daily newspapers have been reporting figures about the number of job offers from Australia, Asia, Canada which could not be answered because employers require some command of English which potential Tunisian candidates do not have (*Echourouk,* Friday, August 19th, 2011).

What should be noted after this overview of the different linguistic policies in postcolonial Tunisia is the fact that inconsistent and shifting linguistic policies, designed under the pressure of the times, in order to respond to the political demands of some communities, may have negative results. What has added to the lack of consistency in all the linguistic policies in Tunisia before January 2011, was the absence of representative institutions where political debates over these issues might take place and where consensual decisions might be taken. Will the situation in Tunisia evolve after getting rid of dictatorship? It is too early to give a reliable answer to the question. One may only observe the current debate on the linguistic issue during this transitional period.

It seems that most parties are aware of the importance of English in the world of today. It is the status and the rank of the language in relation to French which is at stake. The section below sums the arguments in favour of giving English a special position on the linguistic map that will undoubtedly change after the January uprising.

I.4. English as a Lingua Franca

English as a global language is one of the most remarkable phenomena of the late XXth and early XXIst centuries. Several linguists have traced the evolution of English as a World/International language (Pennycook, 1994; Crystal, 1997; Kramsch, 2000). They have given political, economic reasons for the spread of English worldwide. The political and military predominance of the U.S.A after World War II paved the way for a substantial economic and cultural influence that displaced other languages including French and German. English has become the standard for international communication. The collapse of the Soviet Union in the early 1990s accentuated the trend for a New World order dominated by one Super Power and One Super Language. No country in the world could afford isolation, let alone a small and under-resourced country such as Tunisia.

English has become the official language particularly in the worlds of business and science. The evidence that English has acquired such a status even in Tunisia has been asserted by Battenburgh (1996), Walters (1999), Daoud (2007), and Labassi (2008; 2009a; 2010). Walters (1999, p. 34) for instance, showed that, in Tunisia, "English is certainly audible and visible in a range of situations (the media, the tourist trade, business and advertising)". Europe, China, let alone developing countries, were no exceptions. Linguistic policies all over the world had to cope with this linguistic reality (Labassi, 2008). Some writers admit that what is taking place is linguistic imperialism (Philipson, 1992; Fairclough, 2001), while others might call it linguistic realism (Jabeur, 1999; Friedrich, 2007; Labassi, 2008). This divide, as will be argued later, separates the two major conflicting linguistic projects in Tunisia after the uprising of January 2011.

Crystal (1997) asserts that 85% of international organizations in the world make official use of English, at least 85% of the world's film market is in English, and some 90% of published academic articles in some academic fields, such as linguistics, are written in English. It is estimated that 75% of all international communication in writing, 80% of all information in the world's computers, are in English. Crystal (1997) argues that English is spoken as a native language by nearly four hundred million people and has become a *lingua franca.* If speakers with a lower level of language fluency and awareness were included, the overall total would be 1,000 million. English is recognized as undoubtedly the most important. Graddol (1997) notes that one in five people now speaks English, to some degree of competence, and that the number is growing. More recent figures place English second after Chinese in number of users (*Maniére de voir,* Februray, March, 2008, p. 64). Second and foreign language speakers will soon outnumber those who speak it as a first language. English has become the language to learn for the increasingly mobile international community. This is a fact that seems to be irreversible. Will Tunisian Anti-Americanists (Arab Nationalists, Islamists, and Anti-Imperialists) make the distinction between Anti-Americanism and Anti-Anglicism? I believe that much will depend on the extent of their presence in state institutions after democratic elections.

Friedrich (2007) argues that a *lingua franca* has always existed (Latin, Arabic). But one should admit, today, that the status of English as an international language has reached levels never attained by Latin or Arabic. The reasons need not be explained. The other difference is that English is threatening the very existence of other languages. The exclusive use of English in some domains has reached some exasperating dimensions. Burchfield has noted that

> English has also become a *lingua franca* to the point that any literate, educated person on the face of the globe is in a very real sense deprived if he does not know English. Poverty, famine and disease are instantly recognized as the cruelest and least excusable forms of deprivation. Linguistic deprivation is a less easily noticed condition, but one nevertheless of great significance (Burchfield, 1986. In Swales, 1993, p. 283/84).

This reality has been criticized (Philipson, 1992; Pennycook, 1994) without being altered. The suggestions made by critical linguists (Philipson, 1992; Pennycook, 1994; Canagarajah, 1996) are too distanced from some non-Anglophone environments. Post 1/14 Tunisia is a case in point as will be discussed in the following section. But all the parties cannot deny hard facts. Cursing English will not alter these facts, neither will a rhetoric of condemnation as most Nationalists, some Islamists, anti-Imperialists/ Americanists have, so far, been engaged in.

But if the attitudes of the community of scholars around the world towards the hegemony of English are examined, one would find that they have shifted from denunciation (Philipson, 1992; Pennycook, 1999; Swales, 1997) to effective recuperation (Widdowson, 1994; Seidlhofer, 2000; Llurda, 2004; Friedrich, 2007; Labassi, 2008). It seems that the community of scholars has opted for a pragmatic attitude toward English as the medium of interaction. The rhetoric of resistance to English as an instrument of imperialism (Philipson, 1992; Pennycook, 1999; Canagarajah, 1996; 1999) has been replaced by an instrumental attitude toward the language. Seidlhofer (2000) rightly proposes a functional and realistic attitude, and Labassi (2008) argues for responsible uses of English. It seems that scientists prefer a single language, even if it is not their own. Rogerson-Revell (2008, p.106) confirmed this pragmatic attitude in the context of business:

> This pragmatic view is frequently reflected in business and management. For instance, commenting on the choice of English, as corporate language in the multinational engineering and telecoms firm Siemens AG of Germany, Bernhard Welschke, head of European policy at the Federation of German stated that "German companies are very pragmatic...They value a single language for business, even if it is not their own.

It seems then, that the use of English as the official language of communication in international academic conferences has become a noticeable phenomenon, to the extent that it has triggered several reactions of exasperation. English as the medium of knowledge production is occupying the written, oral and electronic spheres. It seems that the debate over which language to use in education has become obsolete, as most nation states are using their national language. However, the validation of the results of research, whether through publication or in international conferences, the language is most of the time English. When Japanese, Italian, French, Egyptian, and Russian organic chemists, or medical doctors meet, the language they use to interact is most of the time English (Labassi, 2009a).

Tunisian political parties will have to take these facts into consideration and avoid the sterile rhetoric of condemnation which might satisfy the popular anti-American feeling, but would fail to respond to the real needs for the language "of the enemy" in the worlds of business, education and particularly research. The hegemony of English has led other non-Anglophone countries to revise their linguistic policies and invest in the teaching of English. One would hope that the future decision makers in Tunisia will listen to experts in these environments, and call upon them in order to evaluate the real needs, design programs, and advise.

Labassi (2010) made the claim that given the status of English in the world of today, each country has to define its priorities in relation to this language, and the place it should occupy in relation to first and second languages. Labassi (2010) agrees with Celani (2008, p.413) who calls for an instrumental relation with English: "The well-balanced construction of critical social awareness regarding language and particularly regarding the role of English in the contemporary world should be the major aim to be achieved". The same opinion is held by Salager-Meyer (2008) who believes that investing in the teaching of English for Academic Purposes, for instance, would be profitable to the community of researchers in non-Anglophone environments. She makes the claim that: "the English proficiency of a nation's scientists was an even stronger correlate of publication output than funding" (Salager-Meyer, 2008, p. 124).

But what are the emerging views concerning the issue of language, and particularly English for the reasons mentioned above, held by the different political groups in Tunisia today? The following section is an overview of the on-going debate over the issue of language in Arabo-Franco-Anglicized Tunisia. In the aftermath of the 1/14 uprising, there are, as will be argued in the following section, passionate, and sometimes irreconcilable discourses. The examination of these discourses may show that there are two main conflicting projects: A Nationalist/Islamist/Anti-Americanist project and a Modernist Moderate Leftist Project.

II. Current Conflicting Projects in Post 1/14 Tunisia

In today's Tunisia, one may tentatively claim that there are two conflicting social projects, with shifting and, at times, "unnatural" alliances among the defenders of the two projects. But, given the unexpected and unpredictable changes that have taken place in the country, one may only propose a very cautious interpretation, since the situation changes on a daily basis; as it is commonly witnessed during "revolutionary" periods. The positions of the different actors on the political scene are shifting very rapidly, and political actors have to react to unpredictable events. Taking risky decisions is sometimes less harmful than taking no decision. Most political leaders of the left, as well as the right, are making claims that are soon denied under the pressure of the street, sudden events or pragmatic and temporary alliances.

What are the announced projects of the different political parties in post 1/14 Tunisia. It is probably too early to distinguish the major differences between linguistic projects proposed by old and new political parties. So far, more than one hundred political parties have been given legal permission. One of the gains of the "Revolution" is the freedom of speech that Tunisians experience, not without some transgressions. However, there are lines that political groups should not cross, if they wish to remain on the scene. One of the red lines not to cross is the issue of Arabic as the language of identity. The first article of the constitution, drafted after independence, states that Tunisia is a republic, its religion is Islam and its language is Arabic. As a consequence, all the political parties, including the extreme left (Leninists, Stalinists, Trotskysts, Maoists) are calling for keeping the first article in the 1959 constitution (the first constitution drafted after the independence of the country in 1956).

Even secular parties seem to be in a tight corner. Should they stick to secularism and run the risk of being the easy target of their opponents and particularly Islamists, or join what seems to be a national option? Debate among the members of the secular group, advocators of modernism, is till underway, and may add to the divisions among the minority of Modernist Democrats. In other words should they be faithful to the main principle in their ideology which is the separation of politics and religion, and run the risk of adding to their isolation, or make a necessary compromise in order to remain on the political scene? It seems that Modernist Democrats have not reached a consensual answer to this question.

But let's first see the main principles which distinguish the two conflicting projects, and particularly the issue of language in Tunisia after 1/14. As argued earlier, there are two main projects: An Arab Nationalist/Islamist/Anti-Americanist project and a Modernist Democratic project.

II.1. The Arab Nationalist/Islamist/Anti-Americanist Project

Anti-Americanism has often been accompanied by an anti-Anglicism. The defence of the national language is most often accompanied with a suspicious attitude toward those who are defending the cause of French or English.

According to Arab Nationalists, defenders of "Other Languages" are the allies of colonialists. According to Anti-Americanists, made mainly of the Extreme Left, defenders of English are the pawns of American imperialists.

Islamists and the Extreme Left draw on different ideologies; Islamism and Marxism, but they have one thing in common: priority is given to the national language and are calling for Arabization at all the levels of education. They have a suspicious view of those who defend the West, its culture, its language(s) and its values, including democracy in the case of the extreme Islamist Right (*The Tahrir Party:* The Liberation Party). Even though this group is made of parties belonging to opposing ideologies, they hold the same views concerning the issues of language and identity. The representatives of this ideologically heterogeneous group in *the Commission for the Realization of the Objectives of the Revolution, Democratic Transition and Political Reforms* (An advisory commission created after the 1/14 events, and includes the unelected representatives of the main political parties, some associations of the civil society, all the regions, families of martyrs, and some public figures) defended the cause of Arabic and the Arab identity of Tunisia.

For Arab Nationalists, Islamists and Anti-Americanists, no concession will be made as to which language should prevail. They believe that former colonizers and the former ruling party encouraged French at the expense of Arabic, and conclude that the outcome has been the spread of a western way of life, and the emergence of an uprooted generation who is not proud of its Arab culture, religion and glorious history. Their political project aims at correcting this deviation which is, according to them, the cause of backwardness in this part of the world. The remedy to all the political problems according to Islamists is cultural. The main slogan of Islamists, not only in Tunisia, but also in the rest of the Arab World is: "Islam is the solution". They believe that time has come so that the national language, the language of the Koran (the Islamic sacred book), becomes the first language in the country, and that no other language should compete with Arabic. Sciences, should be taught in Arabic, and if they are elected they will implement a policy of Arabization at the primary secondary and tertiary levels of education.

Priority is given to Arabic, but it seems that the attitude of the different parties in this group towards foreign languages, breeds fear and suspicion. I believe that a policy of Arabization may create generations; the only discourse that appeals to them is that of fundamentalists, whose utter adversaries are those who do not consider that the West is evil (Labassi, 2008). As argued earlier, this policy of Arabization, in addition to other factors, implemented in neighboring Algeria, has led to the spread of fundamentalism and a devastating civil war ended only by the taking over of power by the army.

For Arab Nationalists, whose main project is the unification of all the Arab countries, the issue of Arabic is crucial. They believe that Arabic is what unites Arabs. They blame colonialists for creating frontiers, that they wish to abolish, and for trying to eradicate Arabic and replacing it by French in former French colonies, such as Tunisia. They join Anti-Imperialists from the extreme left whose project is fighting colonialism and American-imperialism. The West has colonized the Arab world by using the weapon of language. Time has come to strike back, reduce the impact of foreign languages; the language of imperialists and boost Arabic.

One is tempted to say that this discourse is legitimate. Liberated nations feel the need to regain their identity and speak their language. However, this should go without a rhetoric of hostility and hatred. One can be proud of one's language, culture without necessarily placing oneself in a position of confrontation. Mutual trust, dialogue, respect of the "Other" are often absent in the discourse of this political group. It is true that the position of Western governments, their support of former and surviving dictators, wars in Iraq and Afghanistan, unresolved conflicts and particularly the Palestinian problem, exacerbate this rhetoric and legitimize it in the eyes of angry Arab populations, whose call for democracy should not be tainted with a call for revenge on former colonizers.

II.2. The Bilingual Middle Class Modernist Project

Modernist Democrats' greatest fear is fundamentalism. Soon after 1/14 several secular moderate leftist parties, as well as independent anti-Islamist activists held several meetings to discuss the possibility of creating a Modernist/Anti-Islamist Front. They were aware of the threats of fundamentalism to their way of life. What should be noted was that women were among the most active. It is true that Tunisian women have rights that females in the rest of the Arab world could not even dream of: the right to vote, to marry non-Muslims, to divorce, to drive cars (even if this might sound sarcastic), not to mention the fact that polygamy is forbidden. Therefore, they felt that they had more to lose than their male comrades, if Islamist gain power in the country.

It is the *Ettajdid Party* (The Renovation Party, former Tunisian Communist Party) who first called for the union of the left. Some centre left parties answered the call among them *El Wifaq*, *The Leftist Socialist Party* as well as some independent individuals who were active in *The General Tunisian Labor Union*, and in the associations of the civil society; particularly the *Association of Democratic Women* and the *Tunisian League for the Defence of Human Rights*. This group is now organized under the banner of the *Modernist Democratic Pole* (*Pole Democratique Moderniste*), commonly known as the PDM.

The main slogan on the 14th of January, 2011, on Habib Bourguiba Avenue (the main avenue in the capital Tunis), and in front of the Ministry of the Interior was *"Dègage";* a French word meaning "get out" and shouted at Ben Ali. It shows the profile of some of those who took to the streets on that final day of Ben Ali's rule. The majority of demonstrators, on that day, is bilingual, which means that most of them belong to the educated middle class. It is the interests of this same class that the project of the *PDM* is defending. What this political group fears most is another type of dictatorship under the name of Arabism, Fundamentalism or anti-Imperialism. The *PDM* was founded primarily to counter the project of Arab Nationalists, Islamists and the Extreme Left. Some Meetings were organized in order to propose to the last group to join the family of the left. Some joined for some time (*The Movement of the Nationalist Democrats*, and the *Party of The Nationalist Democratic Action*), but soon left. It seems that the positions of moderate leftists and extreme leftists are irreconcilable, particularly concerning the relations with the West, its values, its culture and its languages.

What justifies the position of moderate leftists who suffered under the former regime, and who had no possibility to break the walls built around them by a subdued media, would not forget that English was, at the peak of oppression, their life saving boat. Labassi (2008) relates how university teachers resorted to English to break the walls of silence. The strike of university teachers was a revealing case: During a very long and unconventional strike carried by Tunisian university teachers (May, June, 2005), English was used to seek support from other trade unions around the world. University teachers refused to correct exam papers; an action that was very daring and was considered by the authorities as civil rebellion. There was a great tension and the authorities were afraid of contagion. At that time, no local daily newspaper (In French, Arabic and English) accepted to publish the motions of the trade union addressed to the public opinion to justify the militant action and seek support. The same subdued newspapers published regularly the attacks of the authorities; some went as far as depicting strikers as traitors, and asked the authorities to take severe measures against them.

Walters (1999: 35) rightly noted that: "English is used in the broadcast media, which in Tunisia are state owned and state controlled to a greater extent than in times past". In a more recent article, Champagne (2007) gives an informative view of the state of the media in Tunisia under Ben Ali, and condemns the unethical attitude of the mercantile West who "is willing to overlook repressive regimes as long as they remain open to US investment" (Champagne, 2007, p. 205).

Trade unionists were left with one choice; addressing themselves to international unions to break the walls of isolation. That was how they discovered the benefits of using English. The only instrument that would help them talk to potential supporters capable of exerting some pressure on local authorities. One would understand that the step taken by trade unionists was intelligent and efficient. The outcome of the strike confirmed this. The repressive measures taken by the authorities could have been much worse. English for Solidarity Purposes responded to the needs of an isolated community of strikers. The "language of imperialism" was used by the small community of university teachers, who are, to a large extent, anti-imperialists, to win the crucial fight for a better life. They were left with no choice but address themselves to the larger community of colleagues at the international level, through the medium of English.

It seems that those who are now calling for the importance of teaching foreign languages and particularly English have learnt the lesson the hard way. It may explain the fact that they are the most ardent defenders of opening to the rest of the world, and warning against the dangers of utter Arabization. They are reminding their opponents that language is not neutral, but it does not carry one message. English is not the sole property of imperialists and hegemonists, as anti-imperialists, freedom fighters may use English to strike back (Labassi, 2008). It seems that Modernist Democrats are making the claim that depoliticizing the issue of language is not realistic. However, the single sided opinion that language is "good" or "bad" in itself, as their opponents seem to suggest, is unrealistic, if not naïve. One may remind some opponents that the liberation movements of the early twentieth century in the region used the language of the colonizer to resist colonization (the first Tunisian national newspaper, mouthpiece of the national party, was written in French: *L'Action Tunisienne*).

The position of the moderate left towards English seems to be less hostile and more constructive. They seem to have learnt the lesson of the past and are condemning the deliberate link between anti-Americanism and anti-Anglicism. Moderate Democrats are proposing less hostile attitudes towards English.

They seem to be aware of the fact that English has become a world language and could be used to speak to the world. In the case of Arabs, English could be used to contribute to universal knowledge and correct a stereotypical image of their culture in the West (Labassi, 2008). English has been used by Tunisian bloggers to condemn the former regime. Some reporters have gone as far as calling the uprising in Tunisia as the "digital Revolution".

Labassi (2008) ,argues that correcting the image of Arabs is vital, and particularly at these times of fear, suspicion and mutual misunderstanding. He maintains that some recent post 9/11 writings do not reach the desired objective of proposing a less biased image of Arabs and their religion. Correcting this vision goes necessarily through a production of some more balanced texts in English.

The use of English by secular Arab thinkers has become a necessary step towards the spread of a more objective image of Arabs and Islam. The spread of anti-fundamentalist writings will reduce the over-presence of Muslim fundamentalists who may use English to propagate a hostile vision of the West and its culture. One might go as far as saying that English may spare us the horrors of future clashes. These clashes will be unavoidable if we do not reverse the trend. It is a mutual effort, but I believe that it is up to Arab secular intellectuals to make the most. More than ten years ago, on the occasion of a conference on "English in North Africa" organized by the Tunisian Society for Anglo-Saxon studies (TSAS) Jabeur (1999, p.21) recommended a broader use of English:

> English can be used to revamp local cultures and various forms of expression by empowering them to transcend national borders. It can also be used to bring the world home, thus creating more ample opportunities for intercultural communication, exchange and interaction.

More than ten years later, and after a promising uprising, the risk of a move backward exists. The attitudes towards English have grown more negative as a result of recent events.

Reversing the trend is much more difficult, yet, unavoidable, if we want to live in a less confrontational world. The new status of English in the world is, by far, the most important incentive for a wider practice of teaching the language in Tunisia. The need that several communities inside the country feel for English is the potential that advocators of modernity should draw on.

III. POTENTIAL ALTERNATIVES

This section assesses the possible orientations that the projects, detailed above, might follow in the near future. There are viable options, some of which are still wishful thinking, but their realization will depend on the results of the first democratic elections which will, hopefully, be held in the country on October 223rd, 20011. Because Tunisians will elect a Constitutional Council, the main mission of which is to draft a new constitution, the issues of identity, language, education, who Tunisians are, and how they will position themselves in relation to the rest of the world, and particularly the West, is of great importance. The constitution will provide the legal framework within which all these issues will be negotiated for the coming decades.

I believe that some questions, related to the issue of language and identity, members of the Constitutional Council will address, include the following:

1. How can Tunisians be better consumers/contributors to knowledge? Again, the issue of language, and particularly English, will be unavoidable, if a serious debate takes place. Non-Anglophone communities, and particularly Francophone North Africans, cannot be more visible contributors to knowledge because most of them, for the time being are poor consumers of knowledge. Lack of mastery of English is a major obstacle to consumption and production of knowledge (Labassi, 2009b). Most data banks testify of the poor contribution of countries where English is not the medium of instruction, even in disciplines which do not require costly equipment. The best periodicals on Islamology are owned by well-known publishers in the West (Sage Publications, Blackwell, Elsevier, Pergamon). Serious writings on contemporary political, theoretical and strategic issues are published in English.
2. Will the question of which language to use in particular domains be left to the community of its users? Many scholars in non-Anglophone countries are aware that a mastery of English a *sine qua non* condition for any possible cultural *renaissance*. North Africans and Arabs do have the economic conditions for economic development, and huge steps have been achieved in this respect (high literacy rates, longer life expectancy compared to other African countries) but lack the culture which should precede any lasting and engrained *renaissance*. Some scholars who belong to different disciplines; hard and human sciences, share the belief that English could be one of the instruments

for a long-awaited *renaissance* in this part of the world (Labassi, 2008). The advent of English as an essential tool for academic production, particularly at the age of computer, leaves no choice to scholars from non-Anglophone environments. Given the pace at which knowledge is disseminated, it seems that there is no time for a debate on which medium is best. Indeed, scientists in non-Anglophone environments did not wait for politicians to advise them on this issue. They are reminded daily, that their survival depends on being operational in English. Reading and writing English have become unavoidable conditions for joining academic communities in almost all disciplines (Labassi, 2008).

3. Will the new post-revolutionary regimes invest in knowledge? Will they propose a new economic deal and review priorities? Labassi (2010) argues that while education and research are top priorities, often as important as national security, in developed countries, developing and underdeveloped countries invest in internal security; the budget of interior ministries, in some totalitarian regimes, exceed by far the budget allocated to research. Nowadays, Research, requires huge funds that some nation states are not providing and that fragile private sectors cannot offer. US, the UK and France devote 2% of their Gross Domestic Product (GDP) to research, while developing countries devote less than 0.5% (Salager Meyer, 2008).
4. Will the issue of language and particularly English be approached from the angle of national interest? Will the future rulers allow a less impassionate debate over the issue of foreign languages, and implement a more responsible policy which will use taxpayers money wisely? So far the Tunisian state has paid for English courses to undergraduate students who do not see the need for it because they are taught through the medium of French, and write exam papers in French. However, potential researchers and professionals who have to read a literature which is, up to 90% in some disciplines in English, are not offered courses in English. Will the new democratically elected government correct the trend and implement a more responsible policy? Time will tell. It is too early to know where the current debate and the conflicting options, as discussed earlier, will lead the country. I hope that Tunisians will choose the most realistic, and the least adventurous option.

CONCLUSION

What recent writings in newly-born Peace Sociolinguistics propose in order to overcome the trap, in which Arab Nationalist, Islamist and Anti-Imperialists may lead us, is interesting. Friedrich (2007, p.73), a leading figure in Peace Sociolinguistics believes that: "An emphasis on peace, rather than on linguistic war, is a much-needed counterpart to the overheated discussions around language and dominance". One may add that a state of war will not end because we refuse to see it. A state of linguistic war exists, denying it will not serve peace. However, the debate over linguistic wars should shift perspectives. We should get rid of the narrow vision of oppressed and oppressors. In this respect, Pratt's proposal, although made more than twenty years ago, seems to be timely. Pratt (1987, p.61) proposed to stand between

> a critical knowledge of the workings of domination and dehumanization on the one hand, and of egalitarian and life-enhancing practices on the other [...] One would want to avoid, in the case of linguistics of contact, a utopian impulse to joyfully display all humanity in tolerant and harmonious contact across all lines of difference, or a dystopian impulse to bemoan a world homogenised by western media or run only by misunderstanding or bad intentions.

Labassi (2008) argued that the way out of the trap is not only condemning the hegemonic nature of English, but for non-native speakers of English, to negotiate a less fragile status and invent more original and "responsible" uses of English. In other words get rid of the rhetoric of victimization or hostility, and construct a more aggressive stand. But in the particular case of Tunisia, one has to admit that successive Tunisian governments have invested in French. The gradual disappearance of this language would be a great loss for the whole community. French should be viewed as; yet another wealth that the country, for historical, geographical and economic reasons, should keep investing in. The private sector is compensating, but only in the case of the privileged few, for the absence of a balanced, accountable, and consensual national linguistic policy. A national and public linguistic policy should attribute a special status to French; otherwise the country will witness an acceleration of a low quality public sector, and a better quality private education, thus adding to other exacerbating inequalities which, by time, will constitute additional sources of anger and frustration.

I believe that the success of future linguistic policies will depend on the extent of involvement of all the stakeholders who will not be active unless they participate in the process of decision making. The participation of teachers' and parents' representative bodies in the design of future linguistic policies will contribute to a more accountable linguistic policy. Linguistic and educational policies are related to issues of democracy and quality of governance. The consequences of deficiencies in these domains will have long term consequences on the political profile of future generations.

The linguistic issue is at the heart of any societal/cultural project, particularly in Arab Muslim countries. A consistent, and realistic management of the place of Arabic in Tunisia is possible. The country is mono-ethnic, and enjoys well-anchored legal rights for women. Educated middle class activists are active in non-governmental associations to protect some threatened civil liberties. These associations had been authorized by the government until the middle of the 1990s in an attempt to counter the spread of Islamism. After 1/14 they are engaged in the same battle. Their demands are the same, but their opponents have changed. They fought against a ruthless dictatorship with the support of a subdued media. Today they are fighting the same battle, and most of the media is not on their side.

Labassi (2009a) mentioned the fact that Tunisia is a small country (population: 11 Million), and its industrial sector is not well developed. The country relies heavily on tourism, and most exporting industries do not rely on highly-qualified graduates. Therefore, the state, even after 1/14, will remain the main employer. These factors are constraining in terms of investment in the training of highly-qualified professionals who should have some command of foreign languages, and particularly English.

Political parties should also be reminded that no Tunisian university is listed among the top 500 in the world. Future governments will have to promote the quality of research in order for Tunisian universities to be visible at the international level. Investing in the teaching of foreign languages, and particularly English, for the reasons mentioned above, is a *sine qua non* condition (Salager-Meyer, 2008). Political parties should attempt feasible targets, which take into consideration social realities, is a step in the right direction. The ultimate condition would be to set clear overall objectives, and to leave the details of their implementation to field agents. In a country with limited resources, the pedagogy of the possible is more than timely. Unrealistic programs might respond to the rhetoric of politics, but fail to answer the real needs of the country.

But what are the most urgent challenges in post 1/14 Tunisia?

It seems that those who have been united against dictatorship are now divided as to what to do after overthrowing Ben Ali. As mentioned earlier, there are two major clear positions. The moderate left, and the extreme left are divided, as has always been the case in Tunisia and which has resulted, among other factors, in the successive failures of this political family. They do not agree on priorities, and on the evaluation of the situation. Moderates believe that time has come to negotiate with what is left of the ruling party and the constitutional bodies of the First Republic. We need time to discuss the foundations of the new republic. The judicial corps, the constitution, the representative bodies, the code of the press and election have been reformed on several occasions by the former dictator to secure his total control of power as well as the supremacy of his party.

We know that the former ruling party was a state in the state. I believe that its legal dismissal is only the first step in the eradication of a system of governance created by this party. The dismantling of this system of governance needs time. The former ruling party plagued the administration, most associations in the civil society, the press, the labour union, the judicial branch, and the internal security bodies. Those who believe that burning its headquarters will solve problems should remember how members of former communist parties have regained all spheres of activities after 1990. The democratically elected Vladimir Putin is a former agent of the KGB, the national security agency of the Soviet Union.

The regime of Ben Ali has not left many options to those who wish to have a say in the future of Tunisia. What happened was unexpected. Those who are speaking today to the press were banned from public spaces. Everybody is learning on the spot, and reacting to a new situation. I believe that we should be vigilant but realistic. Tunisia's neighbours; Algeria and Libya are still ruled by oppressing regimes. The Tunisian uprising has already reached neighbouring Libya and may reach other Maghreb countries (Algeria, Morocco, Mauritania) whose people live under the same conditions, and whose demands for better living conditions and freedom are similar to what triggered the uprising in Tunisia. Their people may be tempted to copy the Tunisian experience. East Germans and Roumanians were surrounded by democratic regimes, and the communist republics were retarding the European project. This, partly explains the success of changes which swept across Eastern European countries. However, in this part of the world, there is no serious political or economic project at the level of the Maghreb. This is probably one of the serious threats to the success of the Tunisian uprising.

Whether this uprising would lead to the emergence of a modern democratic regime depends on many factors:

1. The degree of maturity of the new political parties? Will they transcend petty political manoeuvring, and reach a consensus on priorities during the transitional period. Will they postpone their ideological differences and engage in the construction of the democratic institutions which will contain and control political peaceful confrontation.
2. The capacity of the young generation to change stands: from utopia to realism. Will they accept to join existing parties or create their own, or will they be tempted to play the game of the "continuous revolution"? Extremists from the right and the left are now trying to recuperate this young, impatient, educated but unemployed generation (there are 170.000 unemployed young Tunisians who graduated from Tunisian universities during the last two decades). It is true that the discourse of extremists is more appealing to those who have nothing to lose. One of the top priorities on the agenda of the future government is employment of this highly qualified labor force.
3. Have Tunisian Islamists changed? Time has come to test this. Is the Tunisian Islamist branch really different from Islamist groups in the other Arab and Muslim countries? Have they learnt the lessons of the past? Have they cut links with international Islamism with its ramifications? Their leader, Rached Ghannouchi, who has spent more than twenty years in London, has been in contact with Islamist leaders from Pakistan, Afghanistan and less with Islamists from Tunisia because they were in prison. Will this reality influence the political program of the *Nahdha* (The Islamist party) in Tunisia or will local militants impose their own views? Will local militants who have spent years in Ben Ali's prisons, and who have been released recently, and participated with other political parties, including the left, in peaceful actions against the regime (hunger strikes, demonstrations etc…) accept the rules of the democratic game? Has the leader, who might have lost touch with his troops, regain control of the movement or, will local leadership who has better knowledge of the real forces, and who has learnt to negotiate with opponents and allies, redefine priorities? In a nutshell, have Islamists become more realistic and got rid of the ambition to islamize the country, and exclude all the other forces who have just helped them overthrow dictatorship? Will the

left live the same experience as *Tuda* and *Fidaiyi Khalk* (Leftist Iranian parties eradicated after the Iranian Revolution) in Iran? The future of the Tunisian experience will largely depend on this. Are Islamists ready to accept the rules of the game: Democracy, secularization of the state? Will they resist the temptation of using mosques for political propaganda?

4. Will Europe as a closer continent with historical and economic ties, and the US as a superpower with strategic interests in the region, revise their plans for the region and accept to deal with an "unexpected" event and change plans? How are American think tanks watching this experience? Will the US encourage or abort a process of democratization in this part of the world?
5. The few last weeks has taught us a lesson: external variables are important, but internal mechanisms remain determinant. Will the internal front be united? Will the different parties agree on short term projects?

Many people believe that the street can govern. It was the voice of the street which was misheard by Ben Ali that caused his fall. The creation of *Local Councils for the Protection of the Revolution* might lead to the dismantling of the local state bodies (municipalities, police forces, tax collecting administrations). The extreme left which is the driving force behind these councils might be tempted to create a state above the state. History reminds us that "revolutionary committees" are the recipe for dictatorship. The Soviet Union, China, and Iran are good examples. Comrades Stalin and Mao, as well as brother Khomeini have their disciples in this part of the world. The Tunisian "revolution" might not be an exception, if moderate democrats are not backed by democrats in other parts of the world who do not wish to see other Soljenitsins and Musavis.

References

Battenburgh, J. (1996). English in the Maghreb, *English Today, 48,* 3-12.

Canagarajah, A.S. (1996). Non-discursive Requirements in Academic Publishing, Materials, Resources, of Periphery Scholars, and the Politics of Knowledge Production, *Written Communication, 13,* 435-472.

Canagarajah, S. (1999). *Resisting Linguistic Imperialism in Language Teaching.* Oxford: Oxford University Press.

Celani, M. (2008). When Myth and Reality Meet: Reflections on ESP in Brazil. *English for Specific Purposes, 27,* 412-423.

Champagne, J. (2007). Job Seekers and Enterprise Incubators: Educational reform inTunisia. *Changing English, 14,* 201-215.

Crystal, D. (1997). *English as a Global Language.* Cambridge: Cambridgem University Press.

Daoud, M. (2000). LSP in North Africa: Status, Problems and Challenges. *Annual Review of Applied Linguistics, 20,* 77-96.

Daoud, M. (2001). The Language Situation in Tunisia. *Current Issues in Language Planning, 2,* 1-52.

Daoud, M. (2007). The language Situation in Tunisia. In R Kaplan, & R Baldauf (Eds), *Language Planning and Policy in Africa,* (pp: 256-277), NY: Multilingual Matters *Essabah,* Thursday, April, 24th, 2008.

Evans, S. (2008). Disputes and Deliberations over Language Policy: The Case of Early Colonial Hong Kong. *Language Policy, 7,* 47–65.

Fairclough, N. (2001). *Language and Power.* London: Longman.

Friedrich, P. (2007) English for Peace: Toward a Framework of Peace linguistics. *World Englishes, 26,* 72-83.

Graddol, D. (1997). *The Future of English.* London: Oxford University Press.

Hemissi, H. (1985). Some Aspects of ESP in Tunisian Higher Education. Unpublished Ph.D Thesis. Tunis: University of Tunis.

Jabeur, M. (1999). English, Globalization and Tunisia. Proceedings of the TSAS Conference on "English in North Africa". Tunis: TSAS Innovation Series.

Jrad, N. (2004). La Politique Linguistique dans la Tunisie Poscoloniale. In Ouvrage Collectif, *Trames de Langues* (pp. 525-544). Paris: Maison Neuve.

Kramsch, C. (2000). *Context and Culture in Language Teaching.* Oxford: Oxford University Press.

Labassi, T. (1995). ESP: A Market-oriented Approach. Paper presented at The Second ESP Maghreb Conference. Sfax, Tunisia, Faculty of Letters.

Labassi, T. (2008). On Responsible uses of English: English for Emancipation, Correction and Academic Purposes. *Changing English, 15,* 407-414.

Labassi, T. (2009a). Current Linguistic Pressures in Franco-Arabo-Anglicized Tunisia. *Cahiers de Tunisie, 200,* 11-21.

Labassi, T. (2009b). Periphery non-Anglophone Scholarship in English-only Journals : Conditions of a Better Visibility. *Changing English, 16,* 247-254.

Labassi, T. (2010). Two ESP Projects Under the Test of Time: The Case of Brazil and Tunisia. *English for Specific Purposes, 29,* 19-29. *La Presse.* April 27th, 2008.

Llurda, E. (2004). Non-native-Speaker Teachers and English as an International Language. *International Journal of Applied Linguistics 14,* 314-323. *Manière de Voir* . Februray, March, 2008.

Nunan, D. (1999). So You Think that Language Teaching is a Profession. *TESOL Matters, 9,* 1-12.

Pennycook, A. (1994). *The Cultural Politics of English as an International Language.* London: Longman.

Philipson, R. (1992). *Linguistic Imperialism.* Oxford: Oxford University Press.

Pratt, L. (1987). Linguistic Utopias. In N. Fabb.; D. Altridge.; A. Durant.; & A. Mac Cabe. (Eds) *The Linguistics of Writing,* (pp. 48-66), NewYork: Metheun.

Rogerson-Revell, P., (2008). Participation and Performance in International Business Meetings. *English for Specific Purposes 27,* 338-360.

Salager-Meyer, F. (2008). Scientific Publishing in Developing Countries: Future Perspectives. *Journal of English for Academic Purposes, 7,* 121-132.

Seidlhofer, B. (2000). Mind the Gap: English as a Mother Tongue vs. English as a Lingua Franca. *Vienna English Working Papers 9,* 51–69.

Swales, J. (1993). The English Language and its Teachers: Thoughts Past, Present, and Future. *ELT Journal, 47,* 283-291.

Swales, J. (1997). English as Tyrannosaurex rex. *World Englishes 16,* 373-382.

Tollefson, J. W. (Ed.). (2002). *Language Policies in Education: Critical Issues.* Mahwah: Lawrence Erlbaum Associates.

Tossa, M. (1995). Happy Few Hours, *Jeune Afrique, 6,* 38.

Walters, K. (1999). "New Year Happy": Some Sociolinguistic Observations on the Way to the "anglicization" of Tunisia. Proceedings of the TSAS Conference on "English in North Africa". Tunis, TSAS Innovation Series).

Widdowson, H. (1994) The Ownership of English, *TESOL Quarterly, 28,* 377-88.

In: Tunisia: Economic, Political and Social Issues ISBN: 978-1-61942-157-8
Eds: M. Pusatieri and J. Cannamela

Chapter 2

ELECTRICITY FOR GROWTH AND JOBS IN TUNISIA: EXPLORING THE NUCLEAR AND RENEWABLE ELECTRICITY OPTIONS

Peter Schmidt**, Johan Lilliestam, Daniel Fürstenwerth, and Antonella Battaglini
Potsdam Institute for Climate Impact Research (PIK), Potsdam, Germany

ABSTRACT

In order to continue its socio-economic development and to solve its probably most pressing problem, the unemployment, Tunisia needs economic growth. Many factors need to be fulfilled for this to happen, most of them are not easy to achieve. One of the most important factors is to make sure that the electricity supply keeps pace with economic activity –without electricity, growth, and consequently job creation, will be slowed down. Tunisia's present power system is almost exclusively based on fossil fuels, which are imported at an ever-increasing, over time possibly unsustainable, level. Hence, two alternative pathways to a continued and increased dependency on fossil fuels for power generation have emerged: nuclear and renewable power. In this chapter, these two alternatives are explored, discussed and compared with respect to their financial, technical and socio-economical impacts and viability. We look

* Corresponding author: Phone: +49 331 288 2031, Email: pschmidt@pik-potsdam.de

in detail at the issues of investment needs and feasibility, the fit of the options with the existing electricity infrastructure system, the effects on local industry and economy, and fulfilment of seawater desalination needs. We conclude that the nuclear option is hardly viable, as it constitutes too large an investment, its techno-economical characteristics do not fit the small Tunisian power system, and the socio-economic benefits of nuclear power are few. The prospects for renewables are better, although many significant challenges remain: as renewables projects are of a more decentralised nature, they are more attractive investments than nuclear power, the expansion plans are embedded in an international investment context, and they fit better with the existing power system. However, renewables are too expensive to be a real alternative to fuel desalinisation plants in the short term. Most importantly, a well-designed policy effort to support renewables holds the potential of significant job creation and the emergence of a new Tunisian industry, with strong positive socio-economic effects.

INTRODUCTION

In early 2011, a rapid and radical transformation started in Tunisia: After the desperate act of self-immolation of a young, unemployed graduate student, a massive wave of protests sparked the country. After several days of violent clashes between government forces and protestors, the broad public opposition managed to break down the government of Ben Ali. While the country may have embarked on a path towards more democracy, uncertainty about Tunisia's future remains and many problems have yet to be solved. Among others, Tunisia must maintain its impressive economic growth of the past decade, or even increase it, especially in order to significantly reduce unemployment, which was one of the main reasons for the upheaval. Many factors need to be fulfilled for this to happen, most of them are not easy to achieve. One of the most important factors is to make sure that the electricity supply keeps pace with economic activity. A sufficient, affordable and secure electricity supply system will not directly induce economic growth and will not automatically create employment effects. Without it, however, the Tunisian economy will slow down and remain behind its opportunities with strong negative effects on employment, contentedness and social cohesion.

As the Tunisian power system is almost entirely based on fossil fuels which increasingly need to be imported, the issue of the future electricity system ranks high on the policy agenda and has already triggered debates about alternative electricity sources. Principally, two options are discussed:

nuclear and renewable power. As it cannot afford to do everything, Tunisia stands at a crossroads: will it continue down a gas-based business-as-usual path, or will it embark on a nuclear development, or will it opt to make use of its large renewable resources?

This choice is an important one, with implications to be felt immediately and in the decades to come. Hence, it is necessary to examine the new sources for electricity generation more in detail in order to understand the drawbacks and opportunities they are associated with. This is the aim of the present chapter: to explore, discuss and compare these alternative paths and to point to what could be the most beneficial path for Tunisia to cope with soaring electricity demand to fuel its growing economy in the future.

In the following section, we describe the Tunisian power sector and the main drivers for electricity consumption, thereby highlighting some of the main problems of the current power supply and a business-as-usual outlook. In section three, we examine the nuclear and renewable power futures, which are described in section 3.1, by looking at financial, technical and socio-economic aspects. In concrete terms, we will focus on four factors: investment needs and feasibility (section 3.2), the fit of the options with the existing electricity infrastructure system (3.3), effects on local industry and economy (3.4), and fulfilment of seawater desalination needs (3.5). Before we conclude in section five, we present a discussion of our main findings in section four.

Characterisation of the Current Power System

Power System Status Quo

The Tunisian power mix is typical for North Africa and is characterised by the abundance of fossil fuels in the region. Today, the Tunisian electricity supply is almost entirely based on gas power (89%), flanked by oil power (11%) and minimal shares of wind (0.25%) and hydro power (0.25%), see Figure (IEA, 2011).

This is similar to its neighbour countries (Libya 60% oil, 40% gas; Algeria 97% gas, 3% oil) and other countries throughout the fossil fuel-producing North Africa and Middle East region, but completely different from, for example, Europe or the US, where electricity supply is based on coal, gas and nuclear power. The Tunisian power demand in 2009 was 12 TWh, produced by a power plant fleet of 3.2 GW installed generation capacity (EIA, 2010).

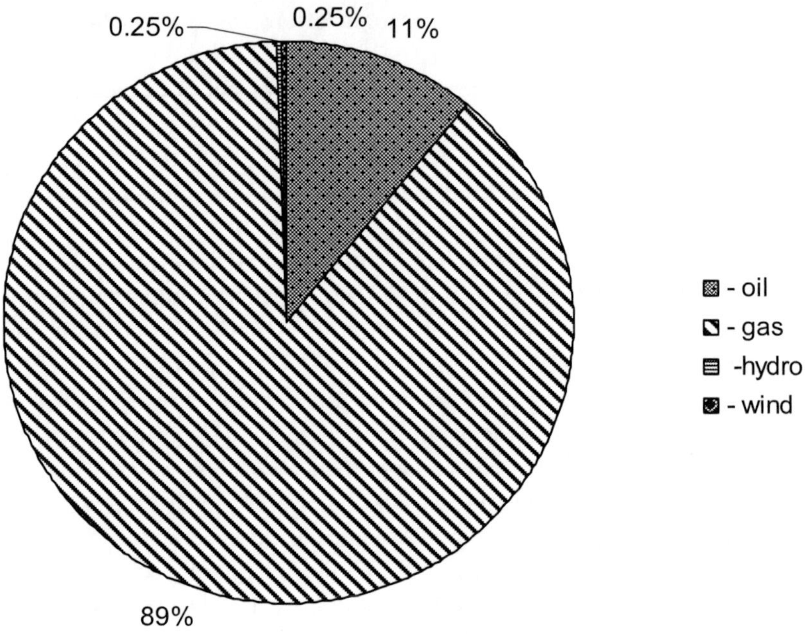

Source: IEA, 2011.

Figure 1. Power mix of Tunisia (2008).

Tunisia has electricity interconnections[1] to its neighbours and its grid is synchronous with Algeria, Morocco and the European ENTSO-E area via AC cables across the Strait of Gibraltar. The Tunisian interconnection capacity has been expanded in recent years and consists of 4 medium- and high-voltage lines to Algeria with a total capacity of 420 MW (thermal limit), of which around 200 MW are commercially available (MED-EMIP, 2010). Despite this, Tunisia is self-sufficient in electricity, with only very small net amounts of electricity flowing across the border. As a consequence, the utilisation of the interconnectors is low: on a yearly average, the load factor is between 5 and 9% (MED-EMIP, 2010). Tunisia also has two 200 kV interconnections to Libya with thermal limits of 300 MW (AFESD, 2011) or 570 MW (Red Eléctrica, 2010). These are currently not in use due to synchronisation and stability problems (ENTSO-E, 2010).

[1] The data about the size of the remaining interconnections in North Africa varies between sources. When there is disagreement, upper and lower ranges are given, together with the source for each number.

Thus, Tunisia currently has active interconnections amounting to 13% of its installed generation capacity – clearly higher than the interconnection ratio of other regions, like the EU. The Tunisian interconnection share may increase to around 20-25% once the lines to Libya are operational. Currently, the only link between the Maghreb and Europe are the two AC cables connecting Morocco to Spain, of 600-900 MW (ENTSO-E, 2011) or up to 1400 MW thermal limit (AFESD, 2011). Tunisia is thus indirectly connected to Europe, via the Algerian-Moroccan link of 470 MW thermal limit (with 240 MW commercially available capacity) and could theoretically, though hardly practically, trade electricity directly with Spain (MED-EMIP, 2010).

In the last years, initial steps have been taken towards liberalisation of the power market. Whereas the monopoly for power production was removed in the mid-1990s, and private companies can now respond to tenders and apply for generation licenses. However, the state-owned gas and electricity supplier STEG (Société Tunisienne de l'Electricité et du Gaz) still benefits from its former monopoly status in a highly concentrated electricity generation market. The transmission and distribution systems have not been liberalised as of yet (Brand and Zingerle, 2011).

Drivers for Electricity Demand: Socio-Economic Progress

The second principal characteristic of the Tunisian power sector is its very rapid growth that continues to be primarily driven by its rapid socio-economic development, steadily growing population, economic modernisation and seawater desalination. These drivers are described below.

Figure 2 shows the development of the Tunisian GDP, foreign direct investment (FDI), population and electricity consumption over the last 30 years. Electricity demand has increased by 3-11% per year, adding up to a growth of some 550% over the entire period: from 2.2 TWh/a in 1980 to 12.5 TWh/a in 2008 (EIA, 2010). The electricity demand is strongly correlated with GDP growth and, although a slight decoupling can be observed in the last few years, it is highly probably that GDP growth will continue to drive the electricity consumption. Thus, it remains a central task for the electricity sector and policy to keep pace with the increasing demand, as electricity consumption is still only around 1,100 kWh per person and year, which is very low compared to the 6,700 kWh per person and year consumed in the EU (Eurostat, 2010).

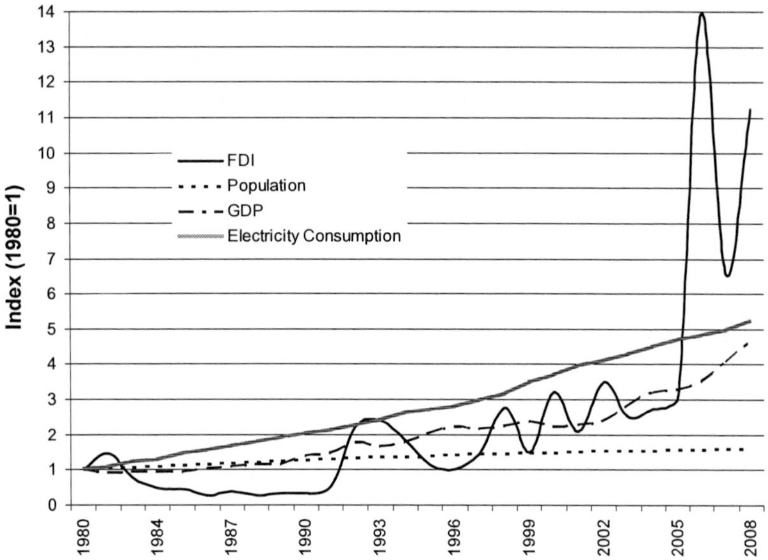

Source: WB, 2011a.

Figure 2. Index (1980=1) of Growth of FDI (net), population, GDP (current US) and electricity consumption (kWh) in Tunisia 1980-2008.

As Figure 2 highlights, Tunisia has had an impressing economic development over especially the last 10 years, with GDP growth rates of 4-6% per year (Global Finance, 2011; WB, 2011a).

There is no official economic data for the impacts of the revolution on the economy and the existing, highly preliminary and uncertain, assessments show a very mixed picture, with expected real GDP growth of -2.5% to +3.6% in 2011. The African Development Bank expects economic growth in 2012 to be at +2.4% to +4.2% (Verdier-Chouchane et al., 2011).

Overall, the short-term economical effects of the upheaval are difficult to assess, but the longer-term prospects for Tunisia remain positive, as soon as stability is restored: in the long term, a return to growth of around 5% per year seem reasonable and realistic. The current Tunisian GDP per capita – US$ 4,200 – is one of the highest in Africa following its steady increase, especially during the last decade. The distribution of wealth is uneven, and the Tunisian Gini index (45) is a high mid-field value compared to other countries on its level of development[2](UNDP, 2010), indicating a relatively unequal wealth

[2] To be compared with Algeria (35) or Morocco (41). A lower Gini index indicates a more equal income distribution.

distribution, something that may have played an important role in the 2010-2011 upheaval. At the same time, the population has been steadily growing over the last three decades. Total population was 10.5 million in 2010 and is projected to increase to 11.6 million, 12.5 million, and 13 million in 2019, 2029, and 2039 respectively (INS, 2011). As shown by Figure 2, even if population has been growing moderately with rates of 1.1-1.2% in the last years, electricity consumption rose disproportionately due to the adoption of energy-intensive life-styles, accelerating urbanisation – some 2/3 of Tunisians live in large urban agglomerations - and positive human development in many areas. The National Institute of Statistics (INS, 2011) reports that, for instance:

- national poverty rate dropped from 7.7% in 1985 to 3.8% in 2009,
- life expectancy increased from 68 years to 74 years between 1987 and 2008,
- infant mortality decreased from 42% in 1994 to 17.8% in 2009.

The former government's economic modernisation programme was targeted at opening and diversifying the national economy, with industry (which currently creates 35% of the GDP) and service sector (42%) becoming the main drivers for growth, coupled with export-oriented economic policies towards Europe (OECD and UN, 2011; Verdier-Chouchane et al., 2011).

The transformation from a low- to middle-income country was accompanied by positive net inflow of foreign direct investment (FDI) over the course of the last 30 years, as shown in Figure 2. Interestingly, the FDI development correlates well with GDP and electricity consumption growth. However, the overall FDI inflow is rather low, just as in most African countries, and highly unstable, as indicated by fluctuations in the last years. Taking into account the current instabilities, a decline in FDI for 2011 is likely and, as long as the political uncertainty remains, no significant and sustained positive changes are expected (Verdier-Chouchane et al., 2011).

Despite these overall positive macroeconomic and socio-economic developments, one of the most urgent problems, unemployment, has not been solved. Total unemployment has been stagnant for more than 10 years, at a level of 14-16%, despite the continuous economic growth (Verdier-Chouchane et al., 2011). In earlier decades, unemployment affected mainly the less-qualified labour force but in the last 20 years, unemployment among young Tunisians with tertiary education exploded from 1.3% in 1989 to 13.6% in 2005 (WB, 2011a). Thus, a rising share of young high skilled labour force has not benefited from the overall positive economic development. According to the African Development Bank (Verdier-Chouchane et al., 2011), this was one of the main drivers for the upheaval of Tunisians in late 2010. This issue remains to be highly problematic and a rapid solution is necessary, or the social instability is likely to remain.

Another potential social and economical stressor is scarcity of renewable freshwater, and the water sector is already a major electricity consumer: in 2007, 10% of the total electricity consumption in Tunisia was attributed to desalination (Jewell, 2011). DLR (2007) projects that the total water consumption of the MENA region will almost double within the next 40 years, driven by largely the same factors that increase electricity consumption: economic growth, social development and population growth. With a total availability of renewable freshwater of 410 m^3/cap/a, Tunisia already today ranks below the water poverty threshold of 1000m^3/cap/a (DLR, 2007: 4). Impacts from climate change are expected to further exacerbate the situation, thereby affecting in particular the agricultural sector, which is still an important employer in the country (Mougou et al., 2011). Even if significant improvements in water management and efficiency were achieved, Tunisia will not be able to match its future fresh water demand without additional desalination projects (Trieb and Steinhagen, 2008). All signs point in a similar direction: towards more desalinisation and Tunisia recently launched a new tender for three desalination projects, which will be based on fossil fuels only (D&WR, 2010). The share of fresh water provided by desalination plants is thus very likely to increase strongly. Projections show that an increase from 1% in 2006 to around 10% in 2016 is probable. If this becomes reality, one quarter of the projected electricity consumption growth up to 2016 will be attributed to an increase in seawater desalination capacity (Jewell, 2011).

Fuelling the Power Sector: Growing Energy Import Dependency

Unlike its neighbour countries, Tunisia does not produce all of its fuel for the power sector domestically, but has to rely on growing imports: in 2009, about a quarter of the gas demand was imported, because the domestic production did not keep up with consumption despite efforts to scale it up (see Figure 3 and 4).

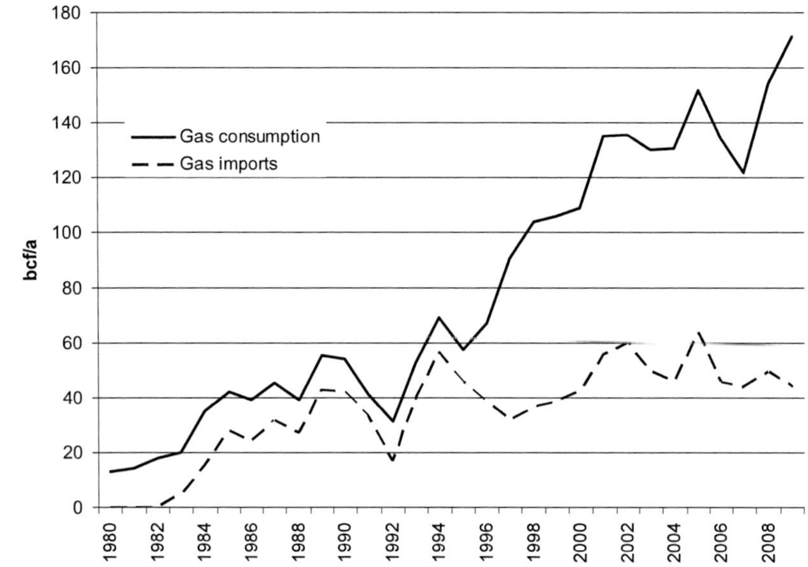

Source: EIA, 2010.

Figure 3. Tunisian gas consumption and gas imports 1980-2009. The gap between the curves is domestic production.

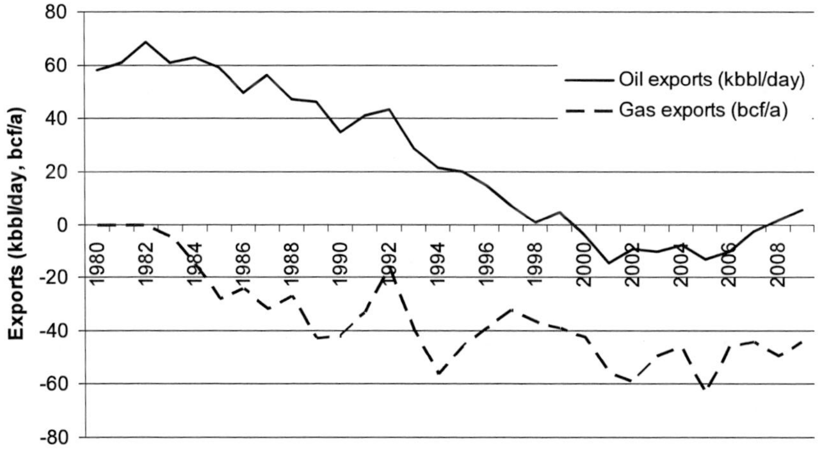

Source: EIA, 2010.

Figure 4. Tunisian oil (kbbl/day) exports and gas (bcf/a) imports (here registered as negative export values) 1980-2009.

Tunisia has been a gas importer since 1983 when the pipeline from Algeria started operations and imports have steadily increased since then. All gas imports come from only one supplier, Algeria.

Over the last 15 years, the Tunisian gas production increased dramatically – more than a 1000% boost between 1995 and 2009.

Hence, although the proven reserves have been rather constant over the last 10 years – the gas R/P quota is currently 18 years (EIA, 2010; BP, 2011) – the gas R/P quota is destined to slump rapidly unless new fields are found. This trend will be even stronger if the added electricity generation capacity continues to be based on gas.

On contrast, as Figure 4 shows, Tunisia is still more or less self-sufficient on oil, although the production has declined generally over the last 20 years, changing the oil sector from being an oil exporter towards becoming an importer. The Tunisian proven oil reserves have been steady in terms of reserves/production quota over the last 10 years after a sharp decline in the 1990s (R/P ratio of 15 years in 2010) (EIA, 2010; BP, 2011). Overall, it is easy to foresee that Tunisia is heading for significant increases in oil imports and massive increases in gas imports in the coming decade, with probably worse impacts on the national economy.

Considering that North African countries are heavily subsidising domestic energy consumption (cf. Supersberger and Führer, 2011), Belloumi (2009: 2749) warns of ever rising subsidies if Tunisia further increases its dependence on fossil fuels.

Together with rising global energy prices, the resulting outflow of urgently needed capital may result in a serious obstacle for the Tunisian economy, disabling the government to pursue the necessary investments in infrastructure, education and social programmes, as seen in other parts of the world, for example in Morocco or Belarus. This, in turn, could convert into a serious threat to economic growth and social cohesion.

Business-as-Usual Outlook: More of the Same

A comparison of the energy consumption trends and GDP growth (see Figure 5) shows that efficiency gains are possible, as the demand growth – especially in the gas sector – has outpaced economic growth. The gas consumption has increased by a factor 12 since 1980, whereas GDP has only increased by a factor 4.5: the gas consumption is increasing much more rapidly than the value created by this increase.

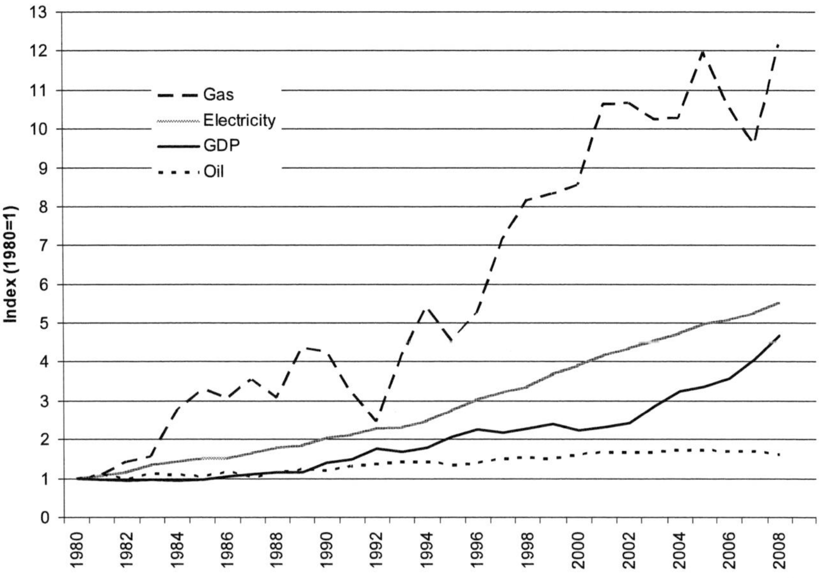

Figure 5. Index (1980=1) of Tunisian consumption of electricity, natural gas and oil, and the Tunisian GDP (nominal) 1980-2009. Source: EIA, 2010; EconStats, 2010.

The same, but to a much smaller extent, applies to electricity, and this has significant knock-on effects on the gas sector as roughly half of Tunisia's gas consumption is used for electricity generation.

A study of the Tunisian National Agency for Energy Conservation (ANME, 2005) reveals that there is much room for savings in aggregate primary energy consumption. Electricity transmission and distribution losses add up to 12.4% in 2008, compared to for example 5% in Spain and 8% in Greece, thus leaving room for efficiency gains (WB, 2011a). Achieving all possible efficiency gains should be the primary aim of any Tunisian energy and electricity policy programme.

Nevertheless, regardless of progress in energy efficiency and demand side measures, Tunisia will need new generation capacity. Projections show an expected electricity demand of some 17 TWh/a in 2015 and 21 TWh/a in 2020, which means an increase of more than 55% compared to 2009 (MED-EMIP, 2010). New generation capacity of 1.8 GW has already been approved and is expected to go online before 2016 (MED-EMIP, 2010). Almost all of this is combined cycle power plants fuelled with natural gas. A significant amount of new capacity will come from the Tunisian-Italian ELMED project, which provides 400 MW for Tunisia and 800 MW generation capacity for

Italy through a 200 km long 1000 MW high-voltage direct current (HVDC) submarine cable link between El Hawari/ Tunisia and Sicily/Italy that is expected to be operational by 2016. While the HVDC connection provides 800 MW of transmission capacity for power from the ELMED power plant, the remaining capacity of 200 MW is reserved for renewable electricity (TERNA, 2011; MAGHREB, 2010a). Current plans indicate the installation of another 1.2 GW by 2020. If these plans materialise, the total Tunisian installed generation capacity will be more than 6 GW by 2020 (MED-EMIP, 2010). This is roughly twice the size of the current Tunisian electricity system.

The increasing electricity demand will require Tunisia to expand and reinforce the electricity networks. A number of initiatives already address the refurbishment and expansion of low- and medium-tension lines in order to reduce electricity losses and prepare for further electricity market integration, but much remains to be done in this area (GAN, 2009).

Summary: Status Quo and Outlook

The Tunisian power sector has, just like the economy in general, grown at an impressive pace in the last decade. There are currently no signals that this may change in the years to come: Economic growth is expected to be at a similar rate, on average some 5% until 2020, once the uncertainty following the revolution has been resolved. This is expected to be accompanied by a sharp increase in electricity demand: electricity demand is projected to have increased to 21 TWh/a by 2020, an increase of more than 50% in only 10 years.

Tunisia's electricity production is based on an increasing amount of fossil fuels, in particular gas, and there will not be any significant changes in the short-to medium term. However, Tunisia may head for difficulties, if its electricity supply is based on increasing shares of imported natural gas. The national gas supplies are unlikely to be sufficient to satisfy the resulting increase in gas demand for very long – the most recent R/P quotas indicate that gas reserves are enough to satisfy the current national gas demand for some 18 years, which is less than the depreciation and economical lifetime of a power plant. Thus, continuing with business-as-usual is likely to cause difficulties for Tunisia. Efficiency measures, especially regarding electricity end-use efficiency, transmission and distribution system efficiencies, but also power plant-level efficiency, will be of great importance. Nonetheless, Tunisia will need more electricity generation capacity to keep up with demand if its economy is to continue growing to help reducing unemployment. While natural gas will play an important role in Tunisia's future electricity supply, discussions about alternatives, especially nuclear power and renewable power, have emerged and appear to be real policy options for the future of the Tunisian power supply.

TUNISIAN ELECTRICITY FUTURES

Plans and Prospects for Nuclear and Renewable Power

Nuclear Power

Like all North African countries, Tunisia is considering nuclear power as a potential source for the generation of electricity to support its continued economical and social development (UNEA, 2010; WNA, 2011). If all of the nuclear plans that are currently discussed were carried out successfully, nuclear power could supply 9-15% of electricity in North Africa by 2030 (Jewell, 2011).

Tunisia is a member of the International Atomic Energy Agency's (IAEA) regional cooperation programme on capacity building in sustainable energy development planning and the nuclear option has been on the agenda as a real option for the future electricity supply in Tunisia for at least five years. In 2006, STEG was commissioned to conduct a techno-economic feasibility study for the examination of new energy sources for Tunisia in 2030. Although first results are not expected to be published before the end of 2011, rumours about an agreement already made for a nuclear power plant in Kélibia, Cap Bon have been circulating in recent months. The interim government rejected these speculations, and it remains to be seen what the official nuclear plans will be, but there seems to be strong industry support for a nuclear deal (CIGI, 2011; AM, 2011).

A nuclear cooperation agreement in the areas of electricity production and desalination was signed with the French government in 2006. The agreement was extended twice, in 2008 and 2009. The last time it was agreed upon an development aid package of US$ 104 million and the plan to implement a nuclear power plant of 900 MW in Tunisia by 2020 (WNA, 2011; Reuters, 2009). The updated database of the World Nuclear Association (WNA, 2011), however, indicates that the implementation of a 600 MW nuclear plant is currently assessed. Other sources report from a plant with a capacity between 700-1000 MW (CIGI, 2011). Despite these inconsistencies, STEG recently confirmed that nuclear plans of the former government will be further developed in the coming years (KUNA, 2011).

Renewable Power

Facing dwindling domestic fossil resources and rising dependence on imports for electricity production, renewable electricity has emerged as an option, much due to Tunisia's large renewable energy resource base. While the idea of using renewable energy from the deserts to satisfy the rising electricity demand is not new (Gnad and Viëtor, 2011), such thoughts gained new momentum in 2008 when the Union of the Mediterranean (UfM) launched the 'Mediterranean Solar Plan'. This plan's objective is to build 20 GW renewable electricity generation capacity, mainly solar power plants, by 2020 throughout the MENA region in order to provide electricity for the MENA countries, and, through exports to Europe, to contribute to the EU's renewable energy and greenhouse gas emission reduction targets.

One year later, in 2009, the Desertec industry initiative (DII) was founded and set the goal of producing 15% of European electricity demand with renewable power from North Africa by 2050. The total renewable power potential is huge in North Africa and the solar electricity potential alone is assessed to be in the magnitude of 600,000 TWh/a. Besides the €400 billion Desertec vision, a number of other initiatives were launched throughout the last 2 years (Battaglini et al., 2009; Schellekens et al., 2010, 2011: 34). What all these initiatives have in common, is the objective to bring the EU and North Africa closer together in energy policy making and make the enormous renewable power resources available to all countries around the Mediterranean.

Tunisian decision makers have recognised the potential future role of renewables, for example by instituting a subsidiary for renewable energy at STEG. In 2004, a study commissioned by the National Agency for Energy Conservation (NAEC) indicated an accessible potential for renewable power of 81 TWh by 2020 and 220 TWh by 2030 (ANME, 2004).

To create new employment and to highlight Tunisia's ambitions in renewable energy, the former government launched the 'Tunisian Solar Plan' (PST) in late 2009. The PST aims at increasing the share of renewables in total electricity generation capacity up to 4% by 2014 (MAGHREB, 2010b). The plan consists of 40 individual projects, almost all of them public-private partnerships, which are to be implemented until 2016. Besides from reducing consumption in primary energy by 22% until 2016, the PST aims to accelerate diffusion of solar water heating installations, build 120 MW of new photovoltaic (PV) and concentrating solar power (CSP) for electricity production, and to increase the share of wind electricity generation capacity up to 320 MW by 2016. This is rather modest in comparison to the ambitious Moroccan (2 GW solar power by 2020) and Algerian (12 GW renewables by 2030) targets. While a number of smaller PV programmes are to be developed, 2-3 CSP projects are under active consideration, whereof one is already in advanced planning stage (WB, 2011b: 182)[3].

All measures and programmes combined are expected to achieve an overall renewable capacity increase up to some 10%, or 660 MW of new PV, wind and CSP generation capacity by 2020 (FEMIP, 2010: 105). To keep pace with the renewable technology deployment, the PST contains grid capacity expansion measures to allow for integration of 10% electricity from renewables already by 2014 (FEMIP, 2010).

Investment Needs and Feasibility

Nuclear Power

Taking into account the current plans for nuclear power, huge investment is needed for a nuclear power plant (NPP) in the size of 600-1000 MW. The costs for a 1 GW nuclear power plant vary widely and range between $US 1.4-6 billion, and countries without any existing nuclear infrastructure are more likely to face the upper than the lower range costs (IAEA, 2007: 9; 2009:10). Compared with most countries with nuclear power, which are typically wealthy, the Tunisian GDP is rather low.

Tunisia will thus need to rely on FDI for the financing, in addition to relying of foreign know-how (UNEA, 2010). Since official discussions about nuclear power started in 2006, the average FDI has been fluctuating between $US 1.5 and 3 billion (see section 2.2; WB, 2011a):

Tunisia's total FDI is only at the lower cost range of the estimated investment costs for a new NPP, which shows the magnitude of the financing problem for an NPP. The investment climate following the financial and debt crises, and the uncertainty caused by the turmoil in North Africa, exacerbate these problems.

Even if Tunisia has already signed a nuclear cooperation agreement with France, Tunisia's largest FDI partner outside the oil sector, the current

[3] For more details regarding the current status of wind, CSP and PV projects in Tunisia, see FEMIP (2010: 107-109).

investment climate for such huge deals may also lead French investors to rethink their investment strategy.

Renewable Power

The 2016 goals of the PST are very ambitious. While the share of renewables in terms of installed generation capacity has increased slightly since 2008, mainly due to up-scaling of wind farm Sidia Daoud in 2009, the political turmoil has increased uncertainty for investors and renders investments in renewable power more complicated (Verdier-Chouchane et al., 2011).

A total investment of some € 2 billion, wherefrom € 0.6 billion will be provided by the Tunisian government, is expected to be needed for fulfilling the goals, both for heat and electricity, of the PST by 2016 (AM, 2009; UNEP, 2011). Considering that the general energy investment risk in North Africa is high, mainly due to perceived regulatory uncertainty (Komendantova et al., 2009), the political changes have further put large scale long-term FDI on hold (see section 2.2). As long as political and social instability remains, no significant positive changes should be expected (Verdier-Chouchane et al., 2011).

Since the PST is integrated into the vision of the Mediterranean Solar Plan and also considered as a 'mosaic of the Desertec concept' (ZO, 2011), government officials expect to receive sufficient support in terms of funding, training, and technology transfer from European and international partners. This interest is reciprocal, and a number of major supra-national funding initiatives, such as the Clean Technology Fund (CTF), have already declared their intent to become a funding partner for renewable energy deployment in Tunisia (WB, 2011b: 27).

Furthermore, the DII, which consists of many of the biggest potential investors in North Africa, has renewed its declaration of interest for Tunisian renewable electricity projects: Despite the political instability, DII sticks to initially announced plans and aims to build one of its first pilot projects in the country.

Besides the launch of a new office in Tunis, officials from STEG Renewable Energy, the interim government and DII met to clarify on potential power plant sites and to commission a feasibility study about regulation and economics of solar and wind power plants in Tunisia (DII, 2011; ZO, 2011). Furthermore, a cooperation agreement on energy efficiency and renewable energy exports was signed between the French Ministry of Industry and Technology and Tunisian officials in March 2011 (WKO.at, 2011). \

Thus, against many speculations and despite increased uncertainty, it seems that the political changes in Tunisia have not put an end to already ongoing projects and plans. A renewables expansion will not be for free, but there are interested, financially highly potent, investors. Additionally, the EU is supporting renewables technology deployment in North Africa through Article 9 of the Renewables Directive: the renewable part of the ELMED project could be financed through this mechanism.

Fit with Existing Electricity Infrastructure System

Nuclear Power

A nuclear power plant produces baseload electricity, which is in principle relatively easy to integrate into the power system. However, one has to take into account the comparatively small size of the Tunisian system – the peak load was about 2467 MW in 2008 – and the effects of introducing a potential economic cost in case of a breakdown of a nuclear power plant with a size of 600-1000 MW (MED-EMIP, 2010: 42). This single production unit would represent 25-40% of the Tunisian power system if build today. This is highly problematic, as the system must be capable of handling this unit going offline, due to technical problems or maintenance. In large electricity systems, like Europe or the US, this is not an important problem, as each single unit represents a small share of the available generation capacity. In small power systems, however, it is a serious problem, as a shut-down of single large unit removes a large share of the overall generation capacity and the necessary back-up cost increases the system cost, possibly to the point where such large units are economically unfeasible (Supersberger and Führer, 2011).

Although smaller nuclear power plants are commercially available and implemented, such as for instance the 165 MW Pebble Bed Modular Reactor in South Africa, NPPs typically need economies of scale in order to be economically viable: Small NPPs are possible, but expensive. Even the International Atomic Energy Agency, otherwise not known for being overly critical of nuclear power, recognises that it is challenging to achieve an economic design at sizes between 150-400 MW (IAEA, 2007). Thus, the option of building a small NPP is unlikely to provide real benefits for Tunisia, as it is too expensive.

The Tunisian power system will not be able to accommodate a NPP of aforementioned sizes of 600-1000 MW within a timeframe of 10 years from now. As a rule of thumb, a grid capacity of around 10 GW should be provided in order to allow for successful integration of a NPP of 1 GW (Jewell, 2011: 5). Currently, Tunisia has the smallest power system in North Africa with an installed capacity of about 3 GW. By 2020, the system is projected to be expanded to some 6 GW (MED-EMIP, 2010: 46). As described above, Tunisia has grid connections to Algeria and Libya that could make grid integration of large-scale nuclear power by 2020 more feasible by effectively creating a larger power system. However, the North African electricity markets are hardly integrated and there are no strong signs that this is about to happen: hence, a far-reaching market and system integration with the neighbour countries does not seem probable in the coming years (section 2.1). Additionally, Algeria and Libya also have ambitious plans for own nuclear power programmes (Jewell, 2011) which effectively compete with the Tunisian plans, and strongly decrease their interest in nuclear electricity imports from Tunisia.

Renewable Power

If realised, the renewable part of the ELMED project will add a generation unit of up to 100 MW (a CSP plant), which will be the largest single renewable generation unit to Tunisia's power fleet in 2016 (FEMIP, 2010: 108). Hence, the size-related system back-up costs that constitute a large problem for nuclear power will be small for renewables.

Instead, the fluctuating nature of many renewables will create a need for grid expansions to maintain system stability at all times. Concepts for how to handle this exist, such as the SuperSmart Grid concept developed for Europe and North Africa (Battaglini et al., 2009; Battaglini et al., 2010), and these especially emphasize the need for expanded and reinforced transmission grids. Already meeting the targets of the PST requires a significant refurbishment and scale-up of the transmission grid capacity, as a number of more fluctuating sources are to be integrated into the grid and electricity needs to be transmitted from remote production sites to load centres in the densely populated areas in the north-east of the country. This is the same challenge as Europe and other regions with rapidly increasing shares of renewables experience: the systems were designed for dispatchable, thermal power generation, not for remote, decentralised and fluctuating renewables (Battaglini and Lilliestam, 2010; Battaglini et al., 2009).

The PST foresees measures to reinforce the grid to make it able to absorb 10% of electricity from renewables by 2014 (FEMIP, 2010: 105). At the same time, as mentioned above, the Tunisian power system size is projected to double in the coming decade, which requires the power grid to grow at a corresponding pace. Regardless of whether Tunisia opts for a renewable future or not, the grid will need to be massively expanded and reinforced. This holds promise for renewables: if the expansion for grid integration is coordinated with the necessary scale-up to meet the increasing demand, the costs of grid integration can be minimised. This would greatly improve the economic and technical feasibility of a large-scale renewables expansion, but it requires planning and coordination between authorities and companies and is a large institutional challenge.

Effects on the Local Industry and Economy

Nuclear Power

Tunisia does not have any experience with nuclear technology, nor does it, in contrast to other North African countries, have any significant nuclear infrastructure[4]. Developing own knowledge and expertise on nuclear technology takes time, and systematically building this up will likely take too long for domestically engineered nuclear power to play a role in the Tunisian power system before 2020. The nuclear expertise in the industrialised countries was built up over decades, and it is not realistic to expect that the few dominant actors in the nuclear industry are willing to transfer their knowledge to new players (Supersberger and Führer, 2011: 4464).

As nuclear cooperation agreements are already signed with France, it is likely that most, if not all of the technology and know-how needs to be bought and imported from the nuclear-experienced partner. This means that Tunisia would become dependent on external support in terms of knowledge and technology. This is true for any alternative the country is going to opt for in a short-to medium term – Tunisia also does not have any significant experiences in large-scale renewables – but to a different extent. In the case of nuclear technology in North Africa, Marktanner and Salmann (2011: 4484) point to Vernon's life-cycle hypotheses of trade: capital-intensive technologies are developed in the wealthiest countries and are sold to the less-wealthy countries at the end of their product life cycle. Accordingly, there is little prospect that Tunisia could become a technology leader in the nuclear sector, quite in contrast to the prospects in the renewables sector (see below). The nuclear option thus threatens to lock Tunisia into the role of an energy technology

[4] Algeria, Egypt, Libya and Morocco own at least one research reactor. Tunisia has only one research centre for Nuclear Science and Technology, but no research reactor (Jewell, 2011).

importing country which is dependent on others for sustaining its power supply. This has adverse impacts as it causes an outflow of capital by importing foreign technology, and it holds little prospect for additional employment in the local Tunisian industry.

In addition, as the Tunisian domestic uranium reserves are limited (WNA, 2011) and as it does not have – and is extremely unlikely to build – an enrichment facility, gas imports would be replaced by imports of nuclear fuel rods. Such imports are much cheaper and better storable, which increases Tunisian energy security and reduces the capital outflow, but Tunisian energy dependency on other countries would remain high, which may constitute a political obstacle in addition to the described economical ones.

Renewable Power

With the rise of the Desertec vision in the last few years, an increasing number of studies assessing the impacts of large scale CSP deployment in North Africa on the local industry have been published (e.g. Komendantova and Patt, 2010; WB, 2011b). The experiences from ongoing CSP projects in Morocco, Egypt and Algeria give some empirical data, but these experiences do not point in a uniform direction. On the one hand, in Algeria and Morocco, where the participation of local industry has been low, no or very small positive employment effects could be observed. On the other hand, the construction of a CSP power plant in Egypt, with a local manufacturing component of 60 % for the solar fields, improved technical know-how of the local industry and created local employment (WB, 2011b: 11; FEMIP, 2011).

The World Bank (2011b) provides different scenarios for the local manufacturing potential of CSP in the MENA region. World Bank's 'transformation scenario'[5] concludes that with the local manufacturing potential of 5-7 GW of CSP by 2025, 64.000-79.000 new jobs could be created in the MENA countries by 2025. If looking until 2020 only, about 34.000 permanent jobs are expected to be created through the MENA-CTF financing program (WB, 2011b: 4).

Based on the Desertec scenario, Komendantova and Patt (2010: 8) conclude that about 2-3 million job-years could be created until 2050, if 40 % of manufacturing components were produced locally. If all components were

[5] While the 'stagnation' and 'no-replication' scenarios base on rather pessimistic assumptions, the 'transformation' scenario may be too optimistic; assuming a strong development of local industry with 5 GW of CSP by 2020 in MENA-CTF countries and the creation of a 2 GW CSP component export market. For a brief overview about the scenarios' main assumptions, the reader is directed to WB (2011b: 1-2).

manufactured locally in North Africa, the job creation potential of Desertec is up to 6 million induced job-years by 2050. While the potential for directly and indirectly induced jobs and new employment opportunities vary largely, depending on the underlying modelling assumptions, it is clear that the more the local industry is integrated into production processes, the higher the benefits for the North African countries. Thus, due to the decentralised nature of renewable technology deployment, even large-scale renewables, local economic spillovers such as job creation can be expected, although the exact effects depend on the conditions of the projects and the local manufacturing share. In addition, although it is impossible to robustly foresee the precise impacts, the effects of building up new industrial know-how may prove to be an even more important effect for the socio-economic development than the direct job creation.

Considering the current composition of the Tunisia industry, it is clear that a 100% local manufacturing share is unrealistic in the short-term perspective. The main suppliers for solar and wind power equipment are currently located in Europe, the US and China: in the short term, Tunisia would need to buy most of the components for renewable power generation from foreign suppliers. However, if Tunisia opts for the renewables pathway, the domestic industry could be integrated into the supply chain, as some of the necessary industry capabilities are already there and many components are not high-tech. In Tunisia, especially the cable, electrical and electronic industry has been thriving and flourishing over the last years and has achieved a competitive market position (WB, 2011b). Once built up on cheap labour and energy, the Tunisian electronic manufacturing industry and the information-communication technology (ICT) oriented service sector has gained much credit, and throughout the last years the success of these industries was facilitated by joint ventures between local and foreign players (WB 2011b: 107). The Technology Park of Borj Cedria in Tunisia can be taken as an example for technology clusters with focus on renewable energy technologies. The proximity to European markets is clearly an advantage. Chakira cables from Tunisia, to name another example, is already producing cables for PV plants and could adapt production processes to CSP equipment too (WB, 2011b: 119, 182). Whether these effects are achieved or not, it is largely a policy-design issue: if requirement of local industry participation is included in tenders and support schemes for renewables, as is common practice elsewhere, the prospects are good that Tunisia will be able to build up a significant domestic renewable power industry.

Last but not least, due to the large domestic resource potential for renewable electricity, especially from solar but also from wind power, Tunisia can massively decrease its energy import dependence. While gas will play a role in Tunisia's future electricity mix, not least to smooth out fluctuations in electricity supply, the Maghreb country could theoretically completely get rid of imports of natural gas and oil for electricity production in the long term. This would significantly reduce the capital outflow and free domestic capital urgently needed for other infrastructure investments, education and social programmes.

Fulfillment of Seawater Desalination Needs

Nuclear Power

Nuclear power is often regarded as a panacea for fuelling energy intensive seawater desalination projects (Misra, 2007). Cost estimations indicate that nuclear desalination is in the same range as fossil fuelled desalination projects and that nuclear power could provide an economically viable option for Tunisia for solving freshwater scarcity problems (Misra, 2007: 270).

However, nuclear power will not be available soon, due to the long lead times, and the lack of nuclear experience (see previous sections). Hence, nuclear power is not an option to help to alleviate water stress in the short- to medium term (Jewell, 2011). On the other hand, the need for desalination projects will undoubtedly be present also in the longer term, beyond 2020. If nuclear power is available, on commercial terms, and if all the obstacles outlined above are overcome in the more distant future, it may indeed be an option for fuelling desalinisation: for this, the economics of nuclear power is the key determinant.

Renewable Power

Renewable electricity, and in particular CSP, is regarded as an economically viable option for desalination of seawater in a mid- to long-term perspective: studies indicate a cost-reduction potential to € 0.04/kWh and € 0.40/m^3, respectively, over the coming decades (Trieb and Steinhagen, 2008; DLR, 2007). In the short term, CSP-fuelled desalinisation is not economically feasible: it is still much too expensive. In addition to this, the limited experience with different CSP options for desalination is a challenging issue. Also from a technical perspective, one should not expect significant and affordable CSP desalinisation capacity to be available in the MENA region in the next 10-15 years (Trieb and Steinhagen, 2008: 181). Hence, renewable electricity desalinisation faces the same problems as nuclear-powered desalinisation in the short term: it is not feasible before, say, 2025. Until then, desalinisation is likely to continue to be fuelled by fossil energy.

Renewable electricity for desalinisation however shows one important difference compared to the nuclear option. Tunisia is highly unlikely to become a technology leader in nuclear power, but solar power, especially combined with desalinisation, may turn out to be a suitable niche for Tunisian industry. The country will benefit from its status as being a member of MENA-CTF funding initiative that financially supports deployment of CSP power plants in the next years. This opportunity can be seized to gain experience in using CSP for desalination, and aim for becoming a major player on the undoubtedly large future market for desalination technology.

DISCUSSION: TUNISIAN ELECTRICITY FUTURES

Tunisia has developed more or less concrete plans for both nuclear and renewable power as options for its future electricity supply. Both options have benefits, but also face difficulties and obstacles in the way of realisation. These benefits and obstacles, which are of different types and of different magnitudes, are discussed below.

First, attracting funds for the necessary investments is one of the biggest challenges for both options. Especially for nuclear power, but also for renewable power in the medium term, Tunisia will likely need to rely strongly on FDI, as it may not have the financial power to stem these investments itself. Both the former government and also the interim government have been working with both electricity options, but especially for the nuclear plans – which still remain vague already regarding what the plan actually is – the financing seems very difficult: a nuclear project has very high up-front investment costs, high investment risks, and consequentially the international investment community has been more than reluctant to invest in nuclear in the last decades. Given the drawbacks, especially the lack of fit with the existing system (see below) and the uncertainties following the revolution, it seems unlikely that Tunisia will find investors willing to invest in nuclear power on market conditions.

Renewable power has quite different financing prospects. Also for this option, the total up-front investment requirements are high, but it differs in two important aspects. First, the renewables path does not consist of single very large one-shot projects, but of a large number of small projects: this makes each investment smaller, which lowers the risks and makes the investment more attractive. Second, the plans, especially the PST, for renewables are embedded in a wider international context, with financially and politically potent players such as the DII, the EU's Mediterranean plans and the CTF pushing for the deployment of renewable technology in North Africa. Despite the political turmoil throughout North Africa, these plans have been reconfirmed. Exporting renewable electricity to Europe to fund the domestic electricity expansion is an option that is on the table – as seen in the ongoing ELMED project – whereas exporting nuclear power does not appear to be realistic, both due to financing reasons and to acceptability issues in Europe. Thus, the financing climate is much more favourable towards renewables than for nuclear power.

Second, the integration into the Tunisian power system is a major obstacle for both nuclear and renewable power: none of them fit very well with the existing system. However, the obstacles are of different nature. The integration of renewables requires expansion and reinforcement of the power grid, both to facilitate the integration of intermittent sources and to access the often remote production sites for wind power and CSP. Expanding the grid is not a trivial task, and it will add to the already high investment needs. However, the grid must be reinforced anyways to meet the increasing demand: within the next 15 years, the total system size is likely to double in order to cope with rising domestic electricity demand. If the grid integration of renewables and the anyways required grid expansion are coordinated, the grid integration of renewables is still an ambitious project, but the additional costs for renewables can be minimised.

The integration of nuclear power, on the other hand, requires the entire system and the system power demand to increase, which is a completely different issue. The Tunisian power system is currently the smallest in North Africa, and it will remain small for at least the next decade, despite the high expected growth rates. An economically operating nuclear reactor will likely need to be 1000 MW or larger, which corresponds to 40% of the current system size or 20% of the expected size in 2020: providing stand-by back-up power for such a large unit is not economically feasible. The competing nuclear plans in the neighbouring countries, however realistic or unrealistic they may be, make it improbable that Algeria and Libya are willing to buy into a Tunisian nuclear project and completely integrate their systems with Tunisia. Hence, the large size of nuclear power units does not fit the small size of the Tunisian power system: the nuclear option is unlikely to be economically viable due to its system back-up costs, regardless of what the stand-alone levelised generation costs are.

Third, the effects on local industry and economy are also different for the two options. Empirical evidence from around the world, also from North Africa, shows that large-scale renewable technology deployment can stimulate employment, improve competitiveness of the local industry and potentially create a new industry sector. This is due to two factors: first, the decentralised nature of renewables compared to conventional power technologies allows for higher shares of local manufacturing, which is enabled by the second factor, the relative low-tech nature of renewables. Consequentially, job creation and industry policy have also been main drivers for the expansion of renewables in other countries, such as the US, Germany, and Spain. Although Tunisia does not have a significant renewables industry at present, its current industry structure, characterised by small- and medium-sized companies in the manufacturing industry and the information communication technology (ICT)-oriented service sector, is compatible with a roll-out of domestically produced renewable technology: If the policy is right, Tunisia is well equipped to produce the components domestically. This has a number of benefits, among the most important ones are keeping capital within the country and creating jobs in a new, future-oriented industry. This could help to significantly ameliorate the situation in the labour market and reduce unemployment.

On contrast, Nuclear power is unlikely to achieve any of these advantages. It is a highly complex technology: only a few countries in the world have the capacity to build nuclear power stations. Tunisia does not have any nuclear experience, and will need to buy everything from abroad – France seems to be the partner of choice. Thus, none of the job-creation or industry policy advantages that potentially come out of a successful policy for renewables can be expected for the nuclear option. Instead, this option shows some negative effects: Tunisia would, due to its lack of experience, know-how, nuclear infrastructure and fuel, lock itself into further dependence on other countries, an effect with perhaps minor economical, but major political effects.

Fourth and finally, the short- to medium-term desalination needs will neither be addressed by a nuclear nor by a renewable power programme. Nuclear power for desalinisation may be an option in the long term, if the economics are right and the difficulties outlined above are overcome. From today's perspective, it seems highly improbable, but not impossible: History has shown that the decision for nuclear power has not always been an economically and politically rational one. Desalinisation from renewable power is still too expensive, and is therefore not an immediate alternative.

However, renewables-fuelled - especially CSP-fuelled – desalinisation may turn out to be an attractive option for Tunisia, as the market prospects for greenhouse gas emission-free desalinisation are very good: becoming a market leader in this field holds much promise for both job-creation and economic growth in Tunisia.

Conclusion

Despite the many challenges that remain, the comparison between the nuclear and the renewables options has shown that the renewables path is the less complicated and more promising track for Tunisia. The obstacles for nuclear power are very large and difficult to solve, and the benefits are few. The obstacles for renewables are also large, but they can be overcome with a dedicated policy effort, and the potential benefits are large. Importantly, the renewable path is not only more realistic, as it has a better fit to the existing power system and is much more attractive for investors, a targeted policy effort in this direction also offers the potential for Tunisia to build up a new, sustainable and future-oriented industry. This could help to reduce the unemployment, which is probably the most pressing problem in Tunisia today. Hence, the realisation of a renewable electricity development is more probable and more beneficial for Tunisia than a nuclear path.

References

AFESD (2011). Electricity. *Arab Fund for Economic and Social Development* (AFESD), Kuwait. http://www.arabfund.org/default.aspx?pageId=454, (Retrieved: 2011/07/27).

AM (2009). Tunisie : Le Plan Solaire Tunisien : ambitions et mécanismes. African Manager (AM). http://www.africanmanager.com/articles 125657.html#, (Retrieved: 2011/08/24).

AM (2011). Tunisia: *No nuclear power project* in Kélibia. AfricanManager (AM). http://www.africanmanager.com/site_eng/articles/16497.html, (Retrieved: 2011/08/24).

ANME (2004). Energy conservation studies: Strategic study on the development of renewable energies in Tunisia, 2004. *National Agency for*

Energy Conservation (ANME), Tunis. http://www.anme.nat.tn/index.asp?pId=148, (Retrieved: 2011/08/24).

ANME (2005). Etude stratégique sur le développement de l'utilisation rationnelle de l'énergie en Tunisie, 2005. *National Agency for Energy Conservation* (ANME), Tunis. http://www.anme.nat.tn/index.asp?pId=51, (Retrieved: 2011/08/24).

Battaglini, A., and Lilliestam, J. (2010). *On transmission grid governance.* Heinrich Böll Foundation, Berlin.

Battaglini, A., Lilliestam, J., and Knies, G. (2010). The SuperSmart Grid - paving the way for a completely renewable power system. In: H. J. Schellnhuber, M. Molina, N. Stern, V. Huber, and S. Kadner (Eds.), *Global sustainability* - A nobel cause (pp. 290-305). Cambridge: Cambridge University Press.

Battaglini, A., Lilliestam, J., Haas, A., and Patt, A. (2009). Development of SuperSmart Grids for a more efficient utilisation of electricity from renewable sources. *Journal of cleaner production,* Volume 17, 911-918.

Belloumi, M. (2009). Energy consumption and GDP in Tunisia: Cointegration and causality analysis. *Energy Policy,* Volume 37, 2745–2753.

BP (2011). *Statistical review of world energy.* British Petroleum (BP), London.

Brand, B., and Zingerle, J. (2011). The renewable energy targets of the Maghreb countries: Impact on electricity supply and conventional power markets. *Energy Policy,* Volume 39 (Issue 8), 4411–4419.

CIGI (2011). Survey of Emerging Nuclear Energy States (SENES): Tunisia. *Centre for International Governance Innovation* (CIGI). http://www.cigionline.org/senes/tunisia, (Retrieved: 2011/08/24).

D&WR (2010). Three desalination plants for south Tunisia in 2011. *Desalination and Water Reuse* (D&WR). http://www.desalination.biz/news/news_story.asp?src=nlandid=5476, (Retrieved: 2011/08/22).

DII (2011). Desertec: Industry Initiative Dii is stepping up its activities in Tunisia. *Desertec Industry Initiative* (DII). http://www.dii-eumena.com/home/news-single/article/216.html, (Retrieved: 2011/08/22).

DLR (2005). Concentrating Solar Power for the Mediterranean Region. German Aerospace Center (DLR), Institute of Technical Thermodynamics, *Section Systems Analysis and Technology Assessment*, Stuttgart.

DLR (2007). Aqua-CSP: Concentrating Solar Power for Seawater Desalination. German Aerospace Center (DLR), *Institute of Technical*

Thermodynamics, Section Systems Analysis and Technology Assessment, Stuttgart.

EconStats (2010). Tunisia. EconStats, New York. http://www.econstats.com/weo/CTUN.htm, (Retrieved: 2011/07/26).

EIA (2010). Country analysis brief: Tunisia. U.S. *Energy information administration* (EIA), Washington D.C. http://www.eia.gov/countries/country-data.cfm?fips=TS#undefined, (Retrieved: 2011/07/26).

ENTSO-E (2010). ENTSO-E interconnection test with the LEJS synchronous area conducted. *European Network of Transmission System Operators for Electricity* (ENTSO-E), Brussels. https://www.entsoe.eu/index.php?id=42andtx_ttnews[tt_news]=63andtx_ttnews[backPid]=28andcHash=6d6e9a69512a3c4c0f9250224047f84a, (Retrieved: 2011/07/27).

ENTSO-E (2011). NTC matrix. European *Network of Transmission System Operators for Electricity* (ENTSO-E), Brussels. https://www.entsoe.eu/resources/ntc-values/ntc-matrix/, (Retrieved: 2011/07/27).

Eurostat (2010). Energy and transport in figures. *Statistical pocketbook* 2010. Eurostat. European Commission, Brussels.

FEMIP (2010). Study on the Financing of Renewable Energy Investment in the Southern and Eastern Mediterranean Region. Summary Report October-2010. Facility for Euro-Mediterranean Investment and Partnership (FEMIP). *European Investment Bank,* Hamburg.

GAN (2009). Tunisia integrates electricity network between Europe and North Africa. *Global Arab Network* (GAN). http://www.english.globalarabnetwork.com/200910113107/Energy/tunisia-integrates-electricity-network-between-europe-and-north-africa.html, (Retrieved: 2011/08/22).

Global Finance (2011). Tunisia country report. Global Finance, New York. http://www.gfmag.com/gdp-data-country-reports/158-tunisia-gdp-country-report.html#axzz1TDlvZW8s, (Retrieved d: 2011/07/26).

Gnad, O., and Viëtor, M. (2011). Desert Powered Progress: Desertec can integrate the EU with North Africa and the Middle East on many different Levels. http://www.europeanenergyreview.eu/site/pagina.php?id=3095, (Retrieved: 2011/08/14).

IAEA (2007). Considerations to launch a nuclear power programme. *International Atomic Energy Agency* (IAEA), Vienna.

IAEA (2009). Nuclear Technology Review. *International Atomic Energy Agency* (IAEA), Vienna.

IEA (2011). Statistics by country/region. *International Energy Agency* (IEA), Paris. http://iea.org/Textbase/stats/index.asp, (Retrieved: 2011/07/26).

INS (2011). Statistical Information. *National Institute of Statisitcs,* Tunisia. http://www.ins.nat.tn/indexen.php, (Retrieved: 2011/08/22).

Jewell, J. (2011). A nuclear-powered North Africa: Just a desert mirage or is there something on the horizon?. *Energy Policy*, Volume 39 (Issue 8), 4445-4457.

Komendantova, N., and Patt, A. (2010). Employment creation under vertical and horizontal transfer of concentrated solar power technology to North African countries. *Energy Policy* (Submitted December 2010, in review).

Komendantova, N., Patt, A., Barras, L., and Battaglini, A. (2009).Perception of risks in renewable energy projects: the case of concentrated solar power in North Africa. *Energy Policy*, DOI:10.1016/j.enpol.2009.12.008 (online first).

KUNA (2011). Tunisia still keen on nuclear-generated power station. *Kuwait News Agency* (KUNA). http://www.kuna.net.kw/NewsAgencies PublicSite/ArticleDetails.aspx?id=2179858andLanguage=en, (Retrieved: 2011/08/22).

MAGHREB (2010a). ELMED to export green energy to North of Mediterranean. *Maghreb News and Press Reviews.* http://news.marweb.com/economics/elmed-to-export-green-energy-to-north-of-mediterranean.html, (Retrieved: 2011/08/20).

MAGHREB (2010b). Tunisia Solar Plan: Public-Private Partnership for the promotion of renewable energies. *Maghreb News and Press Reviews.* http://news.marweb.com/tunisia/economics/business/tunisia-solar-plan-public-private-partnership-for-the-promot.html, (Retrieved: 2011/08/22).

Marktanner, M., and Salman, L. (2011). Economic and geopolitical dimensions of renewable vs. nuclear energy in North Africa. *Energy Policy*, Volume 39 (Issue 8), 4479–4489.

MED-EMIP (2010). Medring update. Volume I. Overview of the power systems of the Mediterranean basin. Euro-Mediterranean *Energy Market Integration* Project (MED-EMIP), Brussels.

Misra, B. M. (2007). Seawater desalination using nuclear heat/electricity: *Prospects and challenges. Desalination*, Volume 205, 269-278.

Mougou, R., Mansour, M., Iglesias, A., Chebbi, R. Z., Battaglini, A. (2011). Climate change and agricultural vulnerability: a case study of rain-fed wheat in Kairouan, Central Tunisia. *Reg Environ Change*, Volume 11 (1), 137–142.

OECD, and UN (2011). Economic Diversification in Africa: A Review of Selected Countries. *Organization for Economic Co-operation and Development* (OECD) *and United Nations* (UN), Paris: OECD Publishing.

Red Eléctrica (2010). Synchronous or asynchronous? *Status of the ongoing projects. The Tunisia-Libya interconncection.* Red Eléctrica de España, Madrid. http://www.rcreee.info/archive02/med-emip/Mediterranean%20Region%20Pages/MR_Documents/201002%20Brussels-experts_group_meeting/2010_02_08_experts_group_meeting_presentations/Presentation%20Red%20El%C3%A9ctrica%20de%20Espa%C3%B1a.pdf, (Retrieved: 2011/07/27).

Reuters (2009). France seals nuclear, aid deals with Tunisia. http://uk.reuters.com/article/2009/04/23/idUKLN941296, (Retrieved: 2011/08/24).

Schellekens, G., Battaglini, A., Finlay, C., Fürstenwerth, D., Lilliestam, J., Patt, A., and Schmidt, P. (2011). Measuring progress towards 100% renewable electricity in Europe and North Africa. *PriceWaterhouseCoopers* (PWC), London.

Schellekens, G., Battaglini, A., Lilliestam, J., McDonnell, J., and Patt, A. (2010). 100% renewable electricity - A roadmap to 2050 for Europe and North Africa. *PriceWaterhouseCoopers* (PWC), London.

Supersberger, N., and Führer, L. (2011). Integration of renewable energies and nuclear power into North African Energy Systems: Analysis of energy import and export effects. *Energy Policy,* Volume 39 (Issue 8), 4458–4465.

TERNA (2010). *Elmed Project for Tunisia.* http://www.terna.it/default/home_en/the_company/about_terna/terna_group_abroad/growth_abroad/elmed_project.aspx, (Retrieved: 2011/08/20).

Trieb, F., and Müller-Steinhagen, H. (2008). Concentrating solar power for seawater desalination in the Middle East and North Africa. *Desalination,* Volume 220, 165–183.

UNDP (2010). Human development report 2010: *The real wealth of nations. United Nations Development Programme* (UNDP), New York.

UNEA (2010). Energy for Sustainable Development: *Policy Options for Africa.* United Nations-Energy/Africa (UNEA). http://www.uneca.org/eca_resources/publications/unea-publication-tocsd15.pdf, (Retrieved: 2011/08/23).

UNEP (2011). Success Stories: Solar energy in Tunisia. *United Nations Environment Programme (UNEP).* http://www.unep.org/greeneconomy/SuccessStories/SolarenergyinTunisia/tabid/29871/Default.aspx, (Retrieved: 2011/08/23).

Verdier-Chouchane, A., Obayashi, N., and Castel, V. (2011). The Revolution in Tunisia: *Economic Challenges and Prospects,* Economic Brief, African Development Bank (AfDB), Tunis.

WB (2011a). *World Bank Indicators.* http://data.worldbank.org/indicator, (Accessed: 2011/08/22).

WB (2011b). Middle East and North Africa Region Assessment of the Local Manufacturing Potential for Concentrated Solar Power (CSP) Projects. *World Bank (WB)*, Washington.

WKO.at (2011). Tunesien und Frankreich kooperieren im Bereich Erneuerbare Energien. Wirtschaftskammer Österreich (WKO.at). http://portal.wko.at/wk/format_detail.wk?angid=1andstid=606576anddstid=0andtitel=Tunesien%2Cund%2CFrankreich%2Ckooperieren%2Cim%2CBereich%2CErneuerbare%2CEnergie, (Retrieved: 2011/08/23).

WNA (2011). *Emerging Nuclear Energy Countries.* World Nuclear Association (WNA), London. http://world-nuclear.org/info/inf102.html, (Retrieved: 2011/08/19).

ZO (2011). Wüstenstrom: "Kein Rückschlag". Zeit Online (ZO). http://www.zeit.de/2011/13/Wuestenstromprojekt-Desertec, (Retrieved: 2011/08/14).

In: Tunisia: Economic, Political and Social Issues ISBN: 978-1-61942-157-8
Eds: M. Pusatieri and J. Cannamela

Chapter 3

VALORIZATION OF TUNISIAN OLIVES AND JAPANESE CONSUMER PREFERENCE FOR OLIVE OIL

Kenichi Kashiwagi*[*1,2], Junkyu Han[1,3] and Hiroko Isoda[1,3]

[1]The Alliance for Research on North Africa, University of Tsukuba, Japan
[2]Graduate School of Humanities and Social Sciences, University of Tsukuba, Japan
[3]Graduate School of Life and Environmental Sciences, University of Tsukuba, Japan

ABSTRACT

In the face of growing international competitiveness, one of the main challenges for the olive oil sector in traditional olive oil-producing countries such as Tunisia is to open up in non-traditional, emerging markets such as Japan. Many medical and medicinal effects of Tunisian olive oil components on health such as anti-oxidant, anti-aging, anti-allergy and anti-metabolic syndrome have been detected by the multifaced bioassay technique. This chapter investigates olive oil consumption behavior of Japanese consumers and examined their preferences using a sample of 532 consumers living in Tokyo. Six

[*] Address: 1-1-1 Tennodai, Tsukuba, Ibaraki, 305-8572, Japan. Tel: +81-29-853-3982 Fax: +81-29-853-5776, E-mail: kashiwagi.kenichi.fn@u.tsukuba.ac.jp

attributes were chosen in the design of the experiment: country of origin, price, olive oil type, taste, color and component. To reflect the components of Tunisian olive oil, a health attribute represented by a high concentration of polyphenol was explicitly included in the product design. By applying the conjoint technique, a rank-ordered logit (ROL) model and a cross effect model were estimated. Results suggested that Japanese consumers prefer extra virgin and virgin olive oil and sweet taste. While the country of origin when indicated as Tunisia has a negative effect, the preference for olive oil increases if the oil contains a high concentration of polyphenol. As a net effect, the WTP (Willingness to Pay) increased at 202.2 yen for the Tunisian product with a high concentration of polyphenol. Female, elder consumers with a higher educational status and those who frequently use olive oil prefer purchasing olive oil with a high concentration of polyphenol. This chapter verifies the significance of emphasising a health attribute to valorize and increase the export of Tunisian olive oil products to the Japanese market, even though products from Italy and Spain still dominate the market.

Keywords: olive oil; multifaced bioassay; polyphenol, consumer preference; Tunisia; Japan

1. Introduction

Reflecting an increase in the demand for better health and nutrition, olive oil consumption in Japan showed an increasing trend during the last two decades. According to official statistics, Japan has an annual consumption of olive oil of around 30,000 tons. The volume of olive oil imported in Japan gradually increased during the first half of the 1990s and escalated after the mid-1990s (Japan Tariff Association, 1985, 2007). On the other hand, olive oil constitutes an important part of Tunisian export, and accounted for 169,100 tons in 2008 representing 59.8% of total agricultural exports (Institut National de la Statistique, 2008). While Tunisia occupies the fourth position as an olive oil exporter, preceded by Spain, Italy and Greece, the share of Tunisian olive oil in Japanese imports was less than 1% (Japan Tariff Association, 2007). The country of origin of Japan's import diversified during the 1990s; however, 99% of olive oil imports still come from Italy and Spain (Japan Tariff Association, 1985, 2007). Therefore, the main challenge for the olive oil sector in Tunisia is to expand export destinations towards non-traditional emerging markets such as Japan. Improvement in the product quality by valorizing olive oil and the development of bottled exports with a country of origin label (made and bottled in Tunisia) is an important strategy to achieve competitive superiority.[1]

What attributes of olive oil are attractive when developing a competitive product? Traditionally, olives and olive oil seeds grown in the Mediterranean region are known for their high quality and long shelf life. Several studies in biosciences found that olive seeds and olive leaf extracts contain a high concentration of polyphenol, and these studies detected their anti-cancer, anti-oxidant and anti-inflammatory effects (Martin-Moreno et al., 1994; Gerber, 1994; Visioli et al., 1998; De la Puerta et al., 2000; Miles et al., 2005).

As for the Tunisian olive oil, Abaza et al. (2005), Yamada et al. (2008) and Yamada, Han and Isoda (2009) detected many medically effective biological activities, such as anti-allergy, anti-oxidant, anti-cancer and anti-leukaemia properties, in the components of olive oil and the olive leaves. By detecting such useful health properties, Tunisian olive oil may gain the potential to increase its value as being applied to functional foods, cosmetics and for medicinal use to increase exports to a new and emerging market such as Japan.

In fact, a shift in the Japanese consumer preferences from non-virgin to higher quality virgin olive oil was observed during the 2000s (Mtimet et al., 2011). The above-mentioned evidence provided the rationale to include a health attribute in the product design.

Despite the increasing importance of Japan as an export destination, most literature focused on the analysis of consumption and consumer behavior in European consumer markets. While the effects of olive oil on health, diet and better nutrition were frequently emphasized, the health attribute on consumer preference was not examined explicitly. Mili and Rodriguez (2001) assessed the development of international olive oil markets over the next decade; however, they mainly focused on a forecast of the main trends affecting the Spanish olive oil export business.

In a study of non-traditional markets, García, Aragonés and Poole (2002) examined consumer behavior of UK consumers using conjoint analysis. Ronald et al. (2003) explored German consumers' attitudes towards the country of origin as an attribute of olive oil. For Albanian consumers, Chan-Halbrendt (2010) examined their preference for olive oil, reflected through an

---

[1] Most of the olive oil is exported not by bottle but by bulk. The Tunisian government sought to increase bottled olive oil exports up to 10% of total export under the national industrial upgrading program (programme de mise à niveau), however this goal has not been achieved and still only 2% to 3% are actually exported in bottles. See Kashiwagi et al. (2010).

increase in demand and supply in the domestic market. Krystallis and Ness (2003) developed a consumer cognitive map including links between the quality attributes of olive oil, use benefits and consumer values for consumers in Greece; however, they failed to explicitly examine the effects of a health attribute.

In a pioneering study, Mtimet et al. (2009) and Mtimet et al. (2011) investigated consumer behavior using a conjoint analysis and choice experiment approach on the Japanese consumption of olive oil; however, a health attribute of olive oil was not introduced in the product design.

This chapter examined Japanese consumer behavior related to olive oil by using the conjoint technique on a primary data set collected from a survey conducted in March 2011. Based on the evidence provided by Abaza et al. (2005) and Yamada et al. (2008), a health attribute of olive oil, represented by the concentration of polyphenol, was explicitly introduced in the product design.

The objective was to investigate the Japanese consumer behavior related to olive oil, including normal attributes (type, country of origin, taste, color and price) as well as a specific attribute (concentrations of polyphenol) in particular.

This study assumes that a health attribute of olive oil, represented by the concentrations of polyphenol, has a positive impact on increasing Japanese consumer preference, although the impact of the country of origin as Tunisia was not necessarily positive. Therefore, it is possible to assume that Tunisian olive oil has the potential to increase its share of imports to the Japanese market by emphasizing the health attributes.

Although products from Italy and Spain still dominate the Japanese olive oil market, investigating the effect of a health attribute on consumer preference may shed light on valorizing and increasing the exports of Tunisian products to the Japanese market. Facing international competition as a result of the ratification of the free trade agreement with the EU (Euro-Mediterranean Partnership Program), it is particularly important to differentiate Tunisian olive oil from that of Italy and Spain by introducing an attribute of health in the product design.

This chapter is structured as follows. Section 2 reviews physiological functionalities of Tunisian olives by applying the multifaced bioassay technique. The model used in this study and data collection are presented in Section 3. Section 4 discusses the empirical results. The conclusion is summarized in Section 5.

2. Multifaced Bioassay and Functionality of Tunisian Olives

2.1. Physiological Functions of Tunisian Olives

The Mediterranean diet has become widely associated with improved health and well-being as well as protection against cardiovascular diseases and colon, breast and skin cancers. This diet is not only synonymous with increased consumption of fruits and vegetables but also with a high intake of olive oil and olive products. The beneficial effect is attributed to a favorable fatty acid profile and to the presence of polyphenols that are also responsible for the unique flavor and taste of olive oil (Visioli and Galli, 1995).

Also, olive oil is used traditionally in the Mediterranean for skin care ointments and soap manufacturing. The oldest cosmetics were found in the tombs in Egypt. For centuries Egyptian women used ointments produced from olive oil and other plant oils mixed to protect their skin from aging and dehydration caused by the sun. There are mentions in Greek texts about the protective effect of olive oil, a commonly used skin conditioner at the time, and few scientific studies support this. Olive oil is a good emollient and has anti-inflammatory properties and has been known used for treating burns, bruises, insect bites, itch and sensitive skin (Price et al., 1999).

Olive oil contains compounds with potent antimicrobial activities against bacteria, fungi, and mycoplasma. In addition, olive oil has antioxidant and anti-inflammatory activities. It was demonstrated that newly pressed extra-virgin olive oil contains oleocanthal, which is similar pharmacological activity to the non-steroidal anti-inflammatory drug ibuprofen. Although structurally dissimilar, both these molecules inhibit the same cyclooxygenase enzymes in the prostaglandin biosynthesis pathway (Gary et al., 2005). *In vivo* and *in vitro* studies suggest that phenolic compounds in virgin olive oil are effective antioxidants.

In vivo and *in vitro* studies, hydroxytyrosol and oleuropein have been shown to be strong antioxidants (Visioli et al., 1998, 2000). Considerable data on the polyphenols of olive oil, such as flavonoids, have been reported, but few studies have been published on the antioxidant effects of olive oil. The multifaced bioassays were employed to investigate the physiological functions on olive oil and olive leaves, since they are powerful tools for evaluation of functional assessment on foods and plants etc.

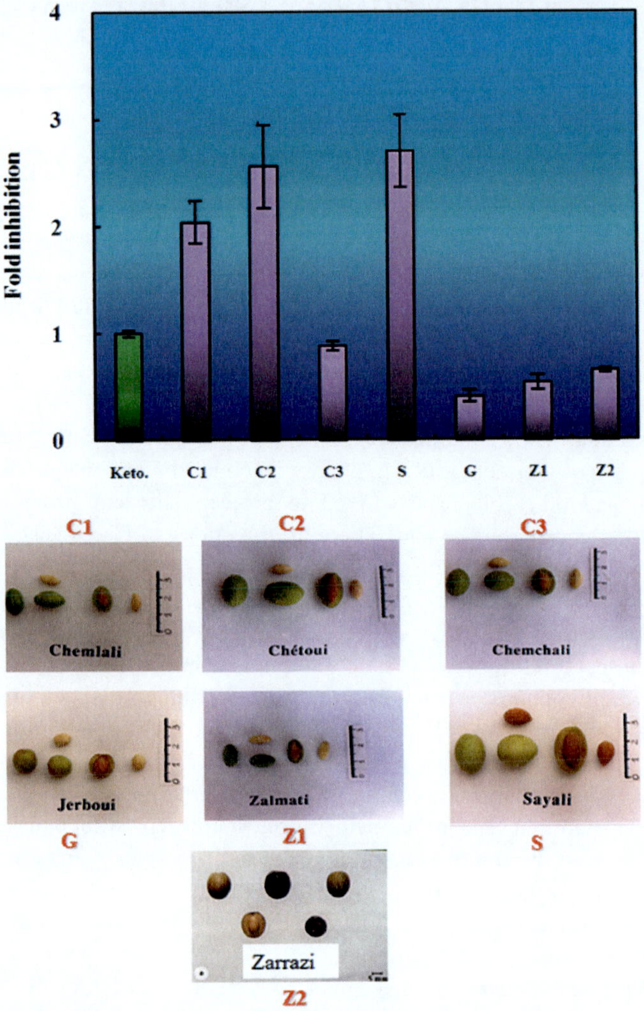

Note: C1: Chemchali, C2: Chemlali, C3:Chetoui, S: Sayali, G: Gerboui, Z1: Zalmati, Z2: Zarrazi.

Figure 1. Effect of various Tunisian olive oil on the b-hexosaminidase release at the antigen- antibody binding stage.

By applying the multifaced bioassays, it was shown that the Tunisian olive oil (*Chemchali*, *Chemlali*, *Chetoui*, *Gerboui*, *Sayali*, *Zelmati* and *Zarrazi*) can inhibit the b-hexosaminidase release from IgE-stimulated RBL-2H3 cells (rat basophilic leukemia) at the antigen–antibody binding stage. Tunisian olive oil can also inhibit the TNF-α and IL-4 production by A23187 plus PMA-stimulated KU812 cells, human basophilic cells (Figure 1). Also, it has provided evidence that virgin olive oil may be beneficial for the treatment or prevention of various types of allergies. Therefore, it is considered that the consumption of olive oil provides protection against allergic diseases.

2.2. Polyphenols in Olives and their Physiological Functionality

The phenolic compounds of olive oil and leaf are a complex mixture of compounds that include 3,4-dihydroxyphenylethanol (hydroxytyrosol), 4-hydroxyphenylethanol (tyrosol), 4-hydroxyphenylacetic acid, protocatechuic acid, caffeic acid and p-coumaric acid, among others (Litridou et al., 1997, Caponio et al., 1999).

The concentration of the phenolic fraction is several times higher in olive leaf than in oil and varies depending on the cultivar and climate (Table 1 and Table 2; Servili et al., 1999; Ryan et al., 2002; Abaza et al., 2005). *In vivo* and *in vitro* studies suggest that these bioactive compounds exhibit powerful antioxidant activity (Visioli et al., 2000; Le Tutour and Guedon, 1992).

One of various phenolic compounds hydroxytyrosol seems to be among the most important ones. It is present in free form and as a constituent of complex molecules such as oleuropein in leaves and fruits. Both hydroxytyrosol and oleuropein have been shown to possess anti-inflammatory, bactericidal and bacteriostatic activities (Yang et al., 2007).

Some in vivo studies on olive leaf have shown that its extract can decrease blood pressure and dilate the coronary arteries surrounding the heart (Tuck and Hayball, 2002).

Moreover, hydroxytyrosol has been shown to have anti-cancer effect on human colon adenocarcinoma HT-29 cells and human promyelocytic leukemia HL-60 cells (Fabiani et al., 2002, 2006), have anti-melanogenesis activity, whereas oleuropein inhibited cell growth of LN-18, poorly differentiated glioblastoma; TF-1a, erythroleukemia; 786-O, renal cell adenocarcinoma; T-47D, infiltrating ductal carcinoma of the breastpleural effusion; RPMI-7951, malignant melanoma of the skin-lymph node metastasis; and LoVo, colorectal adenocarcinoma cells (Hamdi and Hamdi, 2005).

Table 1. The concentrations of major phenolic compounds in extra-virgin olive oil

Phenolic compound	Concentration (mg/kg)
Hydroxytyrosol	14.42 ± 3.01
Oleuropein	2.04 ± 0.78
Oleuropein agycone	14.42 ± 3.01
Tyrosol	27.45 ± 4.05
Apigenin	15.80 ± 4.51

Data expressed in mg/kg SEM

Sources: Servili et al. (1999), Ryan et al. (2002), Abaza et al (2005).

Table 2. The concentrations of major phenolic compounds in olive leaf.

Phenolic compound	Concentration (mg/kg)
Hydroxytyrosol	219 ± 3
Oleuropein	2,231 ± 52
Demethyloleuropein	984 ± 47
Verbascoside	27.45 ± 4.05
Rutin	15.80 ± 4.51
Luteolin 7-o-glucoside	15.80 ± 4.51

Data expressed in mg/kg SEM

Sources: Servili et al. (1999), Ryan et al. (2002), Abaza et al. (2005).

Even though anticancer properties of oleuropein and hydroxytyrosol were confirmed in vitro with different cell lines, studies of their protective effect from breast cancer have not been demonstrated.

Oleuropein or hydroxytyrosol decrease of the number of MCF-7 cells, human breast cancer cells, by inhibiting the rate of cell proliferation and inducing cell apoptosis. Also hydroxytyrosol and oleuropein exhibited statistically significant block of G1 to S phase transition manifested by the increase of cell number in G0/G1 phase (Figure 2) (Han et al., 2009).

Furthermore, apigenin was investigated as a possible cell differentiation inducer and chronic leukemia cells K562 for their pluripotent differentiating potency (Figure 3) (Tsolmon et al., 2011).

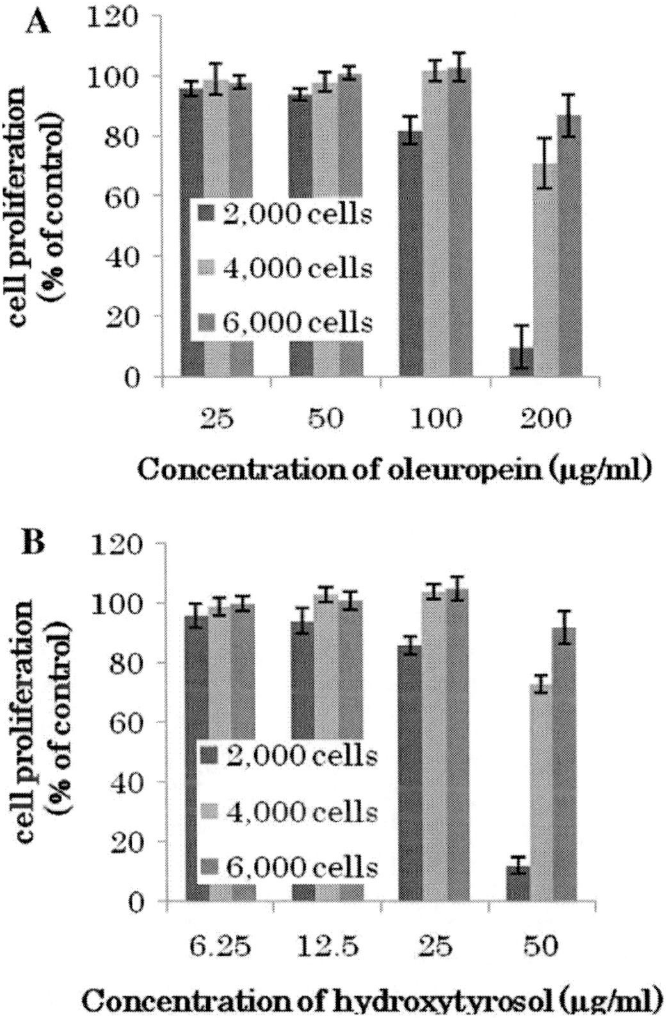

Notes: Influence of initial cell number on the concentration-dependent decrease in viability of human breast cancer MCF-7 cells incubated with oleuropein a and hydroxytyrosol b. Cell viability was determined with the MTT assay. Results (±SD) represent the average of three independent experiments.

Figure 2. Inhibition of MCF-7 cell proliferation.

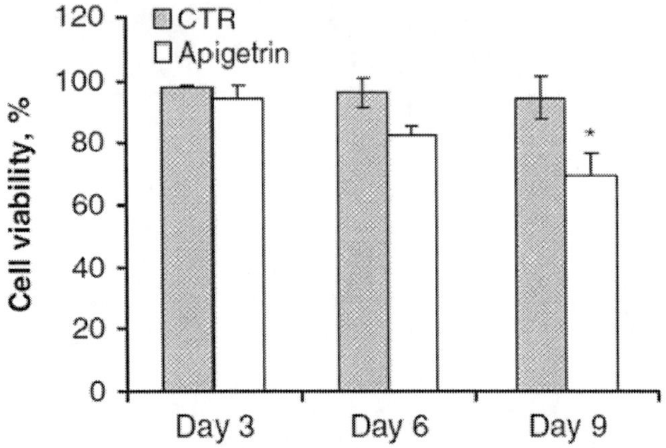

Note: Cell viability was similar to control cells after 3 days with 75 mM apigetrin treatment but subsequent treatments with apigetrin induced reduction in viability of treated cells. Data of three independent experiments are presented.

Figure 3. Cell viability of K562 cells after apigetrin treatment.

2.3. Relationship between Physiological Function and Bitterness in Tunisia Olive Oils

Polyphenols are a structural class of natural, synthetic, and semisynthetic organic chemicals characterized by the presence of large multiples of phenol units (a benzene ring bearing one or more hydroxy group). The number and characteristics of these phenol substructures underlie the unique physical, chemical, and biological (metabolic, toxic, therapeutic, etc.) properties of particular members of the class (Mateos et al., 2004). In the case of virgin olive oils, “polyphenol” mostly refers to hydrolysis products of oleuropein and ligstroside aglycons and related compounds. These compounds are responsible for the oxidative stability of virgin olive oils and are associated with health benefits. Polyphenols also contribute to the organoleptic properties of virgin olive oils and are commonly described as bitter and astringent. Polyphenols have very similar chemical structures, and there is a correlation between the total polyphenol concentration in olive oils and olive oil bitterness (Paul et al., 2003).

Oleuropein, the main component that produces bitterness in olives, is a heterosidic ester of elenolic acid and 3,4-dihydroxyphenylethanol (Panizzi et al., 1960). As the fruit ripens, oleuropein progressively decreases (Amiot et al.,

1986a, 1986b, 1990) and phenolic compounds, such as demethyloleuropein and 3,4-dihydroxyphenylethanol accumulate (Brenes et al., 1995), as does the nonphenolic compound elenolic acid glucoside, which only corresponds to the secoiridoid part of oleuropein (Amiot et al., 1989).

Oleuropein has several pharmacological properties including antioxidant, anti-inflammatory, anti-atherogenic, anti-cancer, antimicrobial, and antiviral, and for these reasons, it is commercially available as food supplement in Mediterranean countries (Impellizzeri et al., 2011). Thus, oleuropein scavenges superoxide anions, hydroxyl radicals and inhibits the respiratory burst of neutrophils and hypochlorous acid derived radicals (Edgecombe et al., 2000). In addition to their antioxidant properties, polyphenolic compounds have been shown to exhibit a range of indirect actions that may be beneficial to health, including the inhibition of enzymes involved in the inflammatory process, the inhibition of platelet aggregation and inhibition of the metabolic activation of procarcinogens.

Table 3. Sensory qualities, taste thresholds, and tentative identifications of components isolated from extra virgin olive oils

main component (tentative identification[a])	sensory qualities
hydroxytyrosol [a]	[a]
tyrosol	sticking astringency, not bitter
deacetoxy-oleuropein aglycon (dialdehydic form)	astringent, bitter, burning/stinging/numbing mostly on tongue (not nearly as strong as that experienced with peak 9)
derivative of oleuropein aglycon	bitter, sour, astringent, sweet, cooling, peppery (tingling tongue)
not identified	bitter, astringent (dry teeth)
derivative of oleuropein aglycon	bitter, astringent, bit burning
deacetoxy-ligstroside aglycon (dialdehydic form)	strong burning mostly at the back of throat, slightly bitter, astringent
isomer of ligstroside aglycon	astringent, bit burning, bitter
isomer of ligstroside aglycon	dry mouth, not bitter
derivative of oleuropein aglycon	bitter, astringent, salt
isomer of oleuropein aglycon	very bitter, very astringent
hydrophobic polyphenols (fractions 70–90)	strong bitter, astringent
very hydrophobic polyphenols (fractions 90–120)	astringent, bitter, bit sour, bit burning, salt

Note: [a]Although synthetic hydroxytyrosol was available, it was not evaluated by the panel because the sample was not of sufficient purity to be safely evaluated.
Source: Paul et al. (2003).

Reflecting above discussed functionalities, the following sections develop a model for the analysis of consumption behavior and make an empirical study using the conjoint technique, explicitly introducing a health attribute of olive oil in the product design.

3. MODEL AND DATA COLLECTION

3.1. Model

The conceptual foundation of conjoint analysis arises from the theory of Lancaster (1966, 1971), which stipulates that utility is derived from the properties or characteristics that goods possess (bundle of attributes) rather than the good per se. The conjoint analysis technique was first developed during the 1970s (Green and Rao, 1971; Green and Srinivasan,1978) and has grown in popularity. Throughout the years, the use of conjoint analysis has been extended to many disciplines such as transportation, telecommunication, environment, marketing and human health. Regarding agro-food products, various studies have used conjoint analysis to explore consumer behavior (Souza and Lucas, 2001; Orth and Krska, 2002; Luckow et al., 2005), Nelson et al., 2005; Feliciano and Albisu, 2006; and Haddad et al., 2007). For olive oil, van der Lans et al. (2001), García, Aragonés and Poole (2002) and Krystallis and Ness (2003) examined consumer behavior in Italy, the UK and Greece, respectively.

Taking into account the nature of the responses (rank ordered) and the discrete character of the dependent variable (which may take the values 1, 2, 3, 4, 5, 6, 7, 8), a rank-ordered logit (ROL) model was selected for data estimation. Random Utility Theory states that the overall utility, $U_{ij,}$ can be expressed as the sum of a systematic (deterministic) component V_{ij}, which is expressed as a function of the attributes presented (olive oil characteristics in our study) and a random (stochastic) component ε_{ij}. Individual i chooses alternative j rather than alternative k if $U_{ij} > U_{ik}$. In probabilistic terms, the equation is given as follows:

$$P_{ij} = \Pr(V_{ij} + \varepsilon_{ij} \geq V_{ik} + \varepsilon_{ik} ; \forall j \neq k \in C_i) , \qquad (1)$$

where C_i is the choice set for respondent i. In our study, the choice set is constant and includes four alternatives. Equation (1) indicates that consumers will choose an option from among a number of choices, in an attempt to achieve maximum utility.

Different discrete choice models are obtained from different specifications of the density function of the error term, which corresponds to different assumptions about the distribution of the unobserved portion of utility. In this research, we assume that the random components are identically and independently distributed type-I extreme values across j alternatives and N individuals, leading to the following multinomial logit (MNL) model (McFadden, 1973):

$$\Pr(j) = \frac{e^{V_{ij}}}{\sum_{k \in C_n} e^{V_{ik}}} \tag{2}$$

In this study, we consider the linear additive form of the utility function V_{ij} for the main effects model:

$$V_{ij} = \beta_0 + \beta_1 x_{ij1} + \beta_2 x_{ij2} + \ldots + \beta_n x_{ijn}, \tag{3}$$

where x_{ijn} is the nth attribute value for alternative j for consumer i, β_n represents the coefficients to be estimated and β_0 represents the intercept or overall mean.

We obtained complete rankings of alternatives for each respondent. We denote the response of respondent i by the vector $r_i = r_{i1},\ldots,r_{iJ}$, where r_{ij} denotes the alternative number that received rank j by a respondent i. Under the above assumptions on utilities, the probability of observing ranking r_i is given by:

$$\Pr(r_i) = \Pr(U_{ir_{i1}} > U_{ir_{i2}} > \ldots > U_{ir_{iJ}}) = \prod_{j=1}^{J-1} \frac{e^{Vir_{ij}}}{\sum_{k=j}^{J} e^{Vir}} \quad . \tag{4}$$

The likelihood function to be estimated is the product of $\Pr(r_i)$ for all respondents. The above expression is known as the ROL model (Chapman and Staelin, 1982). The ROL model can be seen as a series of MNL models: an MNL for the most preferred item, another MNL for the second-ranked item to be preferred over all items except the one with rank 1 and so forth.

The estimate of consumers' Marginal Willingness To Pay (MWTP) for a change in one of the choice attributes (A) from one level (t) to another (s), ceteris paribus, that is, holding all other parameters constant except the attribute for which the MWTP is being calculated, is given by the following equation:

$$\beta_{As} + \beta_p p_s = \beta_{At} + \beta_p p_t \text{, with } p_s = p_t + MWTP \quad , \tag{5}$$

where β_{AS} and β_{At} are respectively the coefficient estimates of levels i and j of attribute A; β_P is the coefficient estimate of the linear price component; and p_t and p_S are respectively the prices corresponding to levels t and s. Equation (5) leads to:

$$MWTP = \frac{\beta_{Ai} - \beta_{Aj}}{\beta_p} \quad , \tag{6}$$

where MWTP is the amount of money consumers are willing to pay to shift from level t of attribute A to level s.

3.2. Data Collection

The survey was conducted by NTT Resonant Inc., which provides Internet research services in Japan. The total number of monitors that the company possessed was 43,973 when this survey was conducted. The Tokyo Metropolitan Government, Department of General Affairs reported that the total population of Tokyo was 13,157,428 in March, 2011, of which the male population was 6,532,645 (49.6%). Randomly selected 3,127 monitors were questioned through a web questionnaire from March 25 to 29, 2011. In total, 532 individuals responded to the questionnaire.

The questionnaire was divided into three blocks. The first block included questions about olive oil consumption and purchase frequency. The use of olive oil, place of purchase and prices were important criteria for choosing olive oil. The second block was composed by a conjoint experiment, whereas the third block included respondents' socio-demographic characteristics. At the beginning of the questionnaire, respondents were asked whether they consume olive oil.

Three response options were provided: 1) Yes, 2) No, but I may use olive oil in the future, 3) No, and I may not use olive oil in the future.

Table 4. Selected olive oil attributes and their corresponding levels

Attributes	Levels
Region of origin	Italy
	Spain
	Tunisia
	Mediterranean
Price (500 ml bottle)	600 Yen
	800 Yen
	1000 Yen
	1200 Yen
Olive oil type	Extra virgin
	Virgin
	Pure olive oil
Taste	Bitter
	Sweet
Color	Green
	Yellow
Component	High polyphenol
	Low polyphenol

These responses generated the response frequencies 375, 63 and 94, respectively. Only respondents who chose responses 1 or 2 (438) participated in the conjoint experiment.

The conjoint cards were described by six attributes: country of origin, price, type, taste, color and component. The choice of these attributes was based on the results of qualitative research on consumer behavior related to olive oil conducted in other countries (Mili and Rodriguez, 2001; García, Aragonés and Poole, 2002; Ronald et al., 2003) and on observations of the Japanese olive oil market and marketing strategies (Mtimet et al., 2009). The choice of the health attribute was based on an analysis of Tunisian olive oil by Abaza et al. (2005) and Yamada et al. (2008). The selected attributes and their corresponding levels are shown in Table 4.

The combination of the six attributes and their corresponding levels resulted in 384 hypothetical products, making respondents' task very difficult. To reduce the number of cards, we used an orthogonal design procedure (SPSS. 13), which resulted in a final design with 16 products. To avoid respondents' fatigue, which could result in biased results, we divided the 16 cards into two different survey versions with 8 cards each through an additional two-level variable. Respondents were asked to rank the eight cards from the most preferred to the least preferred product.

4. Empirical Results

4.1. Japanese Consumer Preference for Olive Oil

Respondents provided their socioeconomic information, such as gender, age, structure of household, level of income and education. They also responded to a series of questions to determine their attitudes towards olive oil, such as consumption and purchase frequencies, purchase criteria and preferences. Selected socioeconomic characteristics of the sample are summarized in Table 5.

Of the respondents, 50.2% were males. The average sample age was 42 years old. More than half of the respondents were married and were living with their spouses. The average numbers of household and children were 2.64 and 0.55, respectively. The medium income was between 4 million and 6 million yen per year. More than 66% of respondents were university graduates. Of the 532 respondents, 375 respondents (70.5%) consumed olive oil, whereas 63 respondents (11.8%) stated that they may use olive oil in the future. Questions regarding purchase frequencies and purchase criteria for olive oil were asked of the 375 respondents, and 438 respondents were asked about their preferences for olive oil, including the conjoint analysis task.

Regarding their consumption pattern, among 375 samples of the survey, 238 respondents, represented 60.8%, consume olive oil every day or some days in a week whereas the rest (39.5%) use it only some days or just a few days in a month. A high proportion of respondents (45.1%) purchase olive oil every three months, followed by respondents who purchase once in six months (21.6%) and once in a month (18.9%). 134 respondents (35.7%) purchase 500 ml size of olive oil while 21.6% of respondents prefer choosing 250 ml. While department stores (18.7%) and foodstuff shops (16.0%) were cited as places to buy olive oil, 84% of the respondents buy olive oil at supermarkets.

Regarding selection criteria, the 438 respondents were also asked to indicate their relative importance of some criteria when purchasing olive oil. Figure 5 presents the consumers' rating each factor from very important (1) to not important at all (5). The percentage of the number of respondents who chose very important and important to the total respondents are plotted on the *Y* axis.

Table 5. Selected sample characteristics of the data of Japanese consumers

Characteristics	Definition	(%)
Gender	Male	50.2
	Female	49.8
Civil status	Single	37.2
	Married	54.5
	Divorces, widow/er	8.3
Education level	Junior high school	0.6
	Senior high school	19.2
	University	66.7
	Professional/tech. school	11.5
	Others	2.1
Household income	income ≤ 2	8.6
(million Yen/year)	2 < income ≤ 4	17.5
	4 < income ≤ 6	23.1
	6 < income ≤ 8	16.7
	8 < income ≤ 10	13.7
	10 < income ≤ 15	13.2
	15 < income	7.1
Age in years	Mean	42.3
	Min./median/max.	16/42/79
Number of persons	Mean	2.64 (1.503)
in household	Min./median/max.	1/2/6
Number of children	Mean	0.55 (0.885)
in household	Min./median/max.	0/2/4

Note: Figures in brackets are standard deviation.

The results suggest that price is the most important attribute considered by respondents, followed by taste, flavor and type. More than 60% of respondents consider healthy attributes (64.6%) and country of origin (61.2%) is also important. On the other hand, less than half of the sample (49.5%) cited a certification for the quality of the product as an important criterion for buying olive oil. Respondents are relatively less sensitive to color, packaging and design of bottle.

Along with the selection criteria, the 438 respondents were asked about their preference of olive oil attributes. More than half of the respondents (56.4%) preferred extra virgin olive oil, followed by olive oil (24.9%) and virgin olive oil (17.8%). The majority of the respondents (76.7%) preferred olive oil produced in Italy (76.7%) and Spain (11.6%) while respondents who chose products of Greece, Turkey and Syria were less than 3%. It is noteworthy that nobody considered olive oil made in Tunisia as a preferable product. As for sensory attributes, 53.7% of respondents showed a higher preference for sweet taste while a bitter taste is less preferable to the Japanese consumer (5.7%). More than half of the respondents (51.8%) prefer yellow color olive oil while green is preferable for the rest 45.4%.

Respondents were also asked about their knowledge of healthy attributes of olive oil. It is interesting to note that 234 respondents, represented 53.4% of the sample, answered that they knew about the healthy effects of olive oil. In addition, this sample of respondents was asked to specify their perceived functionalities of olive oil on health and beauty. Allowing multiple answers, the number of answers and their percentage to respective functionalities are presented in Table 6. Of the 316 answers, 45.9% was composed of the answers of anti-aging, followed by the functionality of anti-metabolic syndrome (29.4%). For the anti-aging effect, most of the answers accounted for an effectiveness in blood thinning. The effect for the promotion of beautiful, smooth and soft skin was also included in this functionality. As for the prevention of metabolic syndrome, a property of olive oil that has an effect of decreasing the level of cholesterol was frequently mentioned. While 10.1% of the answers indicated the functionality of anti-oxidant, consumers have not well perceived the effects for anti-cancer, anti-inflammatory, anti-allergy, anti-melanogenous, anti-viral and anti-microbial.

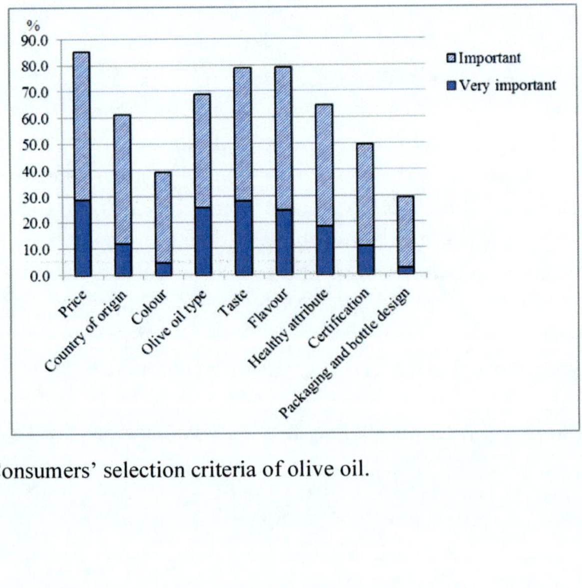

Figure 5. Consumers' selection criteria of olive oil.

Table 6. Consumers' perception of functionality of olive oil

	Number of answers	Percentage
Anti-aging	145	45.9
Anti-metabolic syndrome	93	29.4
Anti-oxidiant	32	10.1
Anti-cancer	1	0.3
Anti-inflammatory	1	0.3
Anti-allergy	0	0.0
Anti-melanogenous	0	0.0
Anti-viral	0	0.0
Anti-microbial	0	0.0
Others	44	13.9
Total	316	100.0

4.2. Results of Conjoint Analysis

The results of the estimations of the ROL model are presented in Table 7. As expected, most of the coefficients of the model, except for color, were statistically significant. First, respondents preferred virgin and extra virgin olive oil compared with olive oil. The estimated coefficient for extra virgin olive oil was more elastic than that of virgin oil. This result suggests that extra virgin oil had a higher probability to be chosen than virgin olive oil. Second, the coefficients for Italy and Spain were positive and statistically significant while that for Tunisia was negative. These results suggest that olive oil from Tunisia had the lowest probability of being chosen compared with the others, whereas that from Italy had the highest probability. This pattern of preference is quite reasonable because, in reality, Italian olive oil had the highest share in the Japanese market. Third, as for sensory attributes, respondents showed a higher preference for a sweet taste rather than a bitter taste, while there was no statistically significant difference between green and yellow olive oil. Fourth and the most important, the estimated coefficient of a high concentration of polyphenol is statistically significant at the 1% level. This result indicates that respondents prefer olive oil with a high concentration of polyphenol, and is consistent with the increasing demand for better health and nutrition. Fifth, as expected, the negative and statistically significant coefficient for price confirmed that the utility of respondents decreased when the price of olive oil increased.

Regarding the estimation of MWTP, respondents increased their preference by 1090.3 yen for extra virgin olive oil compared with pure olive oil. Their preferences increased only by 199.1 yen and 106.5 yen for oil from Italy and Spain, respectively. However, their preference decreased by 236 yen for oil made in Tunisia. While bitter taste resulted in a decrease in preference at 436.2 yen, a high concentration of polyphenol resulted in an increase in preference by 438.2 yen. Focusing on the Tunisian olive oil, the preference decreased by 236 yen compared with preference for the Mediterranean label, but increased by 438.2 yen if the oil contained a high concentration of polyphenol.

Table 7. Estimated parameters and MWTP of the rank ordered logit model (main effect model)

	Coefficient		Standard error	p-value	MWTP
Type [a]					
Virgin oil	0.565	***	0.049	0.000	596.0
Extra virgin oil	1.033	***	0.063	0.000	1090.3
Region of origin [b]					
Italy	0.189	***	0.057	0.001	199.1
Spain	0.101	*	0.057	0.078	106.5
Tunisia	-0.224	***	0.064	0.001	-236.0
Taste: bitter [c]	-0.413	***	0.044	0.000	-436.2
Color: green [d]	0.044		0.042	0.298	46.6
Component: high polyphenol [e]	0.415	***	0.042	0.000	438.2
Price	-0.001	***	0.000	0.000	-
Number of observations	438		LL	-4273.8	

Notes: *, **, *** indicate significant at the 10% level, 5% level, 1% level, respectively.

[a] The coefficient correspond to "pure olive oil" is fixed at 0 as a base.

[b] The coefficient correspond to "Mediterranean" is fixed at 0 as a base.

[c] The coefficient correspond to "sweet" is fixed at 0 as a base.

[d] The coefficient correspond to "yellow" is fixed at 0 as a base.

[e] The coefficient correspond to "low polyphenol" is fixed at 0 as a base.

Table 8. Estimated parameters of the cross effect model

	Main effect	Gender	Age	Income	Number of persons in household	Education	Frequency of use
Type							
Virgin oil	0.492	-0.267 **	0.007	0.182	-0.036	-0.066	-0.060
	(0.314)	(0.135)	(0.006)	(0.139)	(0.053)	(0.136)	(0.131)
Extra virgin oil	1.391 ***	-0.324 **	0.000	0.232	-0.104	0.118	-0.032
	(0.389)	(0.172)	(0.007)	(0.174)	(0.065)	(0.173)	(0.165)
Region of origin							
Italy	-0.287	0.287 *	0.007	-0.070	0.001	-0.156	0.319 **
	(0.367)	(0.158)	(0.007)	(0.160)	(0.061)	(0.160)	(0.152)
Spain	-0.137	0.254	0.007	-0.045	-0.075	-0.246	0.314 **
	(0.371)	(0.156)	(0.007)	(0.162)	(0.062)	(0.158)	(0.154)
Tunisia	-0.627	0.301 *	0.009	-0.173	-0.010	-0.144	0.156
	(0.418)	(0.177)	(0.008)	(0.183)	(0.070)	(0.179)	(0.173)
Taste: bitter	-0.391	0.125	-0.007	0.026	-0.025	0.273 **	0.224 *
	(0.291)	(0.121)	(0.005)	(0.127)	(0.048)	(0.122)	(0.119)
Color: green	0.365	-0.452 ***	-0.002	0.046	-0.022	0.185	-0.207 *
	(0.277)	(0.118)	(0.005)	(0.120)	(0.046)	(0.118)	(0.114)
Component: high polyphenol	-0.268	-0.231 **	0.014 ***	0.132	-0.037	0.224 *	0.236 **
	(0.275)	(0.117)	(0.005)	(0.120)	(0.046)	(0.117)	(0.113)

Table 8. (Continued)

	Main effect	Gender	Age	Income	Number of persons in household	Education	Frequency of use
Price	-0.001 ***						
	(0.000)						
Number of observations 276		LL	-2634.0				

Notes: *, **, *** indicate significant at the 10% level, 5% level, 1% level, respectively.
Figures in brackets are standard errors.

Table 8 shows our estimates for the cross effect model that examined the effect of consumer characteristics on their preferences. Regarding the type of oil, the estimated results suggested that females had a preference for extra virgin olive oil, while males preferred olive oil made in Italy. It is noteworthy that males also showed a preference for Tunisian olive oil while the sign of the parameter in the main effect model was negative. Respondents who frequently used olive oil preferred products imported from Italy and Spain. While respondents preferred a sweet taste (Table 4), those with a higher education status represented by being a university graduate who frequently used olive oil showed a higher probability to choose a bitter taste. While respondents who frequently used olive oil showed a higher preference for yellow olive oil, females preferred green olive oil.

As for the concentration of polyphenol, the estimated coefficients indicate four characteristic effects on consumer preferences. First, females preferred olive oil with high concentrations of polyphenol. Second, the consumption of olive oil with a high concentration of polyphenol was greater for older respondents. Third, respondents with a higher educational status preferred purchasing olive oil with a high concentration of polyphenol. Fourth, the frequent use of olive oil also increased the probability of choosing olive oil with a high concentration of polyphenol.

CONCLUSION

During the last two decades, olive oil consumption in Japan showed an increasing trend, given the dietary and health concerns. Traditional olive oil producing and exporting countries such as Italy, Spain and Tunisia may have an interest in increasing their exports to Japan. This chapter investigated olive oil consumption behavior in Japan and examined consumer preferences using the conjoint analysis. The data used in this study were a sample of 532 consumers living in Tokyo collected in March 2011 through an Internet questionnaire distributed to a panel of Japanese consumers. Six attributes were chosen in the design of the experiment: country of origin, price, olive oil type, taste, color and component. It is noteworthy that the health attributes of olive oil as represented by the concentration of polyphenol was explicitly included in the product design.

By applying the multifaced bioassay technique, many medical and medicinal effects on health, such as anti-aging, anti-metabolic syndrome, anti-oxidant and anti-allergy have been detected in the components of Tunisian olive oil. Particularly, Tunisian olive oil has an anti-allergy effect on IgE-stimulated RBL-2H3 cells through inhibition of TNF-α and IL-4. In addition, hydroxytyrosol, apigenin and oleuropein, the main polyphenols of olive oil, produce bitterness in olive oil. However, it was reported that such polyphenols have anti-oxidant, anti-inflammatory, anti-allergy, anti-atherogenic, anti-cancer, anti-microbial and anti-viral effects. The results of the questionnaire regarding the health attributes of olive oil revealed that the anti-aging, anti-metabolic syndrome and anti-oxidant effects are well perceived by the Japanese consumer.

The results of the estimation by the ROL model suggested that Japanese consumers preferred extra virgin and virgin to olive oil and a sweet taste rather than a bitter taste. While their preferences decreased if the country of origin indicated Tunisia compared with that of the Mediterranean, consumers showed a higher preference for olive oil containing a high concentration of polyphenol. This preference was also consistent with the results of the estimation of MWTP. It is suggested that a high concentration of polyphenol had a WTP of up by 438.2 yen, while the WTP decreased by 236 yen if the products were imported from Tunisia. As a net effect, the WTP increased at 202.2 yen for the Tunisian product with a high concentration of polyphenol.

The estimated results of the cross effect model suggested that females preferred extra virgin and green olive oil. Males preferred olive oil made in Italy, and had a preference for Tunisian olive oil while the overall preference was negative. Respondents who frequently used olive oil preferred products imported from Italy and Spain, and yellow olive oil. While respondents preferred a sweet taste, those with a higher educational status and who frequently used olive oil showed a higher probability of choosing a bitter taste. As for the concentration of polyphenol, female, elder respondents with a higher education status and those who frequently used olive oil preferred purchasing olive oil with a high concentration of polyphenol.

While Tunisia is one of the most important exporters of olive oil in the world, its exports have always been in bulk and directed to the EU market. On the other hand, well-known olive oil producers such as Italy and Spain dominate the Japanese market. However, the obtained results suggests a potential for Tunisian olive oil to increase its share in the Japanese import market by developing a product design with the attributes of extra virgin, sweet taste and a high concentration of polyphenol. From the marketing point of view, a simultaneous indication of Tunisian origin on the label of an olive oil bottle and a health attribute could be a successful strategy, while the main polyphenols, such as hydroxytyrosol, apigenin and oleuropein produce bitterness. Therefore, it is suggested that this strategy can also benefit producers that intend to establish a 'Tunisian brand' of olive oil to be exported not only to the EU, but also to large and emerging markets such as Japan. Although the products of Italy and Spain still dominate the Japanese olive oil market, a designed product emphasizing a health attribute may shed light on increasing exports of Tunisian products to the Japanese market.

ACKNOWLEDGMENTS

The authors gratefully acknowledged that this research was partially supported by JSPS under the Asia Africa Science Platform Program entitled: "Establishment of Integrative Research Base by Humanities and Sciences on Valorization of Useful Plants for Regional Development in North Africa", partially supported by the JICA-JST Science and Technology Research Partnership for Sustainable Development (SATREPS) Project: "Valorization of Bio-resources in Semi-Arid and Arid Land for Regional Development" and by the Grant-in-Aid for Scientific Research (A) entitled: Investigation and Research on Useful Bio-resources in Extremophile Arid Land of North Africa (17255011). Also, the authors thank to Prof. Lokman Zaibet, Prof. Nadhem Mtimet, Ecole Supérieure d'Agriculture de Mograne, Tunisia and Prof. Kiyokazu Ujiie, University of Tsukuba, Japan for their helpful advices for designing the questionnaire and analyzing the data.

REFERENCES

Abaza, L., Taamalli, W., Temime, S. B., Daoud, D., Guteirrez, E., and Zarrouk, M. (2005). *Natural antioxidant composition as correlated to stability of some Tunisian virgin olive oils*. Rivista Italiano Delle Sostanze Gresse, 132, 12–18.

Abaza, L., Talorete T. P. N., Yamada P., Kurita, Y., Zarrouk, M., and Isoda, H. (2007). *Induction of growth inhibition and differentiation of human Leukemia HL-60 cells by a Tunisian Gerboui olive leaf extract*. Bioscience Biotechnology Biochemistry, 71 (5), 1306-1312.

Amiot, M. J., Fleuriet, A., and Macheix, J. J. (1986a). *Importance and evolution of phenolic compounds in olive during growth and maturation*. Journal of Agricultural and Food Chemistry. 34, 823-826.

Amiot, M. J., Fleuriet, A., and Macheix, J. J. (1986b). *Caracte´risation des produits de de´gradation de l'oleuropein (Technological debittering process of olives: characterization of fruits before and during alkaline treatment).* Groupe Phenolic, 364-369.

Amiot, M. J., Fleuriet, A., and Macheix, J. J. (1989). *Accumulation of oleuropein derivatives during olive maturation.* Phytochemistry 28, 67-69.

Amiot, M. J., Tacchini, M., Fleuriet, A., and Macheix, J. J. (1990). *Le processus téchnologique de désamérization des olives: caractérisation des fruits avant et pendant le traitement alcalin.* Sciences des Aliments. 10, 619-631.

Caponio F., Alloggio V., and Gomes, T. (1999). *Phenolic compounds of virgin olive oil: influence of paste preparation techniques.* Food Chemistry, 64, 203–209.

Chapman, R. G. and Staelin, R. (1982). *Exploiting rank ordered choice set data within the stochastic utility model.* Journal of Marketing Research, 19, 288-301.

Chan-Halbrendt, C., Zhllima, E., Sisior, G., Imami, D., and Leonetti, L. (2010). *Consumer preferences for olive oil in Tirana, Albania.* International Food and Agribusiness Management Review, 13(3): 55-74.

De la Puerta, R., Martínez-Domínguez, E., and Ruíz-Gutiérrez, V. (2000*). Effect of minor components of virgin olive oil on topical anti-inflammatory assays.* Journal of Biosciences, 55(9-10), 814-819.

Edgecombe, S. C., Stretch, G. L., and Hayball, P. J. (2000). *Oleuropein, an antioxidant polyphenol from olive oil, is poorly absorbed from isolated perfused rat intestine.* Journal of Nutrition, 130, 2996-3002.

Fabiani, R., De Bartolomeo, A., Rosignoli, P., Servili, M., Montedoro, G. F., and Morozzi, G. (2002). *Cancer chemoprevention by hydroxytyrosol isolated from virgin olive oil through G1 cell cycle arrest and apoptosis.* European Journal of Cancer Prevention, 11, 351–358.

Fabiani, R., Bartolomeo, A. D., Rosignoli, P., Servili, M., Selvaggini, R., Montedoro, G. F., Saverio, C. D., and Morozzi, G. (2006). *Virgin olive oil phenols inhibit proliferation of human promyelocytic leukemia cells (HL60) by inducing apoptosis and differentiation.* Journal of Nutrition, 136, 614–619.

Feliciano, A. and Albisu, L. M. (2006). *A new ready-to-eat dish for a traditional market.* Journal of Foodservice, 17(3), 124-134.

García, M. M., Aragonés, Z., and Poole, N. (2002). *A repositioning strategy for olive oil in the UK Market.* Agribusiness, 18(2), 163-180.

Gary, K. B., Russell, S. K., Diano, M., Lin, J. M., Jana, P., Han, Q., Lee, Ch. H., Amos, B. S., and Paul, A. S. B. (2005). *Ibuprofen-like activity in extra-virgin olive oil.* Nature, 437, 45.

Gerber, M. (1994). Olive oil and cancer. In Hill, M. J., Giacosa, A. and Caygill, C. P. Eds., *Epidemiology of Diet and Cancer (Chapter 13, 263-275).* London: Ellis Horwood.

Green, P. E. and Rao, V. R. (1971). *Conjoint measurement for quantifying judgmental data.* Journal of Marketing Research, 8(3), 355-363.

Green, P. E. and Srinivasan, V. (1978). *Conjoint analysis in consumer research: issues and outlook.* Journal of Consumer Research, 5(2), 103-123.

Haddad, Y., Haddad, J., Olabi, A., Shuayto, N., Haddad T., and Toufeili, I. (2007). *Mapping determinants of purchase intent of concentrated yogurt (Labneh) by conjoint analysis.* Food Quality and Preference, 18, 795-802.

Hamdi, K., and Hamdi, R. C. (2005). *Oleuropein, a non-toxic olive iridoid, is an anti-tumor agent and cytoskeleton disruptor.* Biochemical and Biophysical Research Communications, 334, 769-778.

Impellizzeri, D., Esposito, E., Mazzon, E., Paterniti, I, Di Paola, R., Bramanti, P., Morittu, V. M., Procopio, A., Britti, D., and Cuzzocrea, S. (2011). *The effects of oleuropein aglycone, an olive oil compound, in a mouse model of carrageenan-induced pleurisy.* Clinical Nutrition, 30, 533-540.

Institut National de la Statistique (2008). *Annuaire Statistique de la Tunisie. République Tunisienne Ministrère du Dévelopment et de la Coopréation Internationale, N° 51.*

Japan Tariff Association (1985). *Japan Export & Imports: Commodity by Country, March 1984.* Tokyo: Japan Tariff Association.

Japan Tariff Association (2007). *Japan Export & Imports: Commodity by Country, March 2006.* Tokyo: Japan Tariff Association.

Kashiwagi, K., Mtimet, N., Zaibet, L., and Nagaki, M. (2010). *Technical efficiency of olive oil manufacturing and efficacy of modernization programme in Tunisia.* Paper presented at 3rd Annual Conference of African Association of Agricultural Economists & 49th Annual Conference of Agricultural Economists Association of South Africa.

Kawano, M., Matsuyama, K., Miyamae, Y., Shinmoto, H., Kchouk, M., Morio, T., Shigemori, H., and Isoda H. (2007). *Antimelanogenesis effect of Tunisian herb Thymelaea hirsute extract on B16 murine melanoma cells.* Experimental Dermatology, 16, 977-984.

Krystallis, A., Ness, M. (2003). *Motivational and cognitive structures of Greek consumers in the purchase of quality food products.* Journal of International Consumer Marketing, 16(2), 7-36.

Lancaster, K. (1966). *A new approach to consumer theory.* Journal of Political Economy, 74(2), 132-157.

Lancaster, K. (1971). *Consumer demand: A new approach.* New York: Columbia University Press.

Le Tutour, B., and Guedon, D. (1992). *Antioxidative activities of Olea europaea leaves and related phenolic compounds.* Phytochemistry, 31, 1173–1178.

Litridou, M., Linssen, J., Schols, H., Bewrgmans, M., Posthumus, M., Tsimidou, M., and Boskou, D. (1997). *Phenolic compounds in virgin olive oils: fractionation by solid phase extraction and antioxidant activity assessment.* Journal of the Science of Food and Agriculture, 74, 169-174.

Luckow, T., H. Moskowitz, J. Beckley, Hirsch, J. and Genchi, S. (2005). *The four segments of yogurt consumers: preferences and mindsets.* Journal of Food Products Marketing, 11(1), 1-22.

Martin-Moreno, J. M., Willett, W. C., Gorgojo, L., Banegas, J. R., Rodriguez-Artalejo, F., Fernandez-Rodriguez, J. C., Maisssonneuve, P., and Boyle, P. (1994). *Dietary fat, olive oil intake and breast cancer risk.* International Journal of Cancer, 58, 774-780.

Mateos, R., Cert, A., Pe′rez-Camino, M. C., and Garcı′a, J. M. (2004). *Evaluation of virgin olive oil bitterness by quantification of secoiridoid derivatives.* Journal of the American Oil Chemists' Society, 81, 71-75.

McFadden, D. (1974). *Conditional logit analysis of qualitative choice behavior.* In Zarembka, P. (Ed.), Frontiers in econometrics (105-142). New York: Academic Press.

Miles, E. A., Zoubouli, P., and Calder, P. C. (2005). *Differential anti-inflammatory effects of phenolic compounds from extra virgin olive oil identified in human whole blood cultures.* Nutrition, 21(3), 389-394.

Mili S., and Rodríguez, Z. M. (2001). *Exploring future developments in international olive oil trade and marketing: A Spanish perspective.* Agribusiness, 17(3), 397-415.

Mtimet, N., Kashiwagi, K., Zaibet, L. and Nagaki, M. (2009). *Japanese olive oil consumer behavior: A conjoint analysis approach.* In Sato, F. (Ed.), Consumer behavior (Chapter 2, 27-47). New York: Nova Science Publishers, Inc..

Mtimet, N., Ujiie, K., Kashiwagi, K., Zaibet, L., and Nagaki, M. (2011). *The role of information and country of origin on Japanese olive oil consumer:*

A choice experiment approach. Paper presented for the Congress of the European Association of Agricultural Economists: Change and Uncertainty: Challenges for Agriculture, Food and Natural Resources.

Nelson, R., Jolly, C., Hinds, M., Donis, Y. and Prohete, E. (2005). *Conjoint analysis of consumer preferences for roasted peanut products in Haiti.* International journal of Consumer Studies, 29(3), 208-215.

Orth, U., and Krska, P. (2002). *Quality signals in wine marketing: the role of exhibition awards.* The International Food and Agribusiness Management Review, 4(4), 385-397.

Panizzi, L., Scarpati, M. L., and Oriente, E. G. (1960). *Structure of oleuropein, bitter glycoside with hypotensive action of olive oil. Note II.* Gazzetta Chimica Italiana, 90, 1449-1485.

Paul, A., Johanneke, L. H. C. Busch, Teun de Joode, Anneke G., and Helene A. (2003). *Sensory properties of virgin olive oil polyphenols: Identification of deacetoxy-ligstroside aglycon as a key contributor to pungency.* Journal of Agricultural and Food Chemistry, *51*, 1415–1420.

Price, L., Price, S., and Smith, I. (1999). *Carrier oil for aromatherapy and massage.* Riverhead, England, 166.

Ronald, W., Briz, J., and Felipe, I. D. (2003). *Competing supplies of olive oil in the German market: An application of multinomial logit models.* Agribusiness, 19 (3), 393-406.

Ryan, D, Antolovich, M., Prenzler P., Robards, K., and Lavee, S. (2002). *Biotransformations of phenolic compounds in Olea europaea L.* Scientia Horticulturae, 92, 147–176.

Servili, M., Baldioli, M., Selvaggini, R., Macchioni, A. and Montedoro, G. (1999). *Phenolic compounds of olive fruit: one- and two-dimensional nuclear magnetic resonance characterization of nuzhenide and distribution in the constitutive parts of fruit.* Journal of Agricultural and Food Chemistry, 47:12–18.

Souza, M., and Lucas, M. (2001). *Conjoint measurement of preferences for traditional cheeses in Lisbon.* British Food Journal, 103(6), 414-424.

Tuck, L. K., and Hayball, J. P. (2002). *Major phenolic compounds in olive oil: metabolism and health effects.* Journal of Nutritional Biochemistry, 13, 636–644.

Visioli, F., and Galli, C. (1995). *Natural antioxidants and prevention of coronary heart disease: the potential role of olive oil and its minor constituents.* Nutrition Metabolism and Cardiovascular Diseases, 5, 306–314.

Visioli, F., Bellomo, G., and Galli, C. (1998). *Free radical-scavenging properties of olive oil polyphenols.* Biochemical and Biophysical Research Communications 247, 60–64.

Visioli, F., Galli, C., Plasmati, E., Viappiani, S., Hermandez, A., and Colombo, C. (2000). *Olive phenol hydroxytyrosol prevents passive smoking-induced oxidative stress.* Circulation, 102, 2169-2171.

Visioli F, Galli, C. (2001) *Phenolics from olive oil and its waste products. Biological activities in vitro and in vivo studies.* World Review of Nutrition and Dietetics, 88, 233-237.

Yamada, P., Han, J., and Isoda, H. (2009) *Analysis concerning anti-cancer and anti-allergic activity of olive polyphenol compounds.* Journal of Arid Land Studies, 18-4, 183-187.

Yamada, P., Zarrouk, M., Kawasaki, K., and Isoda, H. (2008). *Inhibitory effect of various Tunisian olive oils on chemical mediator release and cytokine production by basophilic cells.* Journal of Ethnopharmacology, 116, 279-287.

Yang, D. P., Kong, D. X., and Zhang, H. Y. (2007). *Multiple pharmacological effects of olive oil phenols.* Food Chemistry, 104, 1269-1271.

In: Tunisia: Economic, Political and Social Issues ISBN: 978-1-61942-157-8
Eds: M. Pusatieri and J. Cannamela

Chapter 4

INFLUENCE OF ENVIRONMENTAL FACTORS ON ALEPPO PINE FOREST PRODUCTION

Abdelaziz Ayari[1,*], Daniel Moya[2], and Ane Zubizarreta-Gerendiain[3]
[1]National Institute of Research in Rural Geneering, Waters and Forests (INRGREF), Ariana, Tunisia
[2]Escuela Tecnica Superior de Ingenieros Agrónomos de Albacete, UCLM. Spain
[3]Instituto Superior de Agronomia, Universidade Técnica de Lisboa. Departamento de Engenharia Florestal - Tapada da Ajuda, Lisboa, Portugal

ABSTRACT

Mediterranean climate forests product several benefits, such as food, pharmaceutical, cosmetics and other non-food goods. In Tunisia, forest and woodlands cover circa 1.1 million hectares which includes Aleppo pine stands (about 300 000 hectares). Aleppo pine seed production is an important food sub-sector in Tunisia, currently restructured due to the increasing needs of population consumption. Furthermore, the forest and woodlands constitute a source of income in the main inland regions, such as Kasserine, Le Kef, Siliana, Kairouan, Beja and Zaghouan where more

* Corresponding author: Tel.: +216 97 386 516; Fax: +216 71 717 951. E-mail address: abdelazizayari@yahoo.fr

than 96% of Aleppo pine forests are located. The effects of environmental factors on the Aleppo pine production of these forests were evaluated. Bioclimatic zones, stand characteristics and tree measurements (including height and age) were submitted to simple and multiple regression analyses for explaining their interaction on the average seed and cone mass, in addition to the seed production per cone and per tree. Overall, results under simple regression showed longitude and altitude as the most explanatory variables relating average seed production and cone mass. Average cone length showed highly significant relationship with seed number per cone and the cone mass. Moreover, bioclimatic zones, stand density, basal area, tree size and age were linked to cone number and seed mass per tree. However, under multiple regression analysis, longitude was the most explanatory variable for average seed and cone mass, in addition to the seed mass per cone. The average cone length was influenced by the bioclimatic zone and longitude. Total height and age of the tree were the most explanatory variables for the cone number, but these two variables were added to the crown diameter for explaining their influences on the total seed mass per tree. The results have practical implications for the management of Aleppo pine for seed production and subsequent reforestation planning.

Keywords: Aleppo pine; Environmental Factors; Cone Properties; Seed Production

INTRODUCTION

Aleppo pine (*Pinus halepensis* Mill.) is a Mediterranean coniferous tree species with a total forest cover estimated to attain 2.5 million ha (Quezel 2000). In Tunisia, Aleppo pine forests remain the most important of all the country's woodlands with a total forest cover 365,220 ha (DGF 1995). About two thirds of these forests are native stands which are occurring in semiarid areas from northern to central Tunisia. The third remainder is made up of even-aged plantations which were implemented after 1960's (Garchi and Ben Mansoura 1999).

Annual fructification is restricted to Aleppo pine producing cones and seeds massively (Krugman and Jenkinson 1974; Verkaik and Espelta 2006). Aleppo pine shows a dual strategy bearing both non-serotinous and serotinous cones in the canopy (Goubitz et al. 2002) what allows longtime seed storaging strategy but also high potential regeneration in closer areas (Naveh 1974; Trabaud et al. 1985).

Moreover, high seed crops are needed to provide crucial animal food resources for the survival of a wide array of predators, such as insects, birds, mammals (Smith and Balda 1979), and reptiles (Way 2006), whose presence in the forest ecosystem contributes to maintain biotic equilibrium. Worldwide, pine nuts and seeds are also consumed by humans as condiments in a variety of food and additional preparations (Asset et al. 1999).

In Tunisia, others pine nuts and Aleppo pine seeds have historically constituted a basic food staple for local users. The spread of this culinary habit among all the country's population during the last few decades made human consumption the most overwhelming factor calling for continued satisfactory pine cone and seed production. The rising demand for seeds, primarily Aleppo pine's and secondarily Maritime pine's (*P. pinaster*), is driven by an increasingly popular enjoyment for prepare black gravy. The rise in public enjoyment for the consumption of Aleppo pine seeds (Nasri et al. 2004; Sghaier et al. 1997) has extended even to other areas such as eastern Algeria

Several authors (Donahue and Lopez-Upton, 1996; Climent et al., 2008; Ayari et al., 2011a) studying reproduction patterns, found that cone and seed production is strongly influenced by environmental factors, such as climate, geo-positional parameters, stand characteristics and tree size. The climate effect on fructification processes, ranging from strobili primordia differentiation to coning, was attributed to complex interactions including topo-edaphic factors, such as aspect (Despland and Houle 1997; Ayari et al. 2011a) or geographical variables (Mencuccini et al. 1995; Boulli et al. 2001; Harfouch et al. 2003; Ayari et al. 2011a).

In Tunisia, longitudinal changes were related to average seed mass of Aleppo pine (Nasri et al. 2004; Ayari et al. 2011a). Cone and seed production were influenced by stand characteristics and tree size, with a consensus indicating higher crops in stands showing lower tree density (Arista and Talavera 1996; Turner et al. 2007).

In the present study, we aimed to assess the number and the characteristics of cones produced by Aleppo pine trees growing in native stands in Tunisia. The selected characteristics were obtained using the average pine tree which represents the average production in the studied stand. To achieve it, we sampled native Aleppo pine stands located in six Tunisian districts within a wide array of geo-positional coordinates. Seed yields per cone and per tree, were also assessed in relation to the most common environmental factors, stand characteristics and tree size.

Materials and Methods

Study Region and Forest Characteristics

The study region covered most of the native Aleppo pine forests scattered over six Tunisian districts (Figure 1). However, Aleppo pine forests located in other districts were ignored. Likewise, the studied area included the four northern administrative districts (Beja, Le Kef, Siliana and Zaghouan), in addition to the two central districts (Kairouan and Kasserine). The native Aleppo pine stands cover about 1.1 and 12.7% of the district's land cover. These forests are distributed over the northern mountain ranges of the Kroumiries (Le Kef), and the Mogods (Beja), in addition to the Central Dorsale (Zaghouan, Siliana, Kairouan, and Kasserine). They are broken elevations oriented from southwest to northeast ranging from 250 to 1185 m above sea level (asl). Latitudes and longitudes of the study area are comprised between 35.17 and 36.53° N for the former, and between 8.33 and 9.85° E for the latter (Table 1).

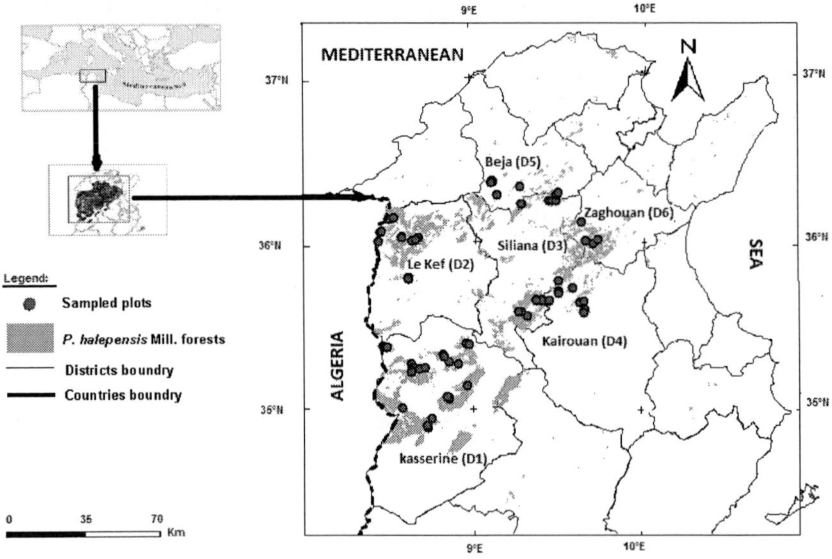

Figure 1. Map showing the Tunisian forests of Pinus halepensis Mill., and the geographic location of all 79 plots used to sample cone and seed production.

Table 1. Range of variability in geographical location and stand characteristics for natural Aleppo pine forests in six Tunisian districts

	Districts						
	D1	D2	D3	D4	D5	D6	
	Kasserine (n= 25†)	Le Kef (n = 16)	Siliana (n = 11)	Kairouan (n = 9)	Beja (n = 14)	Zaghouan (n = 4)	Overall (n = 79)
Geo-positional variables							
Latitude (°N)	[35.17-35.64]	[35.99-36.32]	[35.79-36.42]	[35.80-35.94]	[36.40-36.54]	[36.19-36.30]	[35.17-36.54]
Longitude (°E)	[8.36-8.96]	[8.33-8.61]	[9.30-9.58]	[9.51-9.76]	[9.11-9.59]	[9.74-9.85]	[8.33-9.85]
Altitude (m)	[830-1185]	[250-1000]	[330-900]	[320-630]	[290-770]	[400-730]	[250-1185]
Stand characteristics							
Basal area (m^2ha^{-1})	[4.91-28.40]	[4.98-17.70]	[6.03-18.32]	[3.03-11.55]	[6.48-23.60]	[7.42-11.86]	[3.03-28.40]
Density (t/ha^{-1})	[250-1720]	[340-1910]	[890-1960]	[350-1480]	[440-2050]	[830-2090]	[250-2090]
Shade (%)	[20.38-220.66]	[39.80-290.41]	[86.76-213.40]	[23.04-150.26]	[22.08-239.30]	[53.11-202.31]	[20.38-290.41]

† Sampled plots.

Sampling Procedure

A total of 79 rectangular plots measuring 40 x 25 m were sampled across the study region for the purpose of harvesting all closed mature and over mature cones borne by the average *P. halepensis* tree within each plot. We sampled the reddish/brownish cones as mature cones and closed greyish cones as serotinous cones (Goubitz et al. 2002; Moya et al. 2008). Juvenile cones (greenish/yellowish) and decaying cones (partially or fully opened) were ignored in this sampling. The average tree chosen for cone harvesting was the one presenting an over bark DBH and a total height whose values were the closest to the average of both measurements taken on all the pine trees that were present within a given plot, if not equal to those arithmetic averages (Ayari et al. 2011b). Before to collect cones a year after, an additional sampling was carried to record crown diameter, crown height and age of every average tree (Rondeux et al. 1993).

In all cases, a double recording was insured for all tree measurements that were made in the field. A proportionate allocation of the sampling plots among the various administrative districts was made in relation to the importance of the species forest cover within each one of these geographic entities. Plot selection and delimitation were based on the requirement of the total absence of anthropogenic disturbance, as well as on the necessity of covering a wide array of tree densities. Forest stand characteristics pertaining to total and specific tree density, basal area, and canopy coverage were also determined from field measurements (Ayari et al. 2011a). In the laboratory, all cones harvested from each average tree were individually submitted to the measurement of their length and width, followed by their air dry weight after a 21-day exposure period in a well aerated room (Ayari et al. 2011b). Then, all cones were introduced in an oven set at 45° C where they stayed 5 days in order to induce the opening of their scales. After this treatment, all seeds were carefully extracted, counted and weighed for each cone separately.

Statistical Analysis

Descriptive statistics and simple regression analyses were used to study the effects of the districts distribution and their main characterizing factors on the weight and size of the harvested cones and on the number and mass of extracted seeds.

An overall estimation of the total cone and seed yield per average tree and per stand in each district was also determinate. Multiple regression analyses were carried-out to investigate the relationship linking the aforesaid variables to the geographical variables, the forest stand characteristics and the different measurements taken on the average tree. Regression models were retained when they were significant ($r<0.003$, $p<0.05$). The statistical software package SAS (SAS 2005, Version 9.0) was used to accomplish the aforesaid procedures.

Results

Districts Variability of Stand and Trees Properties

The results showed no significant differences (P-value>0.05) between districts for stand density, diameter at breast height (DBH), average crown height (CrH) and crown diameter (CrD), in addition to the average tree age. By contrast, basal area, shade and total height showed significant differences (P-value<0.05) between the six Tunisian districts (Table 2).

In Kasserine (D1) and Beja (D5), we registered the highest significant values for basal area with 13.64±1.25 m^2 ha^{-1}, and 13.64±1.50 m^2 ha^{-1}, respectively. Likewise, in Siliana (D3) we recorded the highest values for the shade with 144.67±12.68 (%). For the total height, the highest values were found in Beja (D3) with 7.71±1.28 m.

Influence of Environmental Factors

Influence of Environmental Factors on:

Cone Production per Tree

Across districts, no significant effect of the geo-positional variables and the registered rainfall on the cone number (CNT) and cone mass (SMT) produced per tree was found (Table 3). Furthermore, among the main environmental factors characterizing the studied forests, only the stand characteristics except the shade and all the tree dimensions were found to be significantly correlated with CNT and SMT borne by the average Aleppo pine tree. Indeed, negative relationships linking basal area and density to CNT and SMT were found, but it was positive with tree measurements. Separately, only districts of Kasserine (D1) and Beja (D5), they showed some significant correlations between cone and seed production (Table 3). However the highest number of cones produced was observed in Beja (D5) with mean value of 171±27cone $tree^{-1}$, followed by Kasserine (D1) and Siliana (D3) with about 139±21 cone $tree^{-1}$ and 102±8cone $tree^{-1}$, respectively (Figure 2a). For CMT, the highest mean values were recorded in D1 and D5 with 2.98±0.42 kg $tree^{-1}$ and 3.05± 0.5 kg $tree^{-1}$, respectively (Figure 2b).

Cone Traits

Results showed that only longitude and latitude had negative significant influence ($p<0.05$) on cone length in Siliana (D3) and Kairouan (D4) with correlation coefficients $r = -0.671$ and $r = -0.694$, respectively. Across districts, longitude had also a negative significant effect on ACL with $r = -0.475$. An overall results showed that, the geographical variables except longitude, the rainfall recorded, the stand and the tree measurements, had no significant ($p>0.05$) effect on the average cone size in terms of length (ACL) and width (ACW) (Table 4). In the contrary, the average cone mass (ACM) showed highly ($p<0.01$) negative significant correlations with longitude ($r = -0.523$) and positive significant correlations with altitude ($r = 0.377$).

For average cone weights, the highest mean values were obtained in Le Kef forests (D2) followed immediately by Kasserine districts (D1), with 26.04±1.29 and 22.59±0.99 g, respectively (Figure 2c). Lower ACM was found elsewhere, with an average value of 15.8±0.97 g in Siliana district (D3) and 19.34±2.52 g in Kairouan district (D4). Moreover, no significant relationship was recorded between ACM and the latitude, the recorded rainfall, the stand and the tree characteristics (Table 5).

For the average cone size, results showed that the longest cones were registered in le Kef forests (D2), followed by those obtained in D1, D5 and D6 where ACL range between 67.84±1.36 mm in D1 and 63.82±1.38 mm in D3 (Figure 2d). Shorter cone length were found in D3 (59.84±1.23 mm) and D4 (62.33±4.12 mm). Similarly, the highest ACW was registered D4 (31.91±0.45 mm), followed by intermediate mean values obtained D1, D2, D3 and D5. The lowest ACW was recorded in D6 with 28.39±0.50 mm (Figure 2e). Concerning the average cone volume (ACV), no significant differences were found between the six Tunisian districts (Figure 2f).

Seed Production

The longitude and altitude occurred the same pattern of variation across districts when the average seed mass (ASM) was analyzed (Table 5). Similarly to ACM, negative correlation coefficient was recorded between ASM and longitude ($r = -0.660$, $p<0.01$), which it was positive with altitude ($r = 0.379$, $p<0.01$). However, no significant ($P>0.05$) relationship was found between ASM on one hand (Table 2), and the latitude, the various rainfall variables, the stand and the tree parameters affecting the forests in Tunisian districts, as shown in Table 5. However, significant differences were observed between districts for ASM (Figure 3a) while the utmost mean value was recorded in D2 (18.85±0.57 mg) and the lowest one was registered in D6 (11.33±0.19). In fact, ASM it's an interesting variables that depends on seed number (SNC) and the seed mass (SMC) per cone. No significant differences were recorded on SNC between districts which ranging from an average minimum of 76±4 seed/cone registered in D1 to an average maximum of 90±6 seed/cone in D5 (Figure 3b). The highest significant mean value of SMC was registered in D2 (1.65±0.08 g/cone), followed by intermediate values recorded in D1, D4 and D5 (Figure 3c) ranging from 1.27±0.07 g/cone to 1.3±0.13 g/cone.

The lowest mean value of SMC was registered in D6 (0.87±0.13 g/cone). Nevertheless, across Tunisian districts results showed that the number of seed per cone is of about 82±12 seeds/cone (Figure 3b) weighing 1.29±0.05 g (Figure 3c). In fact, SNC and SMC were affected by latitude, longitude, the rainfall variables, in addition to the cone size and the cone volume (Table 6). However, the highest correlation coefficient recorded for SNC it was observed with ACW ($r = 0.523$, $p<0.001$). By similitude, the highest correlation registered for SMC it was found with ACL ($r =0.830$, $p<0.001$) and average cone volume ($r = 0.488$, $p<0.001$). Likewise, the number of seeds (SNT) per average tree, and their total weight (SMT), both increased significantly from 4260±1030 seeds weighing 48.8±12.5g in D6, to 14610±2020 seeds weighing 206.2±32.29 g in D5.

Across districts, the average number of seeds produced by the average Aleppo pine tree is of about 9040±750 seeds (Figure 3d) weighing about 137.89±11.24g $tree^{-1}$ (Figure 3e). Theoretically, the total mass of seeds estimated per stand would vary between a minimum of 54.69±9.27 kg ha^{-1} in D6 to a maximum of 163.94±18.89kg ha^{-1} in D5 (Figure 3f).

Evaluation of the Combined Environmental Factors Effect

Under multiple regression analyses, results showed that highly significant ($p<0.0001$) multi-variable model could be obtained, except for ACW and SNC. In fact, the evaluation of the combined environmental factors effect on the cone number per tree (CNT) lead to the following dual-variable model with $R^2= 0.557$ ($F = 6.28$, $p<0.0001$):

$$CNT = -238.453 + 23.921\ H - 1.219\ age \qquad (1)$$

In the same way, results showed after similar evaluation on SMT, the subsistence of a multivariate model explaining the variability of seed yield per tree. The model took into account the total height (H), the crown height and the age with as follow ($R^2 = 0.549$, $F = 6.10$, $p<0.0001$):

$$SMT = 0.719 + 24.963\ H + 18.968\ CrH – 1.543\ Age \qquad (2)$$

By similitude, for cone dimensions only ACM and ACL under multiple regression analyses showed very high significant ($p<0.001$) multivariate models. The multivariate model obtained for ACM offered a mono-variate model using the longitude as explanatory variable with $R^2 = 0.393$ and $F = 3.23$ (Equation 3).

Table 2. Mean values (± standard error) and significant differences between districts for stand characteristics and tree measurements of natural Tunisian Aleppo pine forests

	Districts						
	D1 Kasse-rine (n= 25†)	D2 Le Kef (n = 16)	D3 Siliana (n = 11)	D4 Kairouan (n = 9)	D5 Beja (n = 14)	D6 Zaghouan (n = 4)	Overall (n = 79)
Stand characteristics							
Basal area (m^2ha^{-1})	13.64±1.25 **a**	11.03±1.09 **ab**	11.85±1.19 **ab**	6.83±0.90 **b**	13.64±1.50 **a**	9.57±0.92 **ab**	11.87±0.60
Density ($t.ha^{-1}$)	822±80 **a**	1008±124 **a**	1253±115 **a**	906±146 **a**	935±105 **a**	1295±291 **a**	973±50
Shade (%)	106.06±9.22 **ab**	97.25±15.40 **ab**	144.67±12.68 **a**	69.84±13.05 **b**	111.84±15.49 **ab**	98.93±35.35 **ab**	104.61±6.07
Tree measurements							
DBH (cm)	15.92±1.42 **a**	12.28±0.91 **a**	11.17±0.72 **a**	10.55±0.67 **a**	14.22±1.28 **a**	10.66±0.55 **a**	13.34±0.59
H (cm)	6.95±0.37 **ab**	6.59±0.39 **abc**	5.40±0.27 **bc**	4.75±0.29 **c**	7.71±0.67 **a**	5.78±0.15 **abc**	6.49±0.22
CrD (m)	4.28±0.35 **a**	3.66±0.29 **a**	3.91±0.22 **a**	3.14±0.19 **a**	3.89±0.25 **a**	3.22±0.79 **a**	3.85±0.15
CrH (m)	4.61±0.27 **a**	3.64±0.31 **a**	3.18±0.20 **a**	3.11±0.21 **a**	4.79±0.48 **a**	3.54±0.56 **a**	4.02±0.16
Age (yr)	51±6 **a**	51±4 **a**	39±2 **a**	35±3 **a**	36±3 **a**	39±3 **a**	44±2

† Sampled plots. Acronyms; – *DBH*: diameter at breast height; – *H*: Total height; – *CrD*: Crown diameter; – *CrH*: Crown height. Horizontal lines: Different letters means differences among districts forests.

Table 3. Influence of geographical variables, Bioclimatic effect, rainfall variables, stand characteristics and tree measurements on total cone per tree (CNT) and total seed mass per tree (SMT) in six Tunisian districts where the Natural Aleppo pine forests are occurred

	Districts													
	D1 Kasserine (n= 25†)		D2 Le Kef (n = 16)		D3 Siliana (n = 11)		D4 Kairouan (n = 9)		D5 Beja (n = 14)		D6 Zaghouan (n = 4)		Overall (n = 79)	
	CNT	SMT	CNT	SMT	CNT	SMT	CNT	SMT	CNT	SMT	CNT	SMT	CNT	SMT
Geo-positional variables														
Latitude (°N)	-	-	-	-	-	-	-	-	0.665**	0.849**	-	-	-	-
Longitude (°E)	-	-	-	-	-	-0.768**	-	-	-	-0.635*	-	-	-	-
Altitude (m)	-	-	-	-	-	-	-	-	-	-	-	-	-	-
Bio-Climatic and rainfall variables														
BC effect	-	-	-	-	-	-	-	-	-	-0.795**	-	-	-0.241*	-0.247*
Rain (2003-2004)	-0.549**	-0.502	-	-	-	-	-	-	-	0.922***	-	-	-	-
Rain (2004-2005)	-	-	-	-	-	-	-	-	-	0.785***	-	-	-	-
Rain (2005-2006)	0.445*	0.415*	-	-	-	-	-	-	-	-0.594*	-	-	-	-
Mean rain (03-06)	-0.403*	-	-	-	-	-	-	-	-	0.751**	-	-	-	-

Table 3. (Continued)

Tot rain (03-06)	-0.402*	-	-	-	-	-	-	-	-	0.753**	-	-	-	-
Stand characteristics														
Basal area (m^2ha^{-1})	0.411*	0.400*	-	-	-	-	-	-	-	0.692**	-	0.995**	0.381**	0.460**
Density (tha^{-1})	-0.581**	-0.525**	-	-	-	-	-0.744*	-	-0.664**	-0.654*	-	-	-0.441**	-0.422**
Shade (%)	0.536**	0.579**	-	-	-	-	-	-	-	-	-	-	-	-
Tree measurements														
DBH (cm)	0.619**	0.568**	-	-	-	-	0.756*	-	0.573*	0.797***	-	-	0.585***	0.604***
H (cm)	0.674***	0.619**	-	-	-	-	-	-	-	0.715**	-	-	0.550***	0.628***
CrD (m)	0.737***	0.719***	-	-	-	-	-	0.757*	-	-	-	-	0.563***	0.492***
CrH (m)	0.538**	0.499*	-	-	-	-	-	-	-	0.778**	-	-	0.504***	0.605***
Age (yr)	0.503*	0.433*	-	-	-	-	-	-	-	0.693**	-	-	0.313**	0.326**

† Sampled plots, * p<0.05; **p<0.01; ***p<0.001. Acronyms; – *CNT*: Cone number per tree; – *SMT*: Seed mass per tree;– *DBH*: diameter at breast height; – *H*: Total height; – *CrD*: Crown diameter; – *CrH*: Crown height. Horizontal lines: Different letters means differences among districts forests.

Table 4. Influence of geographical variables, Bioclimatic effect, rainfall variables, stand characteristics and tree measurements on the average cone mass (ACL) and the average seed mass (ACW) in six districts of Tunisia where the Natural Aleppo pine forests are distributed

	Districts													
	D1 Kasserine (n= 25[†])		D2 Le Kef (n = 16)		D3 Siliana (n = 11)		D4 Kairouan (n = 9)		D5 Beja (n = 14)		D6 Zaghouan (n = 4)		Overall (n = 79)	
	ACL	ACW	ACL	ACW	ACL	ACW	ACL	ACW	ACL	ACW	ACL	ACW	ACL	**ACW**
Geo-positional variables														
Latitude (°N)	-	-	-	-	-	-	-	-	-	-	-	-	-	-
Longitude (°E)	-	-	-	-	- 0.671*	-	- 0.694*	-	-	-	-	-	-0.475**	-
Altitude (m)	-	-	-	-	-	-	-	-	0.647*	-	-	-0.986*	-	-
Bio-Climatic and rainfall variables														
BC effect	-	-	-	-	-	-	-	-	-	-	-	-	-	-
Rain (2003-2004)	-	-	-	-	-	-	-	-	-	-	-	-	-	-
Rain (2004-2005)	-	-	-	-	-	-	-	-	-	-	-	-	-	-
Rain (2005-2006)	-	-	-	-	-	-	-	-	-	-	-	-	-	-

Table 4. (Continued)

Mean rain (03-06)	-	-	-	-	-	-	-	-	-	-	-	-	-	-
Tot rain (03-06)	-	-	-	-	-	-	-	-	-	-	-	-	-	-
Stand characteristics														
Basal area (m^2ha^{-1})	-	-	-	-	-	-	-	-	-	-	-	-	-	-
Density (tha^{-1})	-	-	-	-	-	-	-	-	-	-	- 0.991**	-	-	-
Shade (%)	-	-	-	-	-	-	-	-	-	-	-	-	-	-
Tree measurements														
DBH (cm)	-	-	-	-	-	-	-	-	-	-	-	-	-	-
H (cm)	-	-	-	-	-	-	-	-	-	-	-	-	-	-
CrD (m)	-	-	-	-	-	-	-	-	-	-	-	-	-	-
CrH (m)	-	-	-	-	-	-	-	-	-	-	-	-	-	-
Age (yr)	-	-	-	-	-	-	-	-	-	-	-	-	-	-

† Sampled plots, * $p<0.05$; $^{**}p<0.01$; $^{**}*p<0.001$. Acronyms; – *ACL*: Average cone length; – *ACW*: Average cone width; – *DBH*: diameter at breast height; – *H*: Total height; – *CrD*: Crown diameter; – *CrH*: Crown height. Horizontal lines: Different letters means differences among districts forests.

Table 5. Influence of geographical variables, bioclimatic effect, rainfall variables, stand characteristics and tree measurements on the average cone mass (ACM) and the average seed mass (ASM) in six districts of Tunisia where the Natural Aleppo pine forests are distributed

	Districts													
	D1 Kasserine (n= 25†)		D2 Le Kef (n = 16)		D3 Siliana (n = 11)		D4 Kairouan (n = 9)		D5 Beja (n = 14)		D6 Zaghouan (n = 4)		Overall (n = 79)	
	ACM	ASM	ACM	ASM	ACM	ASM	ACM	ASM	ACM	ASM	ACM	ASM	ACM	ASM
Geo-positional variables														
Latitude (°N)	0.523^{*}	-	-	-	-	-	-	-	-	-	-	-	-	-
Longitude	-	-	-	-	-	-	-	-	-0.587*	-	-	-	-	-
(°E)													0.523^{**}	0.660^{**}
Altitude (m)	-	-	0.536^{*}	0.541^{*}	-	-	-	-	0.556^{*}	-	-	-	0.377^{**}	0.379^{**}
Bio-Climatic and rainfall variables														
BC effect	-	-	-	-	-	-	-	-	-	-	-	-	-	-
									0.694^{**}	0.616^{*}				
Rain (2003-2004)	-	-	-	-	-	-	0.708^{*}	-	0.642^{*}	-	-	-	-	-
Rain (2004-2005)	-	-	-	-	-	-	-	-	-	-	-	-	-	-

Table 5. (Continued)

Rain (2005-2006)	-	-	-	-	-	-	-	-	-	-	-	-	-	-
Mean rain (03-06)	-	-	-	-	-	-	0.679*	-	-	-	-	-	-	-
Tot rain (03-06)	-	-	-	-	-	-	0.684*	-	-	-	-	-	-	-
Stand characteristics														
Basal area (m^2ha^{-1})	-	-	-	-	-	-	-	-	-	-	-	0.580*	-	-
Density ($t\ ha^{-1}$)	-	-	-	-	-	-	0.690*	-	-	-	-	-	-	-
Shade (%)	-	-	-	-	-	-	-	-	-	-	-	-	-	-
Tree measurements														
DBH (cm)	-	-	-	-	-	-	-	-	-	-	-	-	-	-
H (cm)	-	-	-	-	-	-	-	-	-	-	-	-	-	0.238*
CrD (m)	-	-	-	-	-	-	-	-	-	-	-	-	-	-
CrH (m)	-	-	-	-	-	-	-	-	-	-	-	0.596*	-	-
Age (yr)	-	-	-	-	-	-	-	-	-	-	-	-	-	0.262*

† Sampled plots, * $p<0.05$; ** $p<0.01$; *** $p<0.001$. Acronyms; – *ACM*: Average cone mass; – *ASM*: Average seed mass; – *DBH*: diameter at breast height; – *H*: Total height; – *CrD*: Crown diameter; – *CrH*: Crown height. Horizontal lines: Different letters means differences among districts forests.

Table 6. Influence of geographical variables, Bioclimatic effect, rainfall variables, stand characteristics, tree measurements, and cone dimensions on seed number per cone (SNC) and seed mass per cone (SMC) in six districts of Tunisia where the Natural Aleppo pine forests are distributed

	Districts													
	D1 Kasserine (n= 25[†])		D2 Le Kef (n = 16)		D3 Siliana (n = 11)		D4 Kairouan (n = 9)		D5 Beja (n = 14)		D6 Zaghouan (n = 4)		Overall (n = 79)	
	SNC	SMC	SNC	SMC	SNC	SMC	SNC	SMC	SNC	SMC	SNC	SMC	SNC	SMC
Geo-positional variables														
Latitude (°N)	-	-	-	-	0.745*	-	-	-	-	-	-	-	0.305**	-
Longitude (°E)	-	-	-	-	-0.760**	-	-	-	-	-0.620*	-	-	-	-0.412**
Altitude (m)	-	-	-	-	0.609*	-	-	-	-	0.553*	-	-	-	-
Bio-Climatic and rainfall variables														
BC effect	-	-	-	-	-	-	-	-	-	-0.645*	-	-	-	-
Rain (2003-2004)	-	-	-	-	0.687*	-	0.746*	-	-	-	-	-	0.291**	-
Rain (2004-2005)	-	-	-	-	0.729*	-	0.688*	-	-	-	-	-	0.313**	-
Rain (2005-2006)	-	-	-	-	0.697*	-	-	-	-	-	-	-	0.303**	-

Table 6. (Continued)

Mean rain (03-06)	-	-	-	-	0.709*	-	0.722*	-	-	-	-	-	0.316**	-
Tot rain (03-06)	-	-	-	-	0.710*	-	0.728*	-	-	-	-	-	0.316**	-
Stand characteristics														
Basal area (m^2ha^{-1})	-	-	-	-	-	-	-	-	-	0.549*	-	-	-	-
Density (t ha^{-1})	-	-	-	-	-	-	-	-	-	-	-0.964*	-0.959*	-	-
Shade (%)	-	-	-	-	-	-	-	-	-	-	-	-	-	-
Tree measurements														
DBH (cm)	-	-	-	-	-	-	-	-	-	-	-	-	-	-
H (cm)	-	-	-	-	-	-	-	-	-	-	-	-	-	-
CrD (m)	-	-	-	-	-	-	-	-	-	-	-	-	-	-
CrH (m)	-	-	-	-	-	-	-	-	-	-	-	-	-	-
Age (yr)	-	-	-	-	-	-	-	-	-	-	-	-	-	-
Cone dimensions														
ACL (mm)	-	0.645***	0.550*	0.806***	0.685*	0.651*	0.980**	0.969***	0.703**	0.916***	-	-	0.261*	0.830***
ACW (mm)	-	-	-	-	-	-	0.805**	0.843**	-	-	-	-	0.523***	-
ACV (cm^3)	-	0.399*	-	-	-	-	0.957***	0.975**	-	-	-	-	0.291**	0.488***

† Sampled plots, * $p<0.05$; ** $p<0.01$; *** $p<0.001$. Acronyms; – *SNC*: Seed number per cone; – *SMC*: seed mass per cone; – *DBH*: diameter at breast height; – *H*: Total height; – *CrD*: Crown diameter; – *CrH*: Crown height. Horizontal lines: Different letters means differences among districts forests.

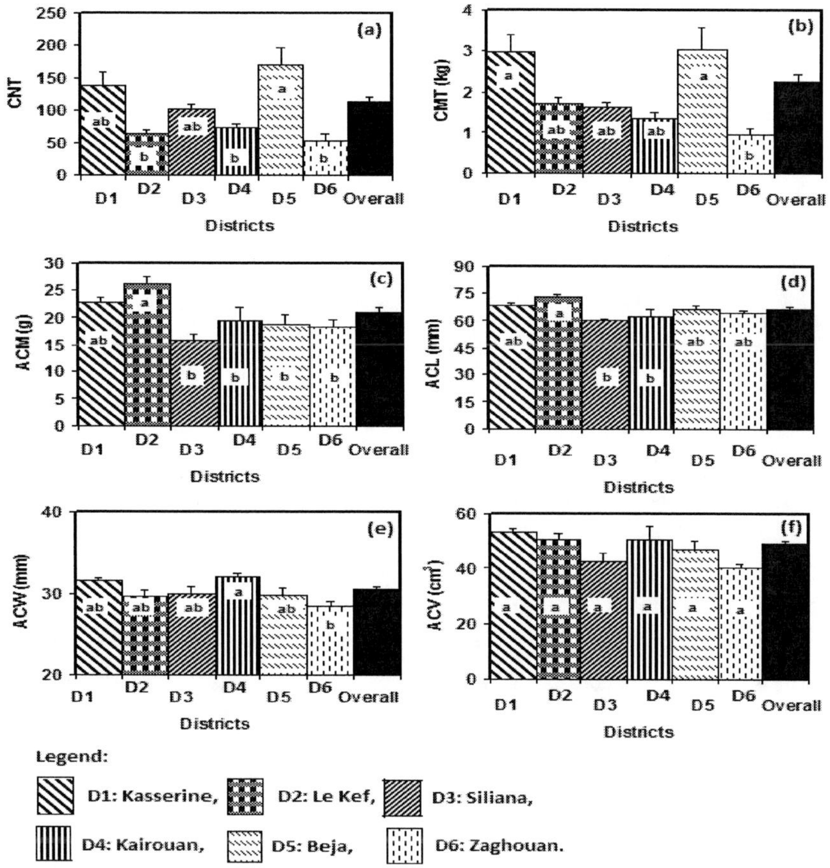

Figure 2. Comparison of the cone production in terme of number (a) and weight (b), in addition to the average cone dimensions (*ACM*: mass (c), *ACL*: length (d), *ACW*: width (e), *ACV*: Volume (f) produced in natural Aleppo pine forests located at six Tunisian districts.

Indeed, the model obtained for ACL presented a bi-variate model using the bio-climate zones and the longitude as explanatory variables with R^2 = 0.416 and F = 3.57 (Equation 4).

$$ACM = -17.975 - 7.612\ Long \quad (3)$$

$$ACL = -142.205 + 2.872\ BC - 9.147\ Long \quad (4)$$

Furthermore, the evaluation of the combined environmental variables on SMC and ASM offered two high significant ($p<0.01$) mono-variate models using only the longitude as an explanatory variable with ($R^2 = 0.329$, F = 2.45) and ($R^2 = 0.516$, F = 5.33) as showed in equations (5) and (6) respectively:

$$SMC = -0.805 - 0.586 \text{ Long} \quad (5)$$

$$ASM = 73.846 - 5.312 \text{ Long} \quad (6)$$

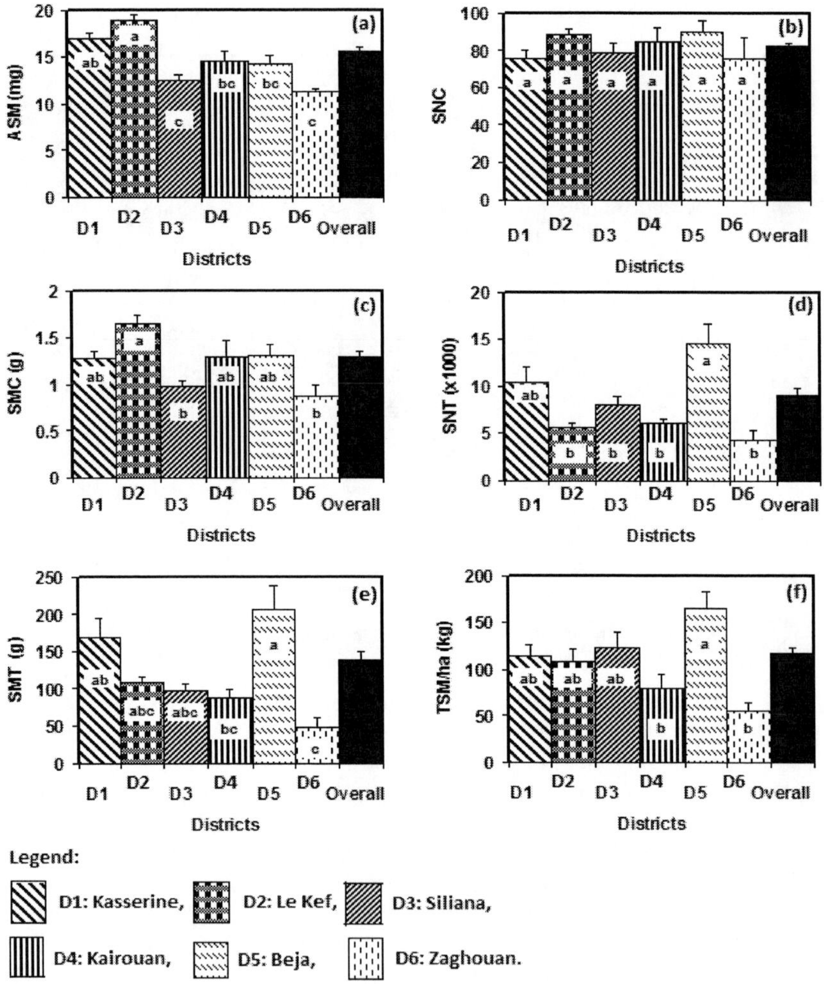

Figure 3. Comparison of ASM (a), the seed production per cone in terme of number (b) and mass (c), and per tree ((d): number, (e); mass), in addition to the prediction of the total seed mass per hectare (f) produced in natural Aleppo pine forests located at six Tunisian districts.

DISCUSSION

Across Tunisian districts where most of the Aleppo pine populations occur, the rainfall variation during the cone growing season period prior to harvesting did not affect the cone and seed production by using the estimation from the average tree representing the stand values. Indeed at the cone level, bioclimatic effect characterizing the study area and rainfall variation registered was not useful in explaining differences observed between districts where D2 offered substantially heavier cones (ACM) enclosing heavier seeds (ASM) than other Tunisian districts. But at tree and stand level, the higher fructification producing the highest amount of cones (CNT, CMT) and seeds (SNT, SMT, TSM ha^{-1}) was observed in D5 due to the combined effect linking mature cone morphology (ACL, ACW, ACV) and amount bear in the canopy (CNT, CMT). However, in D2 we observed less fructification with larger mature cones but in D5 we recorded mainly abundant cone production with small reduction on cone dimension. The tendency was not similar according the ACW values, being ACL more sensitive than ACW. Indeed, similar differences in ACL values were reported by Arista and Talavera (1996) and Donahue and Lopez-Upton (1996) which related it to longitude, total height and crown height of the average tree. Previous researches (Goubitz et al. 2002; Climent et al. 2008) showed that pine tree circumstance invests nutriments primarily in growth and secondarily in fructification. Furthermore, the pine trees developing in high competition have limited resources for fruit development and canopy increase what implies less photosynthetic surface areas (Stephenson 1981). High cone crops and seed yield were recorded in areas with low pine tree density (250 $treeha^{-1}$), which a severe decrease was observed from 750 $treeha^{-1}$. (Ayari et al. 2011b)

By contrast, Harfouche et al. (2003) reported an increase in ASM of the same tree species as a result of geo-positional effect. This result reflects higher fructification processes in northern locations. In the present study, increasing latitudes in Tunisian Mediterranean coast were related to increasing SNC. Latitudinal changes are been related to aridity gradients in the Mediterranean basin (Ayari et al. 2011a). In Tunisia, higher rainfall and soil moisture are found in northern areaass, increasing growth and fructification according we are moving to northwards (Ayari et al. 2011b). Similarly, longitude is related to reproductive characteristics, ACM, SMC and ASM which decreased according higher longitudinal areas. In adittion, longitude was a prevailing factor under multiple regression analyses explaining variability in ACM, SMC and ASM. The altitudinal effect was registered under simple regression analyses on ACM and ASM, in a similar way than Moroccan Aleppo pine forests (Boulli et al. 2001). In neighbouring stands of Algeria, altitudinal effect was not significant on the cone dimensions which could be explained by the fact that only eight locations were sampled (Harfouche et al. 2003).

Under simple regression analyses, the pine tree density and basal area had a significant effect only on CNT and SMT, enhancing production of cones and seeds (Stiell 1988; Arista and Talavera, 1996; Greene et al. 1999). The evaluation of combined environmental factors effects were not showing significant multivariate models when we were using the stand characteristics (obtained under multiple regression analysis). However, we found significant relationships of Further pine tree size on CNT and SMT. The fact that tree-age offered the lowest correlation coefficient value meant that size measurements are more important than age in affecting the tree fructification (Sutton et al. 2002). Numerous studies related cone and seed production to tree size, such as total height (Moya et al. 2008), trunk diameter (Messaoud et al. 2007; Ordonez et al. 2005; Stiell 1988; Sutton et al. 2002; Turner et al. 2007), or both (Oliva and Colinas 2007). Tree crown size is another influencing factor, while larger crowns have higher photosynthetic activity to allocate cone and seed production (Crocker et al. 1975; Sutton et al. 2002). Under multiple regression analysis, only crown height was retained along with H and age only for explaining CNT and SMT.

Conclusion

The latitudes, the ACW, the rainfall variables registered across Tunisian districts showed a significant relationship only with SNC product. Similar significant relationship was also found between CNT and its SMT with stand characteristics and all tree dimensions including age. Longitude was the most used geo-positional parameter for explaining the variability of ACM, ACL, SMC and ASM. Furthermore, it was negatively linked to average cone mass and length, in addition to its total and the average seed mass. Similarly, stand density had a negative effect on CNT and SMT, whereas basal area was positively correlated with both parameters. Indeed, after evaluation of the combined environmental factor DBH and CrD taken from the sampled forest stands had no significant effect on cone and seed production. However, lower forest stand density enhanced fructification, regeneration, growth of wood forest tree species production and pastoral species. Elsewhere, higher basal area showed an increase cone and seed production.

ACKNOWLEDGEMENTS

This research was funded by Agro-Sylvo-Pastoral (INRGREF, Tunisia) and the Tunisian Ministry of Agriculture and Water Resources and also supported by the Spanish I+D+I National Programme CYCIT-AGL 2008-03602/FOR and CONSOLIDER-INGENIO 2010: MONTES (CSD 2008-00040). AGORA Europen project and as well as the Instituto Superior de Agronomia (ISA) are also gratefully acknowledges. The authors would also like to thank the financial support by the Fundación Española para la Ciencia y la Tecnología (FECYT, EX2009-0397) and the FCT (SFRH / BPD / 63979 / 2009).

REFERENCES

Arista M. and Talavera S. 1996. Density Effect on the Fruit-set, Seed Crop Viability and Seedling Vigour of *Abies pinsapo. Annals of Botany* 77: 187-192.

Asset G., Baugé E., Wolff R.L., Fruchart J.C., Dallogeville J., 1999. *Pinus pinaster* Oil Affects Lipoprotein Metabolism in Apolipoprotein E-Deficient Mice. *The Journal of Nutrition* 129: 1972-1978.

Ayari A., Moya D., Rejeb M.N., Ben Mansoura A., Albouchi A., De Las Heras J., Fezzani T., Henchi B. 2011a. Geographical variation on cone and seed production of natural *Pinus halepensis* Mill. forests in Tunisia. *Journal of Arid Environments* 75: 403-410.

Ayari A., Moya D., Rejeb M.N., Ben Mansoura A., Garchi S., De Las Heras J., Henchi B. 2011b. Alternative sampling methods to estimate structure and reproductive characteristics of Aleppo pine forest in Tunisia. *Forest Systems*, In Press.

Boulli A., Baaziz M., M'Hirit O. 2001. Polymorphism of natural populations of *Pinus halepensis* Mill. in Morocco as revealed by morphological characters. *Euphytica* 119: 309-316.

Climent J., Prada M.A., Calama R., Chambel R.M., De Ron D.S., Alia R., 2008. To grow or to seed: Ecotypic Variation in reproductive allocation and cone production by young female Aleppo pine (*Pinus halepensis*, Pinaceae). *American Journal of Botany* 95(7): 1-10.

Croker T.C. and Boyer W. D. 1975. Regenerating longleaf pine naturally. USDA Forest Service, Research Paper SO-105. Southern Forest Experiment Station, New Orleans.

Despland E. and Houle G. 1997. Aspect influences cone abundance within the crown of *Pinus banksiana* Lamb. trees at the limit of the species distribution in northern Québec (Canada). *Ecoscience* 4: 521-525.

DGF (Direction Générale des Forêts) (1995). Résultats du premier inventaire forestier national en Tunisie. Ministère de l'Agriculture, Tunis, 88p.

Donahue J. K. and Lopez-Upton J. 1996. Geographic variation in leaf, cone and seed morphology of *Pinus greggii* in native forests. *Forest Ecology and Management* 82: 145-157.

Garchi S. and Ben Mansoura A. 1999. influence de l'ombrage sur l'accroissement du pin d'Alep à Jbel Mansour. *Les Annales de l'INRGREF*, 3: 89-102.

Goubitz S., Werger M.J.A., Shmida A., Ne'eman G., 2002. Cone abortion in *Pinus halepensis*: the role of pollen quantity, tree size and cone location. *Oikos* 97: 125–133.

Greene D.F., Zasada J.C., Sirois L., Kneeshaw D., Morin H., Charron I., Simard M.J. 1999. A review of the regeneration dynamics of North American boreal forest tree species. *Canadian Journal of Forest Research* 29: 824-839.

Harfouche A., Boudjada S., Chettah W., Allam M., Belhou O., Merazga A., 2003. Variation and population structure in Aleppo pine (*Pinus halepensis* Mill) in Algeria. *Silvae Genetica* 52: 244–249.

Krugman S.L. and Jenkinson J.L. 1974. in Schopmeyer C. S. (tech. coordinator), Seeds of woody plants in the United States. USDA Agric. Washington, DC. *Handbook*. pp. 598-638.

Mencuccini M., Piussi P., Zanzi S.A. 1995. Thirty years of seed production in a subalpine Norway spruce forest: patterns of temporal and spatial variation. *Forest Ecology and Management* 76:109–125.

Messaoud Y., Begeron Y., Asselin H. 2007. Reproductive potential of balsam fir (*Abies balsamea*), white spruce (*Picea glauca*), and black spruce (*P. mariana*) at the ecotone between mixedwood and coniferous forests in the boreal zone of western Quebec. *American Journal of Botany* 94: 746-754.

Moya D., De Las Heras J., López-Serrano F.R., Leone V. 2008. Optimal intensity and age management in young Aleppo pine stands for post-fire resilience. *Forest Ecology and Management* 255: 3270-3280.

Nasri N., Khaldi A., Triki S. 2004. Variabilté morphologique des cônes et graines de pin d'Alep et pin pignon en Tunisie. *Revue Forestière Française* LVI: 21-28.

Naveh Z. 1974. Effects of fire in the Mediterranean region. Fire and Ecosystems (eds Kozlowsky, T. T. and Ahlgren C. E.). Academic Press, New York, pp. 401-434.

Oliva J & Colinas C. 2007. Decline of silver fir (*Abies alba* Mill.) stands in the Spanish Pyrenees: role of management, historic dynamics and pathogens. *Forest Ecology and Management* 252: 84-97.

Ordonez J.L., Retana J., Espelta J.M. 2005. Effects of tree size, crown damage, and tree location on post-fire survival and cone production of *Pinus nigra* trees. *Forest Ecology and Management* 206, 109–117.

Quezel P. 2000. Taxonomy and biogeography of Mediterranean pines (*Pinus halepensis* and *P. brutia*). In: Ne'eman, G., Trabaud, L. (Eds.), Ecology, Biogeography and Management of *Pinus halepensis* and *P. brutia* Forest Ecosystems in the Mediterranean basin. Backhuys Publishers, Leiden, pp. 1–12.

Rondeux J. 1993. La mesure des arbres et des peuplements forestiers. Les Presses Agronomiques de Gembloux, Belgium. pp. 521.

S.A.S. (Statistical Analysis Systems), 2005. SASR User's Guide v 9.0. Statistical Analysis Systems Institute. Inc., Cary, North Carolina.

Sghaier T., Khaldi A., Khouja M.L., Nsibi R. 1997. Estimation du rendement en cônes et en graines du pin d'Alep dans les forêts de Ouergha (Sakiet Sidi Youssef-Tunisie). *Annales des Recherches Forestières Maroc* 30: 84-89.

Smith C.C. and Balda, R.P. 1979. Competition among insects, birds and mammals for conifer seeds. *American Zoologist* 19: 1065–1083.

Stephenson A.G. 1981. Flower and fruit abortion: proximate causes and ultimate functions. *Annual Review of Ecology and Systematics* 12:253-279.

Stiell W.M. 1988. Consistency of cone production in individual red pine. *Forestry Chronicle* 64: 480-484.

Sutton A., Staniforth R.J., Tardif J. 2002. Reproductive ecology and allometry of red pine (*Pinus resinosa*) at the northwestern limit of its distribution range in Manitoba Canada. *Canadian Journal of Botany* 80: 482–493.

Trabaud L, Michels C, Grosman J. 1985. Recovery of burnt *Pinus halepensis* Mill. forests. II. Pine recon-stitution after wildfirere. *Forest Ecology and Management* 13: 167-179.

Turner M.G., Turner D.M., Romme W.H., Tinker D.B. 2007. Cone production in young post-fire *Pinus contorta* stands in Greater Yellowstone (USA). *Forest Ecology and Management* 242: 119-126.

Verkaik I. & Espelta J.M. 2006. Post-fire regeneration thinning, cone production, serotiny and regeneration age in Pinus halepensis. Forest Ecology and Management 231: 155–163.

Way S. 2006. Strategic management of Aleppo Pines on Lower Eyre Peninsula to maximise biodiversity conservation outcomes, Department for Environment and Heritage, South Australia.

In: Tunisia: Economic, Political and Social Issues ISBN: 978-1-61942-157-8
Eds: M. Pusatieri and J. Cannamela

Chapter 5

WHAT CAN THE TUNISIAN REVOLUTION BRING TO AGRICULTURAL WATER SECTOR MANAGEMENT IN TUNISIA?

Aymen Frija[1], Ali Chebil*[2] and Brian Hurd[3]
[1]Higher Agricultural School of Mograne. Mograne, Tunisia
[2]Institut National de Recherches en Génie Rural, Eaux et Forêts, Ariana, Tunisie
[3]Department of Agricultural Economics and Agricultural Business New Mexico State University, Las Cruces, US

ABSTRACT

Tunisia is among countries that face deep and growing water shortages. The water is mainly used in the agricultural sector and many studies show that it is still inefficiently used and allocated despite the deep reforms and institutional innovations brought during the last three decades. In this period, Tunisia is celebrating a peaceful and democratic revolution expected to bring freedom and democracy to the Tunisian population. Many studies (Adelman and Morris, 1967; Adelman and Lohmoller, 1994; Morris and Adelman, 1988; Remmer, 1998) state that democracy and economic growth and development are significantly and positively correlated. By simply introducing democracy into its political

* Corresponding author: Email: chebila@yahoo.es. Tél. : +216 71 719 630; Fax : +216 71 717 951.

and economic system a country can easily gain more growth and wealth. This is a very important statement that should encourage Tunisian people looking forward the economic development of their country through the implementation of new and sustainable democratic political and economic institutions. However, this economic developed will not be realized without higher pressure on natural resources, especially water, which are already suffering from deep shortage and inefficient use.

In this paper, we propose to discuss the possible implications of the Tunisian revolution on the water sector management, with a focus on agricultural water management. Our main objective is to provide guidelines on how to evaluate the future management of the irrigation water sector in the country within the new political context of democratic and efficient economic institutions. Main guidelines of the current agricultural water management tools will be described as well as their limits and potentialities. Then, recommendations and perspectives for future improvement of water management and governance in the country will be provided.

1. INTRODUCTION

Tunisia is among countries that face deep and growing water shortages. The water is mainly used in the agricultural sector (for more than 80%) and many studies show that it is still inefficiently used and allocated despite the deep reforms and institutional innovations brought during the last three decades. In this period, Tunisia is celebrating a peaceful and democratic revolution expected to bring freedom and democracy to the Tunisian population, which was for long time suffering from bureaucratic political and economic system full of unfair formal and informal practices.

Many studies (Adelman and Morris, 1967; Adelman and Lohmoller, 1994; Morris and Adelman, 1988; Remmer, 1998) state that democracy and economic growth and development are significantly and positively correlated. By simply introducing democracy into its political and economic system a country can easily gain more growth and wealth. This is a very important statement that should encourage Tunisian people looking forward the economic development of their country through the implementation of new and sustainable democratic political and economic institutions. However, this economic developed will not be realized without higher pressure on natural resources, especially water, which are already suffering from deep shortage and inefficient use.

In this paper, we propose to discuss the possible implications of the Tunisian revolution on the water sector management, with a focus on agricultural water management. Our main objective is to provide guidelines on how to evaluate the future management of the irrigation water sector in the country within the new political context of democratic and efficient economic institutions. Main guidelines of the current agricultural water management tools will be described as well as their limits and potentialities. Then, recommendations and perspectives for future improvement of water management and governance in the country will be provided based on successful experiences of other similar developed countries.

2. Water Resources and Water Usage in Tunisia

2.1. Water Resources

Annual rainfall averages in Tunisia varies from 1000 mm in the North to 300 mm in the South. Overall water resources in the country are estimated to be around 4700 million m^3 (Mm^3) (Al Atiri, 2007) including 650 Mm^3 of non-renewable resources (13.8 % of the total water resources). Surface water is estimated to 2700 Mm^3 (Table 1). This surface water is mobilized through large infrastructure, mainly 27 large dams, 182 hills dams and 698 artificial lakes. Groundwater resources account for around 43 % of the total water potential. They are estimated to be around 2000 Mm^3, confined within 212 shallow aquifers (containing 719 Mm^3) and 267 deep aquifers. It is estimated that 650 Mm^3 of this resource is mainly located in the south and is non-renewable.

Like surface water, groundwater is characterized by unequal allocation and variable quality in terms of salinity. It is distributed among regions in Tunisia as follows (Ben Abdallah, 2007):

- The north has 55 % of the shallow groundwater resources and only 18 % of the deep groundwater resources
- The centre provides 30 % of the shallow resources and 24 % of the deep resources
- The south provides 15 % of the shallow resources and has 58 % of the deep resources.

Good quality groundwater is only found in 8 % of shallow water and 20 % of deep aquifers. If it is assumed that salty water up to 3 g/l can be used in the agricultural sector and for the production of drinking water, then approximately 36 % of groundwater resources are unsuitable for these purposes (Ben Abdallah, 2007). Another phenomenon, which has a significant effect on water quality, is drought. In periods of drought, the salinity of the water stored in shallow aquifers can reach 3.5 g/l, in some cases due to over-extraction, as resources are drawn down for both drinking and irrigation purposes.

Shallow aquifers in Tunisia were submitted to an increasing pressure during the last two decades. This pressure was particularly higher in coastal (Cap Bon, Sahel, and Gabes) and central (Kairouan) regions (Al Atiri, 2007). They have been the main irrigation source for the private irrigated areas of Tunisia, which cover around 38% of the total irrigated areas in the country. The private irrigated areas are those areas which are irrigated from bore wells and wells that aren't deeper than 80 meters. Moreover, deep aquifers are also used for the irrigation of some public irrigated areas mainly in the Southern oases.

Because of the climatic variation and the growing food demand in the 80's, Tunisian agricultural strategy was based on the extension of the irrigated areas through the investment in large water infrastructure and the use of groundwater. With the extension of old irrigated areas and the creation of new ones, the pressure on groundwater resource was quickly multiplied.

In fact, the number of wells in Tunisia passed from 60415 in 1980 to 128400 in 2000 (groundwater paper), with a total increase of 113% (5.6 yearly). This dynamic was also observed for the equipped (pumping engines, solar energy, etc.) wells which number passed from 23061 in 1980 to 86965 in 2000, with a total increase of 380% (19% yearly) (CITET, 2009).

Table 1. Potential, available, and mobilized water resources in Tunisia (values in Mm3)

	Potential resources		Available resources	Mobilized resources
Surface water	2700	56%	2500	4060, of which 43% of groundwater
Groundwater	2140	44%	2140	
Total	4840	100%	4640	

Source: MAE, 2008.

Efforts were also made in Tunisia to develop non-conventional water resources, particularly desalinized and treated water. In fact, the production cost for these resources is generally very high. Only 5 % (225 Mm^3) of the water mobilized in Tunisia in 2009 was from treated wastewater sources although its supply is increasing annually by 8 %. However, its use is limited to 20 % (Al Atiri, 2009). Treated wastewater water is mainly used in agriculture (feed crops, industrial crops, forests, etc.), the urban sector (irrigation of natural parks, etc.) and the tourist sector (golf courses, hotel gardens, etc.).

This limited use of treated wastewater is mainly due to (i) the existence of available conventional water next to the treatment plants (75 of which are currently operational) which discourages users to use this source of water, and (ii) the limited storage capacity for non-conventional water in the irrigated areas which makes its supply unstable over the agricultural seasons. Moreover, farmers are usually reluctant concerning the use of this water due to its expected impact on their land structure and on the quality of their products.

Tunisia has briny water tables, situated essentially in the south of the country. Reverse osmosis has given this potential water source increased value by making it available for drinking water. Total desalination capacity for drinking water is about 80,000 m3 per day. The desalination of seawater offers a long-term alternative source of drinking water which could contribute as much as 50 Mm3 in 2030.

Thus, desalination of briny and sea waters constitutes an alternative that is more and more attractive as a source of drinking water in areas where water supplies are limited and do not meet standards, notably in the center and the south of the country (Horchani, 2007) .

Table 2. Evolution of water demand by sector in Tunisia.

Sectors	1990		2010	
	Mm^3	%	Mm^3	%
Agriculture	1575	82.1	2540	80.2
Urban	240	12.5	462	14.6
Manufacturing	85	4.4	123	3.9
Tourism	20	1	40	1.3
Total	1920	100	3165	100

Source: Besbes, 2011.

2.2. Water Demand in Tunisia

From 1990 to 2010 total water demand in Tunisia is varied from 1920 Mm^3 to 3165 Mm^3, representing an increase rate of 40 %. This increasing demand is mainly due to the fast growing requirements for water by the agricultural sector (more than 80 % of total water consumption) in addition to improvements in households income and live standards and the development of the tourist sector. Water use for domestic and tourist sectors has doubled during the past two decades.

2.3. Water for Irrigation

The irrigated sector is crucial for the national development. It occupies 7 % of the country's useful agricultural area, but contributes significantly to the development of agriculture. It accounts for 30-35 % of agricultural production value, 95 % of horticultural crops, 30 % of dairy production, 70 % of tree crop production, 22 % of agricultural exports (mainly oranges and dates), and 26 % of total agricultural employment (Al Atiri, 2007).

Irrigated areas have continued to increase in Tunisia during the past two decades (Figure 1). In 2009, they accounted for around 450,470 hectares, of which 49.6 % was in the north, 34.7 % in the centre and 15.6 % in the centre-east of the south (DGEDA, various years).

Despite this increase in irrigated land area, the intensification and occupation rates[1] are still below policy makers' expectations. The intensification rate was approximately 89% in 2009, which is much lower than the potential rate - estimated to be around 130 % (DGEDA,various years).

In 2005, the volume of water used for irrigation was estimated at 1889 Mm^3, with average consumption per hectare of approximately 5500 m^3/year. Consumption reaches 20000 m^3/Ha/year in the oasis. In the north of the country were rain is more abundant, the average consumption is 4000 m3/hectare/year (Horchani, 2007).

Three regimes of management in the irrigated areas could be identified in Tunisia (Figure 2).

[1] Occupation rate = irrigated area / irrigable area; Intensification rate = effectively irrigated areas / irrigable areas

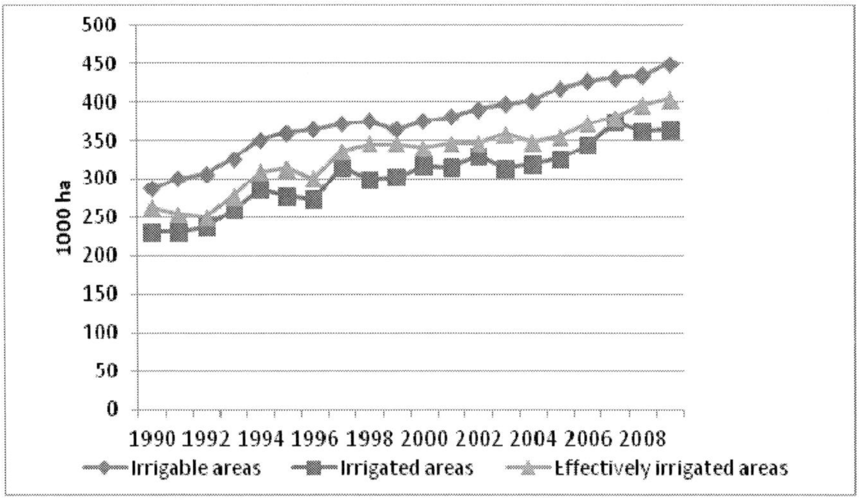

Figure 1. Evolution of the irrigation areas during the past two decade (1990-2009) in Tunisia. (DGEDA, various years).

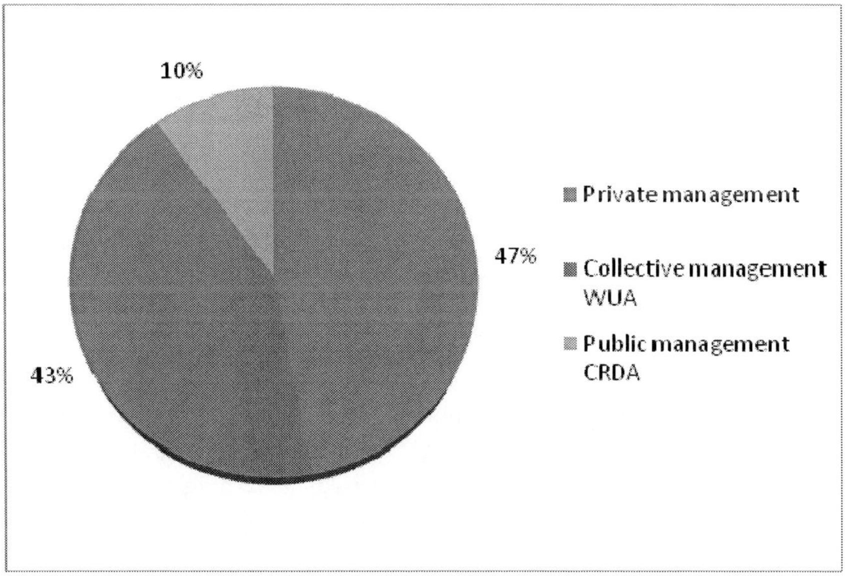

Figure 2. Distribution of the irrigated areas according to the management regime (DGGREE, 2009).

These are the private regime secured by individuals, the administrative regime secured by the CRDA (Commisariats Régionales de Développement Agricole created in the 1990's) and the collective regime secured by the WUAs (Thabet and Chebil, 2006).

- In 2008, private management applies to 47 % of the total irrigated area. It mainly relates to the areas irrigated from superficial aquifers, using a well or other techniques. Farmers in these areas are responsible for the investment and operational costs of their individual water systems.
- Collective management concerns areas that are managed by WUAs. These areas have expanded to cover 43 % of the total irrigated land area in Tunisia in 2008. Collective irrigation networks are set up through public funds, but their management is delegated to the WUA, which fixes the water fees and is responsible for their collection. The WUA also assumes responsibility for investment and the development of irrigation in its areas.
- Public management of large irrigated areas, which constitute around 10 % of the total irrigated lands in Tunisia. This management is still being secured by government agencies (CRDA). Under the Agricultural Reform Law, farmers participate in investment efforts in these areas and pay the total or a part of the O&M costs.

3. Water Institutions: A Theoretical Background

3.1. Water Institutional Structure and Environment

The study of water institutions is not an easy task due to the complicated structure and inter-linkages between their various components. Some distinguish between the water institutional structure and the water institutional environment. Water institutional structure includes the structurally nested and embedded legal, policy and organizational rules governing various facets of water resource management. Water institutional environment, on the other hand, characterizes the overall social, economic, political and resource context within which the water institutional structure evolves and interacts with the water sector. Under certain simplifying conditions, it is possible to provide a visual representation of both the structure and the environment of water institution (Saleth and Dinar, 2004).

The review of the structure of formal and macro-level water institutions is organized within the framework based on institutional decomposition. This framework distinguishes three institutional components, i.e. water law, water policy, and water administration, and highlights a few key institutional aspects under each of three components. As noted already, the ensuing review is focused only on some of the key institutional aspects under each of these three institutional components (Saleth and Dinar, 2004). Figure 1 Depicts a simplified representation of water institutional structure. While figure 1 is largely self-explanatory, a few points require attention. The overall performance of water institutions and their ultimate impact on water sector performance depends not only on the capabilities of their individual institutional components and aspects but also on the strength of structural and functional linkages among them.

The arrow in Figure 1 indicate an illustrative set of linkages possible both within and across the three institutional components. For instance, the legal aspects of how water sources and their relationship with land and environmental resources are treated within water law have linkages with policy aspects such as priority setting for water uses and project selection criteria Saleth and Dinar, 2004).

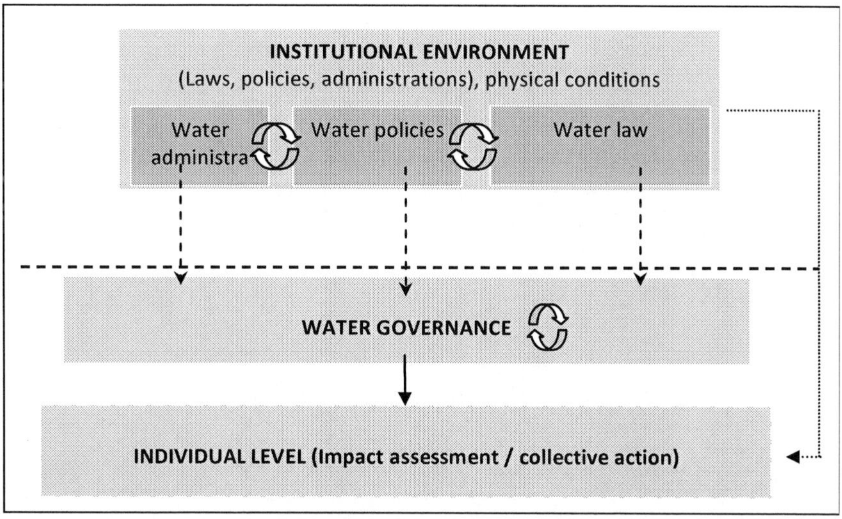

Figure 3. Water sector institutions and interactions.

Thus, as the same previous authors state, a water law that does not differentiate water by its source but recognizes the ecological linkages between water and other resources is more likely to encourage a water policy that assigns a higher priority to environmental imperatives and hydrologicl interconnectivity in project selection. These legal-policy linkages are also important for promoting integrated water resource management. Notably, the legal aspect of water has multiple linkages with many other legal, policy and administration aspects of water. Similarly, the policy aspects pertaining for example to user participation, management decentralization and private sector participation should have strong linkages with other complementary aspects such as the administrative organization and bureaucratization, the ability to raise collective actions and private contributions, etc.

3.2. Water Institutional Change

An important question in the institutional analysis is how institutions and governance structures determine the performance of an economic system. According to North (1990), the fact that institutions affect the performance of economies is hardly controversial. The differential performance of economies over time is fundamentally influenced by the way institutions evolve is also not controversial. One must realize that individuals typically act on incomplete information and with subjectively derived models that are frequently erroneous; Information feedback is typically insufficient to correct these subjective models (North, 1993). Thus, according to North, institutions are not necessarily or even usually created to be socially efficient; rather they (or at least the formal rules, particularly in developing countries) are created to serve the interests of those with bargaining power to create new rules. In a zero transaction cost world, bargaining strength does not affect the efficiency of outcomes; but in a world of positive transaction costs it does and it thus shapes the direction of long term economic growth.

4. Water Institutions in Tunisia

4.1. Water Laws

Water law assumes a central place in the functioning of water institutions as it gives the necessary legal basis to water policy as well as providing an operational framework and powers of enforcement for water administration and its regulatory arrangements (Saleth and Dinar, 2004). From a historical perspective, legislation relating to water resources in Tunisia can be divided into four main contexts[2]:

1) From the first millenium BC until the arrival of Islam, particularly during the Roman period, water resources were managed by building aqueducts for domestic and agricultural use and for water transfer between regions.
2) During the Islamic empire, water was considered to be "God's Gift", and consequently it was declared to be collective property, known as "waqf". In this context, some of the water resources and wells were declared as "waqf" and the public had full access rights to them. However, Islam strongly urged moderation and thriftiness in the use of water, even when performing ablution.
3) The French colonization period (1881-1956) was characterized by the first water Decree favouring the colonists. The Decree of 24 September 1885 defined a public surface water domain, without any reference to groundwater resources. On 24 May 1920, a water committee was appointed. The Decrees which were instituted in 1933, 1935, 1936 and 1938 provided regulations for water use and fixed the charges for this water use; the Decrees of 30 July 1936, 11 January 1945 and 17 March 1949 introduced regulations relating to the Non Governmental Organizations (NGO) involved in water use.
4) The fourth period began with the independence of Tunisia. It was characterized by evolutionary water legislation which related specifically to resource mobilization and exploitation (urban, agricultural, industrial and tourist uses) whilst focusing on water quality and environmental protection of the resource. In order to satisfy water demands from different sectors, a national programme was established to bring into existence many types of hydraulic infrastructure. With the evolution of this plan, hydraulic planning was gradually transformed into an established legislative system. The objectives of this legislative system were to identify the rights and duties of all actors involved in the water field, to preserve water resources, and to ensure its equitable allocation. In 1975, all

[2] Based on Louati et al., 2005.

legislative water documents were updated and promulgated in the Water Code (Law n° 75-16, 31 March 1975).

Since 1975, the Water Code has been continually updated by modifying some legislation and adding new regulations to address socioeconomic and technical requirements. The law n°75-16, 31 March 1975, was largely modified and completed by laws n°87-35, 6 July 1987; n°88-94, 2 August 1988; The law n° 2001-116, 26 November 2001; and law n°2004-24, March 15, 2004. The Tunisian water code is also currently under revision and a new version will soon be ready for validation.

4.2. Water Policies

Water policy relates to the declared statements as well as the intended approach of central government for water resource planning, development, allocation and management (Saleth and Dinar, 2004). It includes statements that not only relate to the overall policy framework but also to specific policy issues such as investment priorities, water transfer, decentralization and private participation, field-level water conservation, and pricing and cost recovery policies.

In Tunisia, the independence of agricultural production from the highly variable climatic conditions was a main objective of policy makers during the 1950's. Accordingly, considerable public hydraulic investment was mobilized in order to control superficial water resources. Nevertheless, this water supply policy was not accompanied at that time by measures that sought to rationalize the growing demand for irrigation water. Policy makers were also facing another challenge due to the increasing competition for water resources created by other sectors (urban water use, manufacturing, tourism). These are considered to be more competitive whilst irrigation water is still being subsidized. Thus, irrigation policies have been shifted since the 1970's from supply towards an irrigation demand management perspective. New policies focus more on organizational and technical tools aiming to reach higher water use efficiencies in all areas of use. In this section, we first review the general, overall aspects of national irrigation water policy in Tunisia during the last three decades, and then provide a detailed description of pricing policies and cost recovery strategies.

From all of the relevant programmes, the following guidelines can be deduced for previous national policy in Tunisia: (1) Investment in projects that aim to improve water use efficiency, (2) enhancement of participation in collective water management, (3) Pricing of water and water services and (4) subsidies and incentives for farmers and the private sector.

4.3. Water Administrations

At the national level, the Ministry of Agriculture and Environment (MAE), through its various departments, is considered as the principal manager of the water sector in Tunisia. However, other ministries, such as the ministry of public health, ministry of public finance, ministry of interior affairs, etc. could also be involved in some management aspects. Main central departments of the MAE that are directly involved in water sector management are:

- General Department of Water Resources (Direction Générale des Ressources en Eau DGRE) which is responsible for monitoring and overall assessment of water resources at the national level;
- General Department of Dams and of Large Hydraulic Projects (Direction Générale des Barrages et des Grand Travaux hydrauliques) which is responsible for the construction of dams (and other large hydraulic projects) and their exploitation in irrigation and other uses.
- General Department of Agricultural Engineering and Water Exploitation (Direction Générale du Génie Rurale et de l'Exploitation des Eaux); This administration is responsible for: irrigation and drainage, rural equipment and development, and (irrigation) water supply for rural populations.

The dissolution during the 1990's of the central "Office of Medjerda Valley Development[3]" (Office de Mise en Valeur de la Vallée de la Medjerda (OMVVM)) and the reinforcement of the CRDA role in regional irrigation development can be considered as major administrative reforms for the Tunisian water sector. Also, the revision, at the same time, of old judicial texts and the implementation of new laws relating to collective water management are important elements in this policy shift.

[3] Central administration which was responsible of all irrigation management tasks at the national level.

Within this context, various other actions were undertaken to improve regional and local management capacities - such as improvements in technical capacity, staff training, and so on. The creation of WUAs as an organizational entity, grouping together all farmers belonging to a given local irrigated area, was the main step in this decentralization process. The aim was to increase farmer participation in decision making and resource management. WUAs are established through government funding and are given responsibility for the collection of water fees as well as service related fees (infrastructure maintenance and so on). The number of WUAs for irrigation water management has risen sharply from about 100 in 1987 to 1064 in 2008 (DGGREE, 2009) managing more than 200,000 ha of irrigated lands (Figure 4).

Many national and regional institutions are involved in the functioning of WUAs (Figure 4). The WUAs are monitored and framed by special regional administrative entities, belonging to the rural engineering division. This latter division provides them with important services, particularly in relation to the technical, administrative and financial training of their staff.

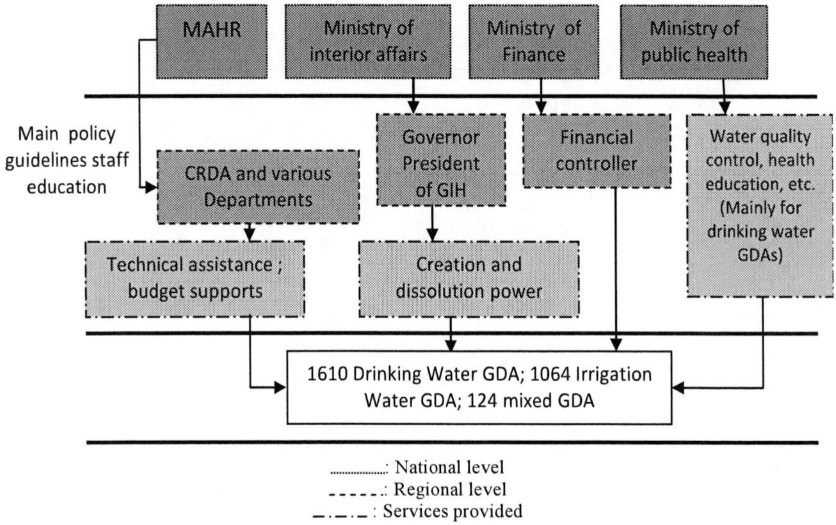

Figure 4. Administrative framework of the Tunisian WUA (GDA).

The responsibilities shared in the irrigated areas between various actors (CRDA, WUA, and farmers) are specified by three types of contract: (1) membership contract: which frames the transactions between the WUA and irrigators. It contains details of the technical and economic dimensions of the irrigation transaction; (2) management contract: which has to be put in place between the WUA and the CRDA. This contract concerns the sharing of maintenance and investment tasks between these two actors; (3) maintenance contract: which can be entered into by any WUA and a private company for doing specific maintenance tasks.

Each year, each WUA is responsible for establishing its own budget. The WUA also has the right to determine the water price and to decide whether the payment basis should be water volume in terms of production or distribution. Furthermore, they estimate the level of projected investments, and operational and maintenance charges. Financially, the WUA perform the following tasks: operation and maintenance of canals, repairs to various infrastructures, functioning of the association and investments. The water charge established by the WUA comprises water buying charges, energy fees, labour charges and maintenance and management fees.

4.4. Limits of Current Tunisian Water Management Institutions

Some major failure factors of irrigation water administration and organizations can be drawn from empirical research and reports already made in the case of Tunisia. These can be divided into three types: Judicial factors: the management contract, that specifies the relationship between the WUA and the CRDA and describes the main responsibilities and tasks of both actors, is not well defined (Bied-Charreton et al., 2004).

In fact, according to the same author, specific conditions under which investment projects have to be undertaken by one or other of the actors, are not well specified.

In addition, the contract duration is not specified and sanctions are not anticipated in cases where some of the contractual obligations are not met. It is broadly mentioned that large irrigation development projects have to be done by the CRDA whilst the “less important” ones are within the remit of WUA. This could be interpreted in different ways and thus lead to some confusion. Currently, the specialist departments of the MAE are working on another draft of this contract in order to clarify it.

Financial and technical factors: technical problems mostly relate to the WUAs and their functioning. WUAs that were created in old irrigated districts are adversely affected by the decay of their irrigation networks and infrastructures.

Renovation places high charges on the WUA. In some other cases, maintenance tasks are neglected by the managers of the WUA, and this can have a negative effect in the medium to long term. These technical factors generally affect the dependability, adequacy and efficiency of the water delivery systems. Problems and misunderstandings between irrigators and the WUA can emerge when these tasks are not well performed (Chraga and Chemakh, 2003).

Another major problem concerns the limited management capacity of the WUAs' administrative members (Ben Salem et al., 2005) who are for the most part, elderly, not well educated or trained (Bied-Charreton et al., 2004). Indeed, the complexity of some tasks requires a higher level of competence and motivation, in addition to the full availability of managers. Also, the "Cellules de promotion des GDA" (CP) that support the functioning of the WUA do not have sufficient means at their disposal and are sometimes incapable of assisting all the WUAs in their regions. In fact, in each CRDA, only one CP is created and is responsible for technical and management assistance for all the existing WUAs in the region.

According to Bied-Charreton et al. (2004) these CPs have around 90 technicians working across all the Tunisian territory and are responsible for supporting more than 2000 WUAs around the country. This rate varies from region to region.

Social factors: many social problems hinder the improvement of WUA performance in Tunisia. The lack of mobilization and motivation of farmers is a major difficulty (Chraga and Chemakh, 2003; Bied-Charreton et al., 2004; Ben Salem et al., 2005). It is not uncommon to find a WUA without a president of the administrative council (Chraga and Chemakh, 2003; Bied-Charreton et al., 2004).

Often, the lack of farmers' confidence in their administrative staff means that collective decisions are not respected or applied (Bied-Charreton et al., 2004). Furthermore, in most cases, the public authorities (CRDA) participate in the choice of WUA president, which makes its legitimacy for farmers weak, and leads to some erroneous perceptions about collective action and the principles of public participation.

In some other cases, the social standing that large and rich farmers have in the association and the special treatment given to meet their demands for irrigation also negatively affect satisfaction and participation by small farmers (Chraga and Chemakh, 2003).

5. Revolution Challenges on Water Institutional Reforms

In general, water resource management is very challenging. Managing water resource involves large transaction costs and serious information deficiencies.

There is a need to design institutions to deal with the peculiarities with water, and to create the right incentives, controls and efficiencies (Crase and Ghandi, 2009).

Many private as well as public investments in water resources failed because of inappropriate institutional factors. There is a need to understanding how rules combine with particular physical, economic and cultural environments to produce appropriate institutions (Ostrom, 1992):

- *Clear objectives*: Good institutions have clear objectives and show clarity of purpose
- *Good interaction*: an important feature of good institutions is good internal interaction among constituents
- *Adaptiveness:* Institutions typically face variation and change in the internal and external environment
- *Appropiateness of scale*: Good institutions are appropriate in scale with respect to their size and scope. If the institution is too large, transaction costs are too high. On the other hand, if the institution is too small, it has very little control over its relevant affairs
- *Compliance ability:* Good institutions demonstrate the required compliance ability. If the rules and processes of the institutions are not followed by a large section of the participants –i.e. compliance is poor-the institution in all likelihood ceases to be effective and meaningful, and transaction costs are high.

Water institutions in Tunisia need to be changed so they allow for good water governance, hence democratic, equitable, efficient and sustainable usage of water resources.

Water institutional reform is now perceived as key for reforms of the water sector. Some of the major institutional reforms that emerge in the Tunisian revolution context are seen as adequate means to ensure good water governance:

➢ The water laws

- *To reform the water code:* The major problems with the current water code is related to the fact that it contains no definition of water rights and water ownership; provisions governing the sale of water and water transfer are highly restrictive; the status of GW rights is left unclear. There is considerable room for modification and clarification of the prevailing water rights system in Tunisia.
- Introduction of a juridical background for an integrated water resources management approach at the national as well as basin level

➢ The water policy

- Testing market mechanisms for irrigation water in some irrigated areas
- Extension of the cost recovery policy by a set of policies which aim to enhance the payment capacity of small farmers (more than 50% of the Tunisian farms are smaller than 5 ha)

➢ The water administration

- Better coordination between state, regions, districts, and sectors
- Stakeholders participation in decision making at the level of their localities
- Decrease in organizational hierarchy in order to make farmers closer to the decision makers
- A formal democratic and trasparent WUS should be established; and special trainings on collective participatory management have to be offered to farmers
- Enhance the technical capacities (extension services and social consultants) of the Tunisian water administration in order to make it more efficient at local levels.

These recommendations and other have to be adapted into a set of complementary measures that garantee the payment capacity of farmers for the water services, the durability of the resource, and the enhancemet of the economic productivity and competitiveness of the Tunisian agricultural products.

Conclusion

In this study, a few suggestions for revamping Tunisian's water institutions are presented in order to improve water sector performance. In summary, water sector and water institutions in Tunisia have a large improvement potential. Among the main measures that can be undertaken in the near future we cite: (i) the settlement of more effective tools for the monitoring and the enforcement of the current existing legislation regarding water resources (especially the groundwater in the prohibited and protected areas); (ii) the extension of WUA experience in managing the shallow and deep aquifers together with the use of appropriate pricing levels and systems; (iii) the proposition of a new legal management contract which could facilitate the management of the irrigation network by the WUA; (iv) the reinforcement of the private sector participation in the management of the hydraulic infrastructure and for the operation and maintenance of secondary irrigation networks at the local irrigation level. The private sector can be more effective than the public administration in providing these services. We remind that currently, operation and maintenance tasks are provided by the regional public administrations; and (v) the enhancement of farmers' capacities for the marketing and transformation of their agricultural products at local levels. This allows the increase of water productivity, and guarantee a higher payment capacities of farmers.

Finally, all of these measures have to be carefully designed and developed in order to fit with the current expectations of the irrigation sector at the national and local levels. they have to be combined into a unique set which can be considered as a more diversified strategy for the management of the agricultural irrigation water. Also, the participation of the local stakeholders and especially irrigators for the design of this strategy is crucial and will be considered as the main challenge for the establishment of a strong and effective water strategy in a period of democratic transition.

References

Adelman, I., & Morris, C.T. (1967). *Society, Politics, and Economic Development: A Quantitative Approach*, Baltimore, MD: Johns Hopkins Press.

Adelman, I. and Lohmoller, J.B. (1994). Institutions and development in the nineteenth century: a latent variable regression model, *Structural Change and Economic Dynamics*, 5 (2), 329–59.

Al Atiri, R. (2007). Evolution institutionelle et réglementaire de la gestion de l'eau en Tunisie, Vers une participation accrue des usagers de l'eau. In : Sami Bouarfa, Marcel Kuper & Abdelhafid Debbarh (eds.), *L'avenir de l'agriculture irriguée en Méditerranée. Nouveaux arrangements institutionnels pour une gestion de la demande en eau.* Actes du séminaire Wademed, Cahors, France, 6-7 novembre 2006. CIRAD, Montpellier, France.

Al Atiri, R. (2009). L'utilisation des eaux non conventionnelles en Tunisie : Problématiques et defis. Actes du séminaire WaDImena, Hammamed, Tunisia, 24 Octobre 2009.

Ben Abdallah S. (2007). The Water Resources and Water Management Regimes in Tunisia; In Laura Holliday (Ed.) *Agricultural Water Management: Proceedings of a Workshop in Tunisia* (Series: Strengthening Science-Based Decision Making in Developing Countries), The National Academies Press, Washington, D.C.

Ben Salem H, Zaibet L.,& Bachta MS. (2005). Performance de la gouvernance de l'eau d'irrigation par les groupements d'intérêt collectifs en périmètres publics irrigués. Actes du séminaire Euro Méditerranéen « Les instruments économiques et la modernisation des périmètres irrigués », 21-22 novembre 2005, Sousse, Tunisie.

Besbes, M. (2011). L'eau en Tunisie : Gestion de la rareté, conjecture de pénuries. Conférence-Débat, INAT, 28 Mai, 2011, Tunisia.

Bied-Charreton, M., Makkaoui, R., Petit, O., & Requier-Desjardins, M. (2004). La gouvernance des ressources en eau dans les pays en développement. Centre d'Economie et d'Ethique pour l'environnement et le développement ; Cahiers du C3ED n 04-01, Janvier 2004.

Centre International des technologies de l'environnement de Tunis (CITET) (2009). *Institutional framework and decision making practices for water management in Tunisia: Towards the development of a strategy for improved groundwater management.* Tunis, Tunisia.

Chraga, G. & Chemakh, F. (2003). Les groupements d'intérêt collectif, un outil stratégique pour une gestion participative de la ressource en eau cas des GIC de Mahdia. *20th European regional conférence of the ICID - Irrigation et gestion concertée des conflits d'usages dans la région euroméditerranéenne.* 17-19 septembre 2003, Montpellier, France.

Crase, L. & Ghandi, V.P. (2009). *Reforming institutions in water resources management.* Cromwell Press; Trowbridge.

Direction Générale des Etudes et de Développement agricole (DGEDA) (various years). *Enquêtes périmètres irrigués en Tunisie.* Ministère de l'Agriculture et de l'Environnement, Tunisia.

Direction Générale du Génie Rural et de l'exploitation des Eaux (DGGREE) (2009). *Rapport de synthèse de la situation des Groupements d'Intérêt Collectif d'irrigation pour l'année 2008.* Ministère de l'agriculture et de l'environnement, Tunisia.

Horchani, A. (2007). Water in Tunisia: A National Perspective; In Laura Holliday (Ed.) *Agricultural Water Management*: Proceedings of a Workshop in Tunisia (Series: Strengthening Science-Based Decision Making in Developing Countries), The National Academies Press, Washington, D.C.

Louati, H., Mellouli, H., & El Echi, ML. (2005). Methodology for the analysis of the organizations and institutions relevant to drought management and mitigation in the Mediterranean : case of Tunisia. *Options Mediterraneennes*, Series B,50, 155-190.

Ministère de l'Agriculture et de l'Environnement (MAE) (2008). *Gestion durable des ressources en eau.* Observatoire Tunisien de l'Environnement et du Developpement Durable, Tunisia.

Morris, C. T., & Adelman, I. (1988). *Comparative Patterns of Economic Development*, Baltimore, MD: Johns Hopkins University Press, pp. 1850–914.

North, D.C., (1990). *Institutions, Institutional Change and Economic Performance.* Cambridge University Press, New York, NY.

North, D.C., (1993).The new institutional development and economics. *Economics Working Paper Archive at WUSTL*, No. ewt-eh/9309002, Washington 1993.

Ostrom, E. (1992). Crafting institutions for self-governing irrigation systems, ICS Press, Institute for Contemporary Studies, San Francisco–California, A publication for the International Center for Self-Governance.

Remmer, K.L. (1998). 'Does democracy promote interstate cooperation? Lessons from the Mercosur region', *International Study Quarterly*, 42 (1), 25–52.

Saleth, R.M. & Dinar, A. (2004). *The institutional economics of water: A cross country analysis of institutions and performance.* Edward Elgar (co-publication with the World Bank) publishing.

Thabet, C.,& Chebil A. (2006). Irrigation Water Pricing in Tunisia: Issues for Successful Water Management Transparency. *Agricultural and marine sciences*, Vol. 11,1, pp. 21-28.

In: Tunisia: Economic, Political and Social Issues ISBN: 978-1-61942-157-8
Eds: M. Pusatieri and J. Cannamela

Chapter 6

IMPORTANCE OF NON-WOOD FOREST PRODUCTS IN TUNISIA

Abdelaziz Ayari*[*1], *Ane Zubizarreta-Gerendiain*[3], *Daniel Moya*[2], *Ali El-Khorchani*[1], *and Abdelhamid Khaldi*[1]

[1]National Institute of Research in Rural Engeneering, Waters and Forests (INRGREF). Ariana, Tunisia
[2]Escuela Tecnica Superior de Ingenieros Agrónomos de Albacete, UCLM. Spain
[3]Forest Research Centre, School of Agriculture, Technical University of Lisbon, Lisbon, Portugal

ABSTRACT

Tunisia is one of the six countries located in Northern Africa, where most parts are deserts or semi-deserts, and covered by drought resistant shrublands. However, forests exits in the northern regions of Tunisia. These forests produce several natural products offering goods and services that are often undervalued. Wood forest products (WFP) and non-wood forest products (NWFP) represent a real employment and income source for the rural population of these forest areas. Local and national incomes of NWFP in Tunisia have a crucial role in comparison

* Corresponding author: Tel.: +216 97 386 516; Fax: +216 71 717 951, E-mail address: abdelazizayari@yahoo.fr.

to WFP. The main WFP is timber for pulpwood, particleboard, fiber-board and cardboard packaging. Similarly, NWFP produced in Tunisia include plant and animal products. The most important NWFP are edible plants, fruits, mushrooms, seeds, oils, cork, fiber, fodder, tannins, resins and gums. Furthermore, animal foodstuffs, is constituted by bush meat, trophy hunting, honey and snails. Important socioeconomic value is also attributed to medicinal and aromatic plants, such as Thymus spp., Laurus nobilis and Rosmarinus officinalis. This review pretends to emphasizes the socioeconomic importance of NWFP produced by these forests. Currently, the WFP are well known and valued while NWFP, even if they are much appreciated, they are undervalued and underestimated.

Keywords*:* Forests; Non-wood forest products; Socioeconomic role; Tunisia; Wood products

INTRODUCTION

According to the Tunisian Development Plan of Forest Resources and Grazing (DPFRG), the forest in Tunisia is a strategic sector in which the state plays a leading role. In addition to the multitude goods and services that forest offers to the local population, forestry sector also has important economic, social and environmental functions that can deeply influence the Tunisian society (Khaldi 2010). The economic role of this sector should be maintained taking into account the conservation of natural resources for future generations (FAO 2001a). Moreover, Tunisia should gradually phase-out some forest management activities to involve, at the same time, the private sector and the rural populations, achieving a new concept of private forests (Gader 2001). Nowadays, Tunisian forest and woodlands cover about 1.1 million hectares (DGF 1995), which are composed by 51.8% of pure forests covering the northern mountainous, 33.8% of scrubland and 14.4% of other forest lands in the centre and the southern country (sliced firewall, ranger station, rocky terrain). All forests are located between humid zones in the north of the country, where temperatures are mild and precipitations frequent, and desert zones in the south with irregular rainfall and a dry summer season (Khessaissia 1997; Ayari et al. 2011a). The most extensive native tree species is Aleppo pine (*Pinus halepensis* Mill.) with more than 36% of the forested area. It is followed by oak (*Quercus* spp., 7%), eucalyptus (*Eucalyptus* spp., 3.4%) and Sictus (*Tetraclinis* spp., 2.6%) (DGF 1995; Ayari et al. 2011b).

Tunisian forests provide a wide range of products and benefits including wood forest products (WFP, i.e. timber and its derivatives) as well as non-wood forest products (NWFP, e.g. edible plants, fruits, mushrooms, seeds, oils, cork, fiber, fodder, tannins, resins, gums). By comparison to NWFP, WFP represent just a small part of all benefits (Croitoru and Merlo 2005). In fact, in Tunisia, NWFP play a significant role in the economy of the local population by providing key subsistence for consume and/or commercialise (Abid 2010). Furthermore, Tunisian forests provide externalities, such as soil protection and conservation, in addition to biodiversity benefits. A previous study (FAO 2001a) revealed that there were more than 800,000 forest users, representing about 100,000 families, with the equivalent of five livestock units per family within the state. Despite this important multi-functionality of the forest there is still lack of information on numerous other benefits. For instance, there is limited information on its socio-economic significance and its ecological impact due to its exploitation (Walter 2001). Rural and local population exert continuous pressure on forest stands through deforestation and overgrazing, leading to progressive forest degradation and declining of profitability (Croitoru and Merlo 2005). Thus, the present work attempts to view the socioeconomic status of natural resources in Tunisian forests.

Background Information on Tunisia

Tunisia is located on the southern bank of the Mediterranean Basin, and it is bordered by Algeria on the west, by Libya on the south and by the Mediterranean Sea on the north and east (Figure 1). The total national population exceeds 10,500,000 (UNESCO 2002). Concerning the topography, Tunisia is mountainous in the north and northwest, plain in the costal area and deserted in the south. Therefore, it has diversity in natural ecosystems and it is very rich in social and cultural heritage (Antipolis 2001). Many empires have played a role in the history of Tunisia ranging from the Phoenicians to French through the Romans, Byzantines, Arabs and Turks (Walter 2001; Room 2006; Taylor 2008). But the origin of the people of Tunisia is Berber, representing actually less than 1% of the total population. They are nowadays confined to the dry part of the country and the mountains in the northwest of the state. Concerning climate, Tunisia has a Mediterranean climate, with cooler season falling between October and May. Usually, summers are hot and dry, while winters are wetter and characterized by frequent rains mainly in the north. The most distinguishing characteristic of the dry summer in Tunisia is its seasonal precipitation regime. In fact, Tunisia is affected by water scarcity and periodic drought. The average temperature range from, 6°C to 14°C in January and from, 21°C to 33°C in August. Moreover, the average annual rainfalls range between 1500 mm/yr in the north and less than 100 mm/yr in the south (Sakiss et al. 1994; Benzarti 1994). The Tunisian forests, woodlands, and scrublands are closely associated with Mediterranean climate zones; therefore the native vegetation is adapted to survive long summer droughts and prolonged wet periods in winter.

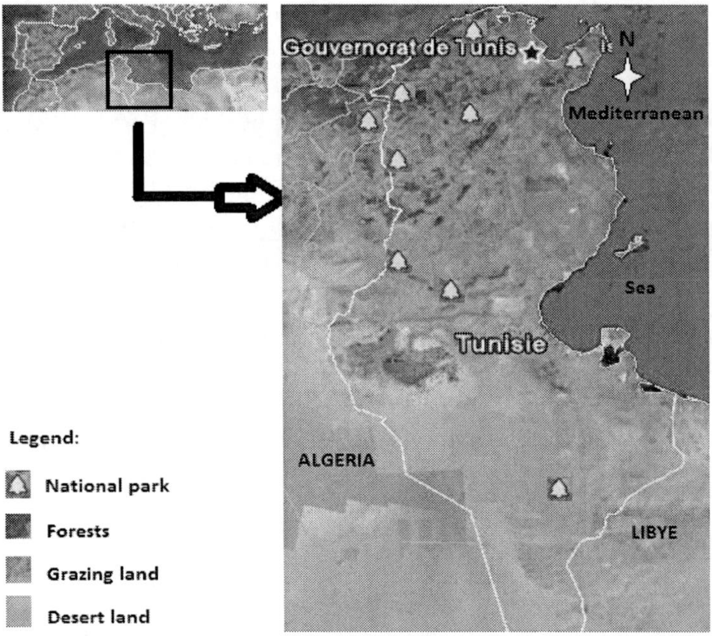

Figure 1. A satellite view of the forests and grazing lands in Tunisia (Source: Google Earth 2011).

Table 1. Forest area distribution in Tunisia

Forests	Surface area (ha)	%
Pure forests	500,826	51.6
Maquis with scrublands	135,062	13.9
Maquis without scrublands	194,849	20.1
Others forest lands (sliced firewall, tracks, rocky lands etc.)	140,080	14.4

Status and Distribution of Tunisian Forests

The total forest cover was reduced from 1,250,000 ha to 500,000 ha between 1910 and 1975 (Posner 1988; DGF 1995). The main factor of this loss is attributed to the massive forest harvesting operation during the colonial period (DGF 1995). A total of 2.7 million ha of grazing lands obtained after intensive cutting of trees and shrubs were put under cultivation between 1890 and 1973 (Posner 1988). Furthermore, the exhaustive grazing by domestic livestock disrupts the natural regeneration and stops the natural replacement of old and dying trees (Boudy 1952). Additional forest cover reduction of 13,000 ha was also recorded between 1975 and 1985. This important reduction was mainly due to poor timber harvesting practices, land clearing for agriculture and grazing as well as high pressure for forest products such fuel wood and forage. In order to conserve and protect some of the important forest areas (Chandoul 1986) and their associated fauna and flora (Chakroun 1986), the Tunisian state has established several reserves and national parks (Figure 1).

According to the national forest inventory realised in 1993, the actual forest cover is about 970,818 hectares due to the successful results obtained after the efforts of the state on reforestation and soils protection (Table 1). The current status of the Tunisian forests is composed with about 502,990 ha and the dominant area species is Aleppo pine that occupies about 363,367 ha (DGF 1995). Concerning, the Tunisian forests structure, only the 30 % of the trees attains the age of maturity. A complementary forest cover is composed by 327,747 ha of maquis and shrub lands.

Main NWFP in Tunisia

In North Africa, a massive quantity of NWFP is exploited by rural communities for direct consumption and/or commercialization as sources of food, medicines and fodder. The main NWFP for the different countries can be found in Table 2. Across Tunisian forests, the NWFP production includes edible plants such as fruits, mushrooms as well as the seeds of *Pinus halepensis* and *P. Pinea*. Essential oils of *Pistacia lentiscus*, *Rosmarinus officinalis*, *Ceratonia siliqua*, *Origanum vulgare*, *Laurus nobilis*, *Argania spinosa*, and *Myrtus communis* are also collected. Furthermore, cork (*Quercus suber*) is one of the main NWFP in Algeria, Morocco and Tunisia (Table 2). Tunisia contributes with about 3% of the world cork production, and its major importer is the European Union (FAO 1994). Beside, in Tunisia cork production spends more than 200,000 working days every year for the local and rural population (Abid 2010).

Other NWFP of major socio-economic importance in Tunisia are fibres (Stipa tenacissima), most important medicinal plants used in the traditional medicine of local and national markets (e.g. *Thymus* spp, *Verbena officinalis*), aromatic plants (e.g. *Mentha pulegium*, *Artemisia* sp., *Eucalyptus* spp.), fodder, colorants, tannins, resins and gums. Tunisia is one of the most important exporting countries of medicinal plant material (USAID 2005).

In fact, in Tunisia and all the Northern African countries, the socio-economic aspects of NWFP provided by forests are often more important than timber production. Livestock production is well supported by forest grazing and fodder that contributed to the livelihood of the local population and the national economy.

Likewise, main animal products, which significantly contribute to the local and national economy in the region, are meat, honey (FAO 1994, Papanastasis 2009) and insecticides (Amri et al., 2010; Releya, 2005). data not available.

Table 2. Main NWFP in northern African countries including Tunisia

Country	NWFP	References
Tunisia	Fodder, aromatic and medicinal plants, Essential oils, grazing, hunting, honey, cork, alfa grass (*Stipa tenacissima*).	Saidi et al. (2009), Rejeb et al. (2006), Coelho et al. (2010), Ben Hassine et al. (2010)
Egypt	Food, Essential oils, medicinal plants, honey, fruits, Grazing.	FAO (1994), FAO (2001b). Papanastasis (2009).
Algeria	Cork (*Quercus suber*).	Djemma et Massaoudene, 2009
Morocco	Cork, medicinal plants, aromatic plants.	USAID (2005).
Libya	-	-
Mauritania	Fruits, fodder, gums, medicinal plants.	FAO (1994)

BENEFITS OF TUNISIAN FORESTS

In all northern African countries (Figre 2), forests productivity is usually computed and compared using the Total Economic Value (TEV), calculated using the direct use values of the products (Croitoru and McGinley 2008).

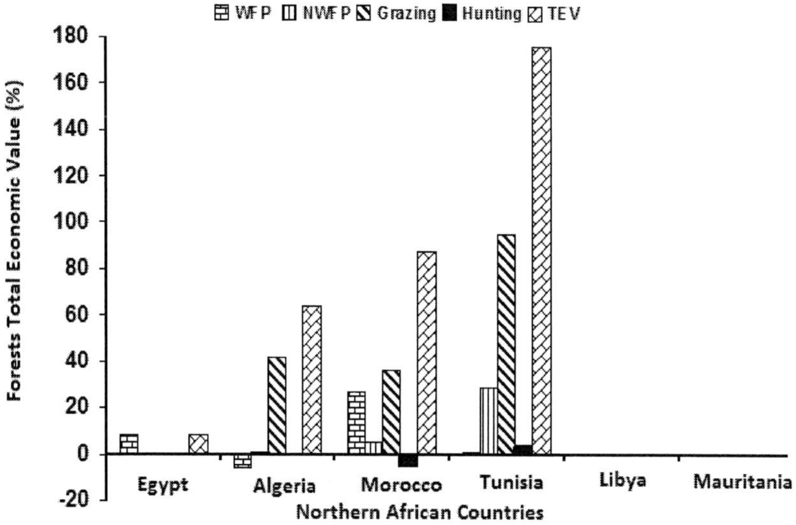

Figure 2. Total economic value of forests in Northern African countries (Source: Croitoru and McGinley 2008).

In addition to hunting and grazing, in general, Tunisia also dominates in NWFP production among all northern African countries (Figre 2). On the other hand, the highest value of WFP benefits was attributed to Morocco (Figre 2). In Tunisia grazing is an important traditional rural activity that represents about 54% of the country's forests TEV, and in total, NWFP represents more than 16% of the national forests TEV. Moreover, Tunisia is the only northern African country with significant benefits coming from hunting, and thus it is considered as a primarily source of livelihood. Overall, the value of hunting in Tunisia is about 1.7% of the country TEV (Figre 2). Most of the NWFP are derived from forests, woodlands and scrubland. The main NWFP encountered in Tunisian forests are the seeds of Aleppo pine and cork with the estimated annual benefits of US$38,571 million and US$17.5 million, respectively (Jalel 2004; Abid 2010). Forest produces additional NWFP such as mushrooms, nuts, seeds, essential oils, honey aromatic and medicinal plants, but they do not give as much incomes as the seeds and the cork. Nonetheless, according to recent reports (Jalel 2004; Abid 2010) the income levels of NWFP are important, giving benefits for local and rural population. For instance, the estimated income values obtained from mushrooms picking and hunting range from US$ 53,571 to US$500,000 (Table 3). Some intermediate values were also recorded with other NWFP such as, essential oils (more than US$150,000 per year), nuts of Pinus pinea (US$334,000 every three years) and snails (US$204,000 per year). By opposite, an over-exploitation of medicinal and aromatic plants as well as overgrazing contributes to the degradation of semi-arid zones through desertification and erosion (Dregne 1986).

Nowadays, in Tunisia, besides the mentioned main NWFP, there are alternative ones that have increased their importance due to their multitude uses in many domains such as food perfumery, aromatherapy, food flavouring (drink), pharmaceutical industry and dietary (Ayari et al. 2011a). The oils used for the cosmetic industry are also very important because of their high quality (Dob et al. 2005).

Furthermore, the chemical composition of the extracted oils by hydrodistillation or by chromatography showed a richness of the lipid fraction compounds characterized by the unsaturated acid (Table4). These compounds are well appreciated either at nutritional level or pharmaceutical uses. The most extracted oil was found to be rich in oleic, linoleic and palmitic acid as ω 6 and linolenic acid as ω 3 (Tlili et al. 2010).

Table 3. Overall NWFP livelihood in Tunisia (Jalel 2004; Abid 2010)

NWFP	Average production (Kg/yr)	Forest zone	Income (US$)
Cork	7,100,000	Subéraie	17.5 million
Oil (*M. communis*)	2,220	Subéraie	150,000
Mushrooms	9,600	Subéraie	53,571-500,000
Nuts (*P. pinea*)	22,000	Subéraie + North-Eastern Forests	112, 000
Hunting	-	State-wide	500,000
Snails	-	Northern Forests	204,000
Seeds (*P. halepensis*)	10,000,000-26,000,000	State-wide	38,571 million

Table 4. Mains products and chemical components of the lipid fraction of the Tunisian NWFP

Flora and fauna Species	Products type	Main chemical components isolated and its frequency	References
Aleppo pine (*P. halepensis*)	Seeds, tannins, needles	*Needles*: α-caryophyllene, α-humulene, aromadendrene *Seeds*: Oleic acid (27.3%) Linoleic acid (48.8%) Palmitic acid (8.75%)	Dob et al. (2005) Cheikh rouhou et al. (2006)
Honey	-		
Stone pine (*P.pinea*)	Nuts, bark, resin	*Seeds*: Oleic acid (38.6%) Linoleic acid (47.6%) Palmitic acid (6.49%)	Nergiz and Donmez (2004)
Rosemary (*Rosmarinus officinalis*)	Essential oil, honey production	*Leaves*: 1,8-cineol (47.5%) Camphor (14.9%) α-pinene (14.1%) borneol (13.2%)	Amri et al. (2010)
Myrtle (*Myrtus communis*)	Essential oil	*α -pinene (>14.7%), myrtenyl acetate (>5.4%)*	Dukić et al. (2010)
Mushrooms	-	-	-
Capper (*Capparis spinosa*)	Fruits, leaves, flowers, honey	*Leaves*: Oleic acid (45.8%), Linoleic acid (25.4%), palmitic acid (15.9%), stearic acid (4.1%)	Tlili et al. (2010)
Walnut (*Juglans regia*)	Nuts	-	-
Peppermint (*Mentha piperita*)	Essential oil, honey, leaves, flowers	-	-
Fodder	-	-	-
Karop (*Ceratonia siliqua*)	Pods	*Fruits*: 1,2-Benzenedicarboxylic acid, camphor, hexadecanoic acid.	Ben Hsouna (2010)
Mastic tree (*Pistacia lentiscus*)	Edible oil,	Oleic acid (55%), Linoleic acid (27%), Palmitic acid 14%.	Mezni et al. (2010)
Snails	-	-	-
Olive tree (*Olea europea*)	Edible oil	*Fruits*: α-pinene (52.7%) 2,6-dimethyloctane (16.6%), 2-methoxy-3-isopropylpyrazine (6.0 %)	Haloui et al. (2010)
(*Schinus molle*)	Fruits, essential oil	*Fruits:* α-phellandrene (46.5%), b-phellandrene (20.8%), α-terpineol (8.4%), a-pinene (4.3%), b-pinene (5.0%).	Bendaoued et al. (2010)
(*Schinus teribinthofolius*)	Fruits, essential oil	*Fruits:* α-phellandrene (34.4%), b-phellandrene (10.6%), α-terpineol (5.6%), α-pinene (6.5%), b-pinene (3.1%).	Bendaoued et al. (2010)
Strawberry tree (*Arbutus unido*)	Fruit, essential oil	-	-

CONCLUSIONS

In Tunisia, NWFP are in many cases more important than WFP. Therefore, NWFP could be used for diversification of the forest activities, helping rural areas with additional economic benefits. Harvesting of these products's increasingly seen as economic activity promoting the traditional use of natural forest resources in the country. Nonetheless, additional NWFP should be harvested or alternative managements should be studied, not to over harvest the most common NWFP, which would lead to a future scarcity, loss of biodiversity and desertification of certain areas. Indeed, these new products could contribute to the creation of additional employment, mainly for rural populations around forest zone.

REFERENCES

Amri I., Hamrouni L., Hanana M., Khouja M.L., Jamoussi B., Lebdi Khaouther. 2010. New biological alternatives based on essential oils to protect the date palm (Phoenix dactylifera) against Ectomylois ceratoniae Zeller. Abstract p92, in Valorisation des produits forestiers non ligneux, 15èmes journées scientifiques de *l'INRGREF,* Gammarth-Tunisie, 28-29 Sep, 2010.

Antipolis S. 2001. Tunisia environment and sustainable development issues and policies. Mediterranean country profiles. Blue plan, pp 69.

Ayari A., Moya D., Rejeb M.N., Ben Mansoura A., Albouchi A., De Las Heras J., Fezzani T., Henchi B. 2011a. Geographical variation on cone and seed production of natural Pinus halepensis Mill. forests in Tunisia. Journal of *Arid Environments* 75: 403-410.

Ayari A., Moya D., Rejeb M.N., Garchi S., De Las Heras J. 2011b. Fructification and Species Conservation on Pinus halepensis Mill. Forests in Tunisia: Managing Structure Using Individual Tree Size In Frisiras Ch. Th. Pine Forests: Types, Threats and Management, In Press.

Ben Hassine D., Ben Ismail H., Jribi C., Khouja M.L., Abderrabba M. 2010. Huile essentielle d'Eucalyptus oleosa: Extraction, composition chimique et activité antimicrobienne. Abstract p22, in Valorisation des produits forestiers non ligneux, 15èmes journées scientifiques de *l'INRGREF,* Gammarth-Tunisie, 28-29 Sep, 2010.

Bendaoued H., Bouajila J., Cazaux S., Rhomdhane M. 2010. Optimization des conditions de l'huile essentielle des fruits de Schinus molle et Schinus teribinthofolius: Détermination de leurs compositions chimiques. Abstract p29, in Valorisation des produits forestiers non ligneux, 15èmes journées scientifiques de *l'INRGREF*, Gammarth-Tunisie, 28-29 Sep, 2010.

Ben Hsouna A., Trigui M., Ben Mansour R., Jerraya M.R., Damak M., Jaoua S. Chemical composition, antimicrobial activity and cytotoxicity effect of essential oil from a North African endemic species Ceratonia siliqua. Abstract p23, in Valorisation des produits forestiers non ligneux, 15èmes journées scientifiques de l'INRGREF, Gammarth-Tunisie, 28-29 Sep, 2010.

Benzarti, Z. 1994. Les variations inetrannuelles de la pluviométrie en Tunisie In:

Boudy P. 1952. Guide du forestier en Afrique du Nord. La Maison Rustique, Paris.

Chakroun M.L. 1986. Le pin d'Alep en Tunisie. CIHEAM, option Méditerranéennes (1), 25-27.

Chandoul H. 1986. La protection des forêts en Tunisie. CIHEAM-option Méditerranéennes (1), 201-203.

Cheikh-Rouhou S., Hentati B., Besbes S., Blecker C., Deroanne C., Attia H. 2006. Chemical composition and lipid fraction characteristics of Aleppo pine (Pinus halepensis Mill.) Seeds cultivated in Tunisia. Food Sci Tech Int, 15(5):407-416.

Coelho J.A., Mechergui Kaouther, Serra M.C., Nunes N.C., Lamine S.B., Boukhchnia S. Khouja M.L. 2010. Composition and antioxidant activities of essential oils from Origanum vulgare L. subsp. Glandulosum (Desf.) Ietswaart from Tunisia. Abstract p20, in Valorisation des produits forestiers non ligneux, 15èmes journées scientifiques de *l'INRGREF*, Gammarth-Tunisie, 28-29 Sep, 2010.

Croitoru L., and McGinley M. 2008. Value of Mediterranean forests, In: *Encyclopedia of Earth.* Eds. Cutler J. Cleveland, Washington, D.C.: Environmental Information Coalition, National Council for Science and the Environment.

Croitoru, L. and Merlo, M., 2005. Mediterranean Forest Values. In: Merlo and Croitoru (Eds.) (2005) Valuing Mediterranean forests: Towards Total Economic Value. CABI Publishing, Wallingford, p. 406.

DGF (Direction Générale des Forêts) (1995). Résultats du premier inventaire forestier national en Tunisie. Ministère de l'Agriculture, Tunis, 88p.

Djema A. and Massaoudene M. 2009. The Algerian Forest: Current Sitauation and Prospects In Valuing and Managing Mediterranean Forest Ecosystems for Non-Timber Goods and Services. *EFI Proceedings* NO. 57, 17-28.

Dob T., Berramdane T., Chelgoum C. 2005. Chemical composition of essential oil of Pinus halepensis Miller growing in Algeria. C.R. Chimie 8.

Dregne, H. E. 1986. Desertification of arid lands. In *Physics of desertification*, ed. F. El-Baz and M. H. A. Hassan. Dordrecht, The Netherlands: Martinus, Nijhoff.

Dukić N.M., Bugarin D., Grbović S., Ćulafić D.M., Gačić B.V., Orčić D., Jovin E., Couladis M. 2010. Essential Oil of Myrtus communis L. as a Potential Antioxidant and Antimutagenic Agents. Molecules 2010, 15, 2759-2770.

FAO, 2001a. Global forest resources assessment. *FAO forestry* paper 140. Rome.

FAO, 2001b. Non-wood forest products of Africa: A regional and national overview, by S. Walter. Working Paper FOPW/01/1. Rome.

FAO. 1994. Tropical palm. Non-wood forest products 10.

Google Earth 2011. GeoEye, Cnes/Spot Image, Digital Globe, Data SIO, NOAA, US Department of geographer, E , Navy, NGA, GEBCO, Europe technologies.

Haloui E., Marzouk Z., Marzouk B., Bouftira I., Bouraoui A., Fenina N. 2010. Pharmacological activities and chemical composition of the Olea europaea L. leaf essential oils from Tunisia. *International Journal of Food, Agriculture and Environment*, 8(1): 204-208.

Khessaissia, B. 1997. Plan d'action de mise en place des AFIC (Groupement GOPA-IGIP). Tunis.La variabilité du climat et l'homme en Tunisie, Hénia, L. (Ed.). GREVACHOT, Université de Tunis I, pp 63-83.

Mezni F., Khorchani A., Boussaid M., Khaldi A. 2010. Etude de la composition en acides gras et de l'activitéantioxydante de l'huile fixe de Pistacia lentiscus dans la zone de Nefza. Abstract p27, in Valorisation des produits forestiers non ligneux, 15èmes journées scientifiques de l'*INRGREF*, Gammarth-Tunisie, 28-29 Sep, 2010.

Nergiz C., Donmez I. 2004. Chemical composition and nutritive value of Pinus pinea L. seeds. *Food Chemistry* 86: 365-368.

Papanastasis P.V. 2009. Grazing Value of Mediterranean Forests In Modelling, Valuing and Managing Mediterranean Forest Ecosystems for Non-Timber Goods and Services. *EFI Proceedings* NO. 57, 7-16.

Posner S.D. 1988. Biologicaldiversity and tropical forests in Tunisia. The Washington D.C. and Tunis offices of the Agency for the International Development, pp 229.

Rejeb M.N., Khouja M.L, Ghrabi Z., Chemli R., Albouchi A., Khaldi A., Dahman M. 2006. Guide des plantes médicinales et aromatiques. ISBN: 9973-9954-3-0, pp129.

Relyea R. 2005. The impact of insecticides and herbicides on the biodiversity and productivity of aquatic-communities. Ecological Applications, 15 (2): 618–627.

Room, A. 2006. Place names of the World: Origins and Meanings of the Names for 6,600 Countries, Cities, Territories, Natural Features, and Historic Sites. McFarland. p. 385.

Saidi Y, Hasnaoui F, Hasnaoui B. 2009. Production Potentiality in fruits, Biomass, essential oils and Medicinal Properties of the Mastic Treeb (Pistacia lentiscus) in Kouroumerie, N-W Tunisia. In Valuing and Managing Mediterranean Forest Ecosystems for Non-Timber Goods and Services. *EFI Proceedings* NO. 185, 195.

Sakiss N., Ennabli N., Slimani M.S., Baccour H. 1994. La pluviométrie en Tunisie a-t-elle changé depuis 2000 ans ?. Recherches de tendances et de cycles dans les séries pluviométriques. Institut National de Météorologie, 283p.

Taylor, I. 2008. Names and Their Histories: A Handbook of Historical Geography and Topographical Nomenclature. *Biblio Bazaar*, LLC. p. 281.

Tlili N., Nasri, N., Saadaoui E., Khaldi A., Triki S. 2010. Caper seeds (Capparis spinosa): New plant sources of unsaturated oil. Abstract p55, in Valorisation des produits forestiers non ligneux, 15èmes journées scientifiques de *l'INRGREF*, Gammarth-Tunisie, 28-29 Sep, 2010.

United Nations Educational Scientific, and Cultural Organization (UNESCO) 2002. Institute for Statistics. World Education Indicators, Paris.

USAID, 2005. Filière des plantes aromatiques et médicinales, note de synthèse in United States Agency for the International developement, pp9.

Walter S. 2001. Non-wood forest products in Africa : A regional and national overview. *FAO Forestry* paper 128.

In: Tunisia: Economic, Political and Social Issues ISBN: 978-1-61942-157-8
Eds: M. Pusatieri and J. Cannamela

Chapter 7

TROPHIC CONDITION OF THE SEVEN MEDITERRANEAN FRESHWATER RESERVOIRS: ENVIRONMENTAL FACTORS AND ZOOPLANKTONIC COMMUNITY

Ikbel Sellami[1*], Asma Hamza[2], Abderrahmen Bouain[1], Lotfi Aleya[3] and Habib Ayadi[1]

[1]Université de Sfax, Faculté des Sciences de Sfax, Département des Sciences de la Vie. Biodiversité et Ecosystèmes Aquatiques. Sfax,Tunisie

[2]Institut National des Sciences et Technologie de la Mer, Centre de Sfax, Sfax, Tunisie

[3]Université de Franche-Comté, Laboratoire de Chrono-environnement, Place Leclerc, Besançon cedex, France

ABSTRACT

Water quality was investigated at seven Mediterranean freshwater reservoirs. Physico-chemical parameters and chlorophyll *a* were measured at all reservoirs to determine the trophic status. The species composition of zooplankton was also studied estimate the trophic level of

* Corresponding author: sellamifss@yahoo.fr, Tel: 00 216 (97) 64 21 80, Fax: 00 216 (74) 27 44 37.

the reservoirs. The environmental parameters indicated an oligo-mesotophic and mesotrophic environments. The presence of zooplankton species known to be indicators of eutrophic status reflected the high trophic condition of the Kasseb, Nabhana and Sidi Saâd reservoirs.

Keywords: Water quality, Mediterranean reservoirs and zooplankton

1. Introduction

The problem of eutrophication of lakes became acute more than 40 years ago and still remains an important problem of limnology. Numerous investigations have shown that the principal criteria of the process of eutrophication such as the elevated concentrations of biogenic elements and suspended organic matter accompanied by a decreased transparency of water; decreased concentration of dissolved oxygen in hypolimnion; intensive development and successive changes in populations of algae, as well as the evolution of faunistic composition towards the dominance of the eurybiontic and widely spread species (Rossolimo, 1964, OCDE, 1982). The species composition of zooplankton is important in determining the trophic level of the reservoirs (Baykal et al., 2006). Therefore, individual species may reflect the level of eutrophication (Rogozin, 2000). The objectives of this work were to study the water quality parameters such as dissolved oxygen, transparency, nutrients (Nitrate, Nitrite, ammonium, orthophosphate and total phosphorus), chlorophyll *a* concentrations and the zooplankton composition in the seven Mediterranean freshwater reservoirs.

A major goal of this study is to determine the trophic status of the seven Mediterranean freshwater reservoirs based on environmental parameters and composition of the zooplankton, to reveal the regular features of eutrophication.

2. Materials and Methods

2.1 Study Site

This study was performed in seven reservoirs (Figure1). Four connected shallow reservoirs are situated in the North of Tunisia (Figure2).

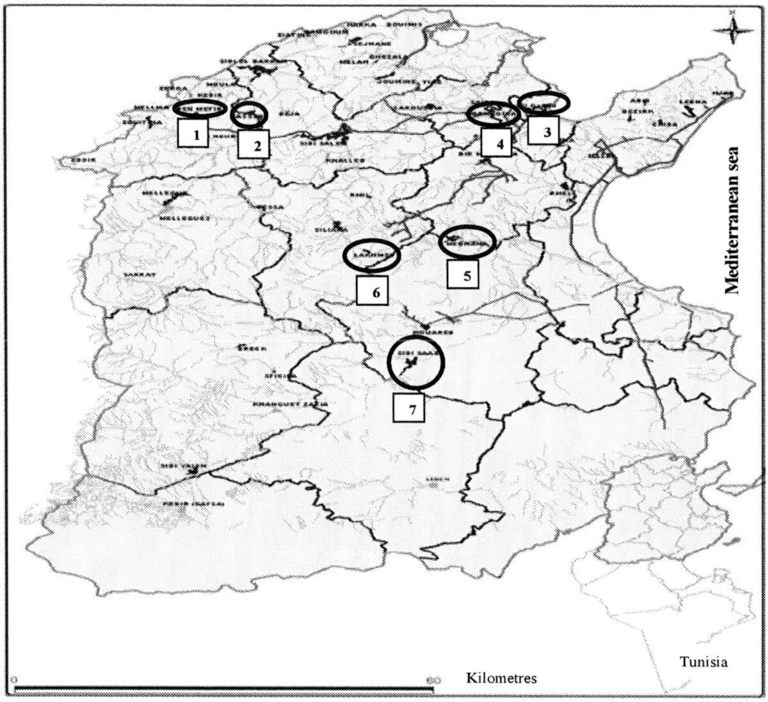

Figure 1. Localization of the studied reservoirs 1: BeniMtir. 2: Kasseb. 3: Ghdir El Goulla 4: Mornaguia 5: Nabhana 6: Lakhmes and 7: Sidi Saâd.

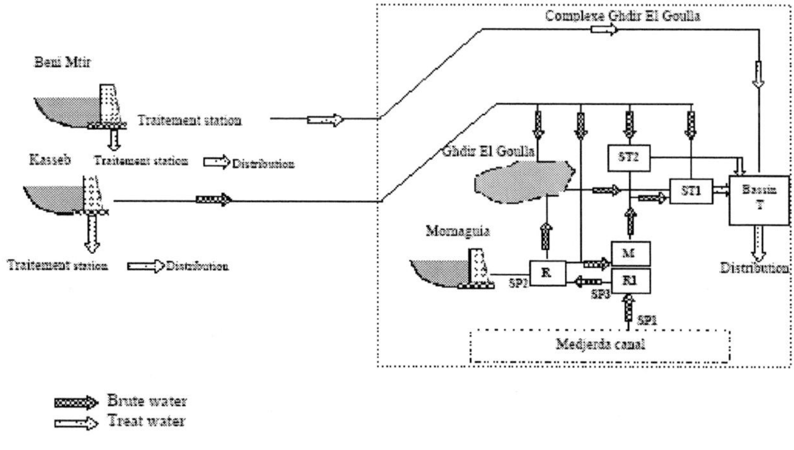

Figure 2. Connected reservoirs.

BeniMtir, Kasseb, Mornaguia and Ghdir El Goulla. The Beni Mtir reservoir is located in about thirty kilometers East of Ain Draham city. The Kasseb reservoir is at 18 Km away from the North West of Beja city; Mornaguia and Ghdir El Goulla reservoirs are located 15 Km away from the South–West of Tunisia.

Three reservoirs are situated in the Center of Tunisia: Lakhmes, Nabhana and Sidi Saâd. The Lakhmes reservoir is located in about fifteen kilometers South- East of Siliana city. The Nabhana reservoir and Sidi Saâd reservoir are situated in about fifty and thirty kilometres South of Kairouan city respectively. The morphometric and hydrologic characteristics of these reservoirs are shown in Table 1.

2.2 Environmental Factors

Monthly samples for physical and chemical analysis were taken with a 1 liter Van Dorn bottle. In Kasseb, Mornaguia and Ghdir El Goulla reservoirs, the water temperature was measured with a mercury glass thermometer graduated in 0.1°C and pH with pH meter type Met Röhm®. The dissolved oxygen concentration was measured by means of Winkler methods (Rodier 1984). Nitrogen was assayed after oxidation to the nitrate form in an alkaline medium, using potassium persulfate.

The nitrate assay was based on the formation, in a concentrated sulphuric acid medium, of a phenol disulphonic acid derivative (D'Elia et al. 1977). The phosphorus concentrations were determined after mineralising the samples using the colorimetric protocol of Murphy and Riley (1962).

In Beni Mtir Lakhmes, Nabhana and Sidi Saâd reservoirs, the water temperature (°C), dissolved oxygen concentration (mg l^{-1}) and pH were measured using a multiparameter probe (Multi 340i/SET). Water transparency was estimated using a Secchi disc. Nutrient concentrations were analyzed by standard colorimetric techniques with an automatic BRAN and LUEBBE type 3 analyzer and were expressed as mg l^{-1}.

Sub samples (0.5 l) for quantification of chlorophyll *a*, were filtered using Whatman GF/C filters (0.45 µm pore size filter and 25 mm- diameter) and the quantity of pigments was determined with a fluorometric using a methanol extraction method.

Table 1. Morphometric and hydrologic characteristics of the studied reservoirs

	Kasseb	Mornaguia	Ghdir El Goulla	Beni Mtir	Lakhmes	Nabhana	Sidi Saâd
Longitude	36° 45’ 30’’ N	36° 44’ N	36° 44’ N	36°43’10’’N,	36°N,	36°03’N,	35° 31’40’’N,
Latitude	09° 50’’E	09° 58’ 50’’ E	09° 58’ 50’’ E	08°44’10’’E	09°22’E	09°54’E	09° 59’ 30’’E
Region	Humid	Semi-arid	Semi-arid	Humid	Semi-arid	Semi-arid	Semi-arid
Construction (year)	1969	1982	1968	1953	1966	1966	1981
Area (ha)	435	150	40	310.6	102	532	1800
Volume (10^6 m^3)	82	15	3	57.6	14	86	209
Uses	Hydro-electricity irrigation drinking water	drinking water	drinking water	Hydro-electricity drinking water	irrigation	irrigation drinking water protection against the violent floods	irrigation protection against the violent floods

2.3. Zooplankton

Zooplankton samples were taken using a 55 µm mesh Juday plankton net and preserved with 4% formalin and stained with Bengal Pink. The zooplankton was enumerated and counted under a binocular microscope type leica in Dolffus chambers (Paterson, 1993). The taxonomic identification was carried out according to Dussart (1969), Koste (1978), Stella (1982), Margaritora (1985), Pourriot and Francez (1986), Korovchinsky (1992). The zooplankton community could thus be described using data expressed in terms of density (ind l^{-1}).

2.4. Trophic Index

Two trophic state indexes were determined; the classical freshwater TSI of Carlson & Simpson (1996) and Burns et al. (2000). TSI was calculated with chlorophyll *a* (mg l^{-1}) and total phosphorus (mg l^{-1}) using the following equations (Carlson & Simpson 1996, Burns et al. 2000):

- TSI_C (Chl *a*) = 9.81 ln (Chl *a*) + 30.6
- TSI_C (TP) = 14.42 ln (TP) + 4.15
- TL_B (Chl *a*) = 2.22 + 2.54 log (Chl *a*)
- TL_B (TP) = 0.218 + 2.92 log (TP)

3. Results

3.1. Environmental Parameters

Water temperature fluctuated between 16.98 ± 6.74°C in Beni Mtir and 21.88 ± 5.86°C in Nabhana reservoirs (Table 2). pH concentrations were relatively constant in the seven reservoirs. Highest values averaging 8.82 ± 1.86 mg.l^{-1}, 8.74 ± 0.86 mg.l^{-1}, and 8.57 ± 0.67 mg.l^{-1} in Kasseb, Ghdir El Goulla and Mornaguia reservoirs respectively. Transparency varied between 1.3 ± 0.34 m Lakhmes and 2.2 ±0.53 m in Nabhana reservoirs. Nitrate is the dominant nitrogen form. Nitrate concentrations fluctuated between 0.13 ±0.1 mg.l^{-1} and 3.1 ± 1.97 mg.l^{-1} in Sidi Saâd and Ghdir El Goulla reservoirs. Orthophosphate concentrations ranged from 0.02 ± 0.015 mg.l^{-1} to 0.059 ± 0.04 mg.l^{-1} in Kasseb and Ghdir El Goulla respectively.

Table 2. Environmental parameters (mean ± SD, standard deviation) in the seven studied reservoirs

	Temperature (°C)	pH	Dissolved oxygen (mg.l^{-1})	Transprancy (m)	Nitrate (mg.l^{-1})	Nitrite (mg.l^{-1})	Ammonium (mg.l^{-1})	Orthophosphate (mg.l^{-1})	Total phosphorus (mg.l^{-1})	Chlorophyll a (µg.l^{-1})
Ghdir El Goulla	21.68□ 5.84	8.07 ± 0.11	8.74 □ 0.86	-	3.1 □ 1.97	0.045 □ 0.04	0.18 □ 0.09	0.059 □ 0.04	0.065 □ 0.039	0.5 ± 0.01
Mornaguia	21 □ 5.25	7.89 ± 0.19	8.57 □ 0.67	-	2.02 □ 1.26	0.049 □ 0.04	0.35 □ 0.42	0.041 □ 0.03	0.087 □ 0.076	0.75 ± 0.1
Kasseb	20 □ 4.67	8.11 ± 0.52	8.82 □ 1.86	-	2.36 □ 2.38	0.1 ± 0.01	0.26 □ 0.15	0.02 □ 0.015	0.081 □ 0.041	0.9 □ 1.05
Beni Mtir	16.98□ 6.74	8.12 ± 0 .74	4.58 □ 2.53	-	0.15 □ 0.1	0.039 □ 0.03	0.03 □ 0.02	0.053 □ 0.02	0.057 □ 0.01	4.94 □ 2.96
Lakhmes	19.47□ 6.21	7.46 ± 0.8	3.3 □ 1.78	1.3 □ 0.34	0.24 □ 0.11	0.074 □ 0.04	0.06 □ 0.02	0.044 □ 0.03	0.049 □ 0.02	4.22 □ 1.71
Nabhana	21.88□ 5.86	8.15 ± 0.69	4.57 □ 1.45	2.2 □ 0.53	0.19 □ 0.08	0.037 □ 0.03	0.05 □ 0.01	0.042 □ 0.01	0.062 □ 0.02	5.71 □ 2.47
Sidi Saâd	19.86□ 7.41	7.8 ± 0.74	4.56 □ 1.3	1.5 □ 0.36	0.13 □ 0.1	0.021 □ 0.01	0.04 □ 0.03	0.046 □ 0.04	0.049 □ 0.02	5.67 □ 3

Table 3. Trophic state index of the seven studied reservoirs

	Carlson et Simpson (1996)				(Burns et al., 2000)				OCDE (1982)
	TSI_C (Chl a)	TSI_C (TP)	TSI_C (SD)		TL_B (Chl a)	TL_B (TP)	TL_B (SD)		
Ghdir El Goulla	39.72	15.84	-		4.46	1.95	-		
Mornaguia	40.12	16.13	-	Oligo- mesotrophic	4.64	2.08	-	Mesotrophic	
Kasseb	40.3	16.06	-		4.71	2.05	-		
Beni Mtir	42.01	15.71	-	Oligotrophic	5.45	1.9	-		Mesotrophic
Lakhmes	41.85	15.55	45.85		5.38	1.82	7.86		
Nabhana	42.15	15.79	46.40	Oligo- mesotrophic	5.52	1.93	7.29	Eutrophic	
Sidi Saâd	42.14	15.55	45.98		5.51	1.82	7.73		

Table 4. Zooplankton species abundance (percentage) found in the studied reservoirs

	Beni Mtir	Lakhmes	Nabhana	Sidi Saâd	Kasseb	Mornaguia	Ghdir El Goulla
Copidodiaptomus numidicus	64	62	65		<1	63	82
Acanthocyclops robustus		1	1	5			
Eudiaptomus sp.					<1	2	5
Acanthocyclops viridis				50			
Acanthocyclops sp.					69	2	8
Cyclops strenuus	1						
Diaphanosoma brachyurum	5	10	22	42	11	26	4
Bosmina longirostris		6	<1		13	5	1
Ceriodaphnia quadrangula	17	9	7		<1	1	
Daphnia longispina	10	1			7	<1	
Keratella quadrata	1	<1	<1	1	<1	1	
Keratella cochlearis		<1	<1				
Hexarthra mira	<1	<1	<1	1			
Filinia longiseta	2	7	<1				
Asplanchna sp.	<1	4	5				
Brachionus urceolaris				1			

Total phosphorus concentrations varied between 0.049 ± 0.02 $mg.l^{-1}$ in Lakhmes and Sidi Saâd reservoirs and 0.087 ± 0.076 $mg.l^{-1}$ in Mornaguia reservoir.

Chlorophyll *a* concentration varied from 0.5 ± 0.01µg l^{-1} to 5.71 ± 2.47 µg l^{-1}. Lower and higher chlorophyll *a* concentrations were observed in the Ghdir El Goulla and Nabhana reservoirs respectively.

Our study shows that the total phosphorus and chlorophyll *a* concentrations indicates an oligomesotrophic or mesotrophic status in Ghdir El Goulla, Mornaguia and Kasseb reservoirs, oligomesotrophic, eutrophic or mesotrophic status in Nabhana, Lakhmes and Sidi Saâd reservoirs and oligotrophic or mesotrophic status in BeniMtir reservoir (Table 3).

3.2. Zooplankton Community Structure

The species *Copidodiaptomus numidicus* was the most dominant species in BeniMtir (64% of the total zooplankton abundance), Lakhmes (62% of the total zooplankton abundance), Nabhana (65% of the total zooplankton abundance), Mornaguia (63% of the total zooplankton abundance) and Ghdir El Goulla (82% of the total zooplankton abundance) reservoirs (Table 4).

The species *Acanthocyclops viridis* (50% of the total zooplankton abundance) and *Diaphanosoma brachyurum* (42% of the total zooplankton abundance) was the most abundant species in Sidi Saâd reservoir and *Acanthocyclops* sp. (69% of the total zooplankton abundance) was the most dominant in Kasseb reservoir.

4. Discussion

In this work we have studied some environmental parameters and the composition of the zooplankton to determine the trophic status of the seven Mediterranean freshwater reservoirs.

Dissolved oxygen is one of the fundamental parameters of lakes, since it is essential to the metabolism of all aerobic aquatic organisms (Wetzel and Likens, 2000). The lowest oxygen concentrations observed in BeniMtir, Lakhmes, Nabhana and Sidi Saâd are most probably related to consumption of oxygen through organic matter degradation in the water column (Brancelj, 2000).

Nitrate concentration in Sidi Saâd reservoir (0.13 ± 0.1 mg.l^{-1}) was low. Low nitrate concentrations resulted from the high concentration of primary producers in this reservoir which caused an uptake of nitrates by aquatic organisms (Trait and Thaler, 2000).

Chlorophyll a is the main photosynthetic pigment. Therefore, its concentration is a representative indicator of the productive processes and development of algae. It is a useful and adequate measure of eutrophication of water bodies. The concentrations of chlorophyll a in the oligotrophic, mesotrophic, and eutrophic water bodies amount to 0–4, 4–10, and 10–100 µg.l^{-1}, respectively (Henderson-Sellers, 1990). According to this classification, the BeniMtir, Nabhana Lakhmes and Sidi Saâd reservoirs are of the mesotrophic type. The Kasseb, Ghdir El Goulla and Mornaguia reservoirs are of the oligotrophic.

The concentration of phosphorus is critical because it is most commonly the limiting nutrient in freshwater ecosystems (Wetzel 1975). The threat of eutrophication in natural waters is heavily dependent upon the external phosphorus loadings (Wetzel, 1975). Total phosphorus concentrations varied between 0.049 ± 0.02 mg.l^{-1} and 0.087 ± 0.076 mg.l^{-1}. The concentrations of total phosphorus indicate the mesotrophic status of the studied reservoirs.

The taxonomic structure of zooplanktonic communities is a good indicator of the state and trophic status of a water body. The majority of species appear in the composition of zooplankton with a small number of species in seven studied reservoirs.

The Kasseb and Sidi Saâd reservoirs were dominated by *Acanthocyclops* sp. and *Acanthocyclops viridis* respectively. Copepods Cyclopoids was observed by some workers (Branco and Senna, 1996) at high trophic levels. BeniMtir, Ghdir El Goulla, Mornaguia, Nabhana and Lakhmes reservoirs were characterized by the abundance of calanoids species *Copidodiaptomus numidicus*. Calanoids occupied a distinct position, in association with more oligotrophic reservoirs (Mornaguia and Ghdir El Goulla). Calanoid copepods were the dominant species under oligomesotrophic conditions (Pinto-Coelho et al., 2005).

The species *Bosmina longirostris* was positioned more closely to Kasseb reservoir. Many studies reported that *Bosmina longirostris* was the abundant species during the periods of increased nutrients inflow (De Eyto, 2001). The species *Diaphanosoma brachyurum* was dominated in Nabhana, Sidi Saâd and Mornaguia reservoirs. This species was generally abundant at high trophic levels (Amoros, 1984).

CONCLUSION

The environmental parameters indicated that the trophic status of the seven Mediterranean freshwater reservoirs fluctuated between oligo-mesotophic and mesotrophic environments. The presence of zooplankton species known to be indicators of eutrophic status reflected the high trophic condition of the Kasseb, Nabhana and Sidi Saâd reservoirs. It is therefore important to prevent the deterioration of these reservoirs, since it is an important drinking water and irrigation supply for Tunisia.

ACKNOWLEDGEMENTS

We would like to express our gratitude to everyone who has contributed to the elaboration of the present investigation.

REFERENCES

Brancelj, A. (Ed.) (2002). *High-mountain lakes in the eastern part of the Julian Alps*. ZRC, Ljubljana.

Amoros, C. (1984). *Introduction pratique à la systématique des organismes des eaux continentales françaises*. Crustacés cladocères. Bulletin Society Linneene Lyon, 72-145.

Baykal, T., Salman, S. & Açikgöz, Ü. (2006). *The Relationship between Seasonal Variation in Phytoplankton and Zooplankton Densities in HirfanlÝ Dam Lake (KÝrßehir, Turkey).* Turkish Journal Biology, 30, 217-226.

Branco, C.W.C. & Senna, P.A.C. (1996). *Relations among heterotrophic bacteria, chlorophyll-a, total phytoplankton, total zooplankton and physical and chemical features in the Paranoá reservoir, Brasília, Brazil.* Hydrobiologia, 337, 171-181.

Burns, N. & Bryers, G. (2000). *Protocol for Monitoring Trophic Levels of New Zealand lakes and Reservoirs.* Lakes Consulting, Pauanui.

Carlson, R.E. & Simpson, J. (1996). *A Coordinator's Guide to Volunteer Lake Monitoring Methods*. North American Lake Management Society, 96 p.

Tait, D. & Thaler, B. (2000). *Journal of Limnology*, 59, 61-71.

D'Elia, C.F., Steudler, P.A. & Corwin, N. (1977). *Determination of total nitrogen in aqueous samples using persulfate digestion.* Limnology and Oceanography, 22, 760-764.

De Eyto, E. (2001). *Chydorus sphaericus as a biological indicator of water quality in lakes.* Verh. int. Ver. theor. angew. Limnol., 27, 3358-3362.

Dussart, B., (1969). *Les copépodes des eaux continentales d'Europe occidentale. Tome II :* Cyclopoides et biologie quantitative, N. Boubée et Cie, Paris, 292 pp.

Henderson-Sellers, B. & Markland, H.R. (1990). *Decaying Lakes, Chichester: Wiley, 1987.* Translated under the title Umirayushchie ozera, Leningrad: Gidrometeoizdat,.

Korovchinsky, N.M. (1992). *Sididae et holopediidae (Crustacea: Daphniiformes).Guides to the identification of the Microinvertebrates of the continental of the word 3.* SPB Academic Publishing, 85pp.

Koste, W. (1978). *Rotatoria.* Die Rädertiere Mitteleuropas. Ein Bestimmungswerk begründet von Max Voigt. Borntrager, Stuttgart, (1), Textband, 673pp, (2), Tafelband, 234pp.

Margaritora, F.G. (1985). *Cladocera.* Fauna d'Italia, Bologna, 399pp.

OECD (1982). *Eutrophication of Water: Monitoring, Assessment, and Control,* Paris.

Pinto-Coelho, R., Pinel- Alloul, B., Méthot, G. & Havens, K.E. (2005). *Crustacean zooplankton in lakes and reservoirs of temperate and tropical regions: variation with trophic status.* Canadian Journal of Fisheries and Aquatic Science, 62, 348-361.

Pourriot, R. & Francez, A.J. (1986). *Rotifères. Introduction pratique à la systématique des organismes des eaux continentales françaises.* Bulletin Mensuelle Société Linnéenne Lyon, 5-37.

Wetzel, R. G. & Likens G. E. (2000). *Limnological analyses.* Springer Verlag, New York.

Rodier, J. 1984. *Analyse de l'eau.* Edition Dunod, Paris, 1135pp.

Rogozin, A.G. (2000). *Specific Structural Features of Zooplankton in Lakes Differing in Trophic Status*: Species Populations. Russian Journal Ecology, 31, 405-410.

Rossolimo, L.L. (1964). *Nakoplenie veshchestva v ozerakh* (Accumulation of Matter in Lakes), Moscow: Nauka, , pp. 5.

Stella, E. (1982). Calanoidi (Crustacea, Copépoda, Cananoida), 14. Consiglio Nazionale Delle Ricerche AQ/1/140. *Guide Per riconscimento delle specie animali delle acqua interne italiane.* Impresa dalla stamperia valdonesa verona, 67 pp.

Wetzel, R. G. & Robert G. (1975). *Limnology.* Philadelphia, Pennsylvania: Saunders College Publishing/Holt, Rhinehart and Winston.

In: Tunisia: Economic, Political and Social Issues ISBN: 978-1-61942-157-8
Eds: M. Pusatieri and J. Cannamela

Chapter 8

EXPLOITATION OF MACKERELS IN THE SAHEL TUNISIAN

Jabeur Chédia**, Mani Yosra, Belhoula Fatma, Khoufi Widien and Bakhrouf Amina

Institut Supérieur de Biotechnologie de Monastir
Laboratoire d'analyse de traitement et de valorisation des produits et des polluants de l'environnement, Tunisia

INTRODUCTION

The fishing of pelagic fish constitutes an important economic activity in the fisheries of Tunisia. Indeed, the production contributes in 2009 to 48% of the national production of the fishery products. It employs approximately 5506 fishermen and utilizes approximately 393 units of fishing whose majority are seiners. The target species in this activity are as well the large pelagic ones belonging mainly to "Scombridés" (like mackerels and tunas) and of small pelagic like the sardine (*Sardina pilchardus*), Sardinelle (*Sardinella aurita*), the anchovy (*Engraulis encrasiculus*). The eastern of Tunisia and particularly the region of Sahel (Figure 1) represented by Monastir, Sousse and Mahdia, is characterized by the activity of fishing of pelagic fish. Thus the production according to the DGPA (General deligation of fishing and aquaculture) in 2009 of small pelagic contributes to 46% of the production of regional fishing

* Corresponding author: Dr. Jabeur Chédia sirsina@yahoo.com.

and utilizes approximately 38, 5% of fishermen. Two mackerel species (Figure 2) are present along the Tunisian littoral; the common mackerel (*Scomber scombrus*) and the Spanish mackerel (*Scomber japonicus*).

The production of mackerel is distributed inequitably between the various areas with 66.41% for the South, 26.53% for the East and 7.05% for the North (Hattour and *al.*, 2004).

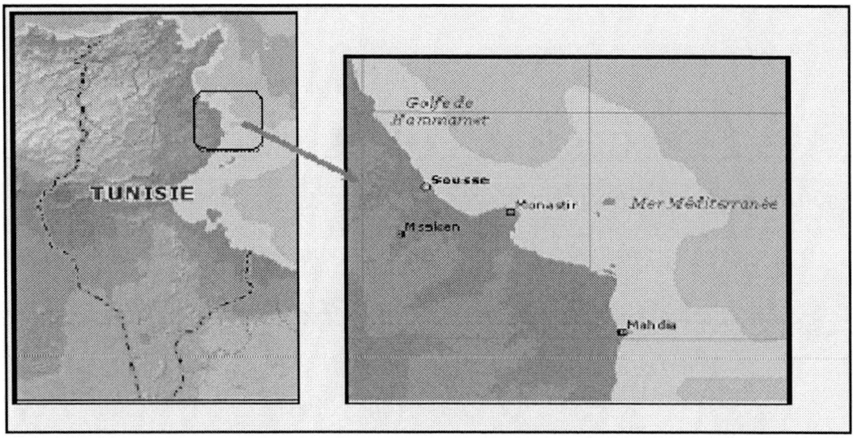

Figure 1. Study area.

Figure 2. Mackerel.

In the area of the Sahel in 2009 it accounts 13% of the national production of mackerel. The production of these species knew during the last decade (2000 to 2009) an important fluctuation with tendencies to a reduction. Fishermen of the area announce a reduction even of the abundance in spite of the use of the better fishing gears following the encouragement of the State for the small pelagic fisheries in 2005. Several methods can be used for the evaluation of the state of marine exploited stocks. Thus, of the mono-specific models like the total models and the analytical models are always applicable. Plurispecific models holding account the interactions between the species and the fishing gears are also possible. The eco-systemic models which are more generals owing to the fact that they integrate, in addition to the biological parameter of species, the effect of environment parameters are also requested. Is added with these types of models and more particularly the methods of echo-sondage used particularly for the small pelagic ones which are applied by the work group of small pelagic in INSTM (National Institute of Sciences and Technologies of the Sea) (Gaâmour and *al.*, 2004). Because of the lack of data we are limited to the use of global models which require only production and effort data that we dispose. In the global models exists several varieties (Laurec and Le Guen, 1981). According to the relationship between the catch per unit of effort (CPUE), definite as the report between the catch and the fishing effort, and the fishing effort (E) we apply one of the varieties. Thus, if the relation is linear it would be the model of Sheaffer, if it is exponential it would be fox model, if it is generalized we apply the model of Pella and Thomlinson. In order to analyze this situation and to try to understand the possible causes of the fluctuations of the production and according to the relationship between CPUE and effort as it is explained below, we made an evaluation of the exploitation of mackerels in the Tunisian East by the global models.

Material and Methods

1. Material

The statistical data of the effort of the three types of fishing (with purse seine, coastal and benthic) and for the three regions (Sousse, Monastir and Mahdia) representing the area of the Sahel Tunisian, the monthly and annual productions were collected from the services of the Head office of Fishing and Aquiculture (DGPA). These statistics are collected on 10 years, from 2000 to

2009. The production is expressed in kg. Two values are given (declared productions and real productions which take account of a factor of correction). We retained the real data constituting the official data. The fishing effort is expressed by three different units: number of day of sea, number of exits at sea and number of flotilla.

2. Methods

After the collect of data we passed to the calculation of CPUE (Catch per Unit of Effort) of each type of fishing (purse seine, inshore fishing and the benthic trawl) for the 3 regions (Sousse, Monastir, Mahdia) separately and in the total area during 10 years. *For example:*

For inshore fishing in Sousse, the coastal CPUE = production (Tons) of inshore fishing (Sousse)/effort of inshore fishing (Sousse). The gear of reference will be retained according to its productivity (which has the highest median of CPUE) to standardized the fishing effort in order to be able to calculate a total fishing effort taking account of the various fishing efforts. By comparing the CPUE of each type of fishing, the purse seine has the maximum of value. It is so retained as a reference gear. Following a comparison between the various units of fishing effort and with an aim of approaching with an effective effort, the choice was related to the number of day at sea which presents more important annual fluctuations. The standardization of the fishing effort is done according to the following formula:

$$Fe = a * F\text{ trawling} + b * F\text{ purse seine} + c * F\text{ inshore fishing}$$

with:

- Fe: standardized effort = effective effort.
- F: fishing effort.
- a, b and c are coefficients of conversion which correspond to the reports of capturability between the gears:

a = average CPUE of benthic trawl/average CPUE of the gear of reference.

b= 1 corresponds to the gear of reference (purse seine).

c= average CPUE of inshore fishing/average CPUE of the gear of reference.

The standardized effort will be used to trace the CPUE according to the effort and thereafter to evaluate the exploitation of the stock of mackerels by global model. The choice of the model is based on the existence of a linear relationship or not between the catch per unit of effort (CPUE=U) and the effective effort of fishing (fe).

The last step consists in calculating the following equation: $Ye = U\infty * f - 1/b * f^2$, to plot the curve of the total catch (Ye) according to the effective effort (Fe) and to determine the Maximum Sustainable Yield (MSY) which is carried out theoretically by the optimum fishing effort (f optimum).

Calculate and the graphs are carried out by the Excel software.

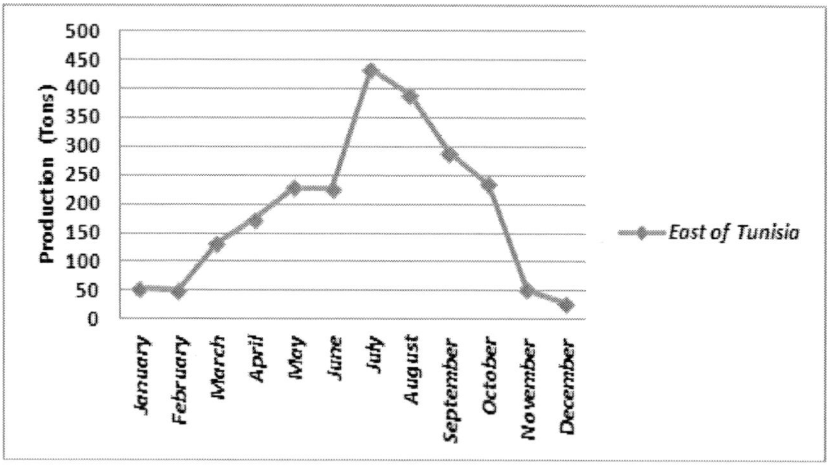

Figure 3. Monthly evolution of mackerel production in the sahel Tunisian.

RESULTS

1. Production and Relation between CPUE and Effort

The monthly fluctuations of the production of mackerel show a presence all the year but with a maximum level in the summer and at the beginning of autumn (May at October) (Figure 3). Evolution of the annual production (Figure 4) shows fluctuations with a tendency of increase between 2000 and 2005 and of reduction between 2006 and 2009. For the catches per unit of effort (Figure 5) a maximum is reached in 2004-2005 followed-up by a fall to reach zero values from 2006.

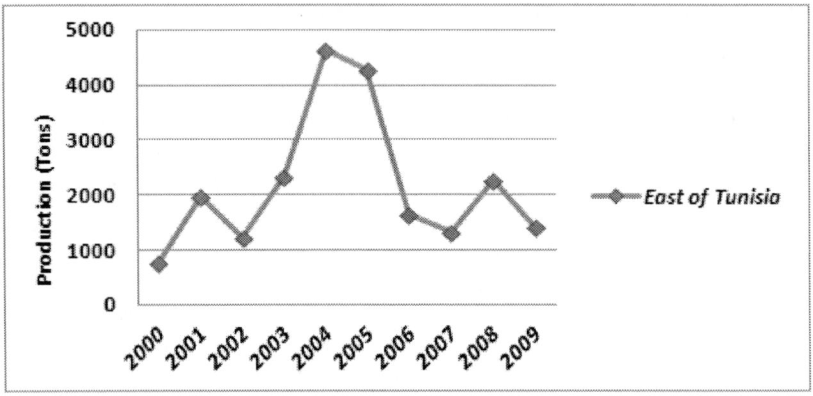

Figure 4. Annual evolution of mackerel production in the sahel Tunisian.

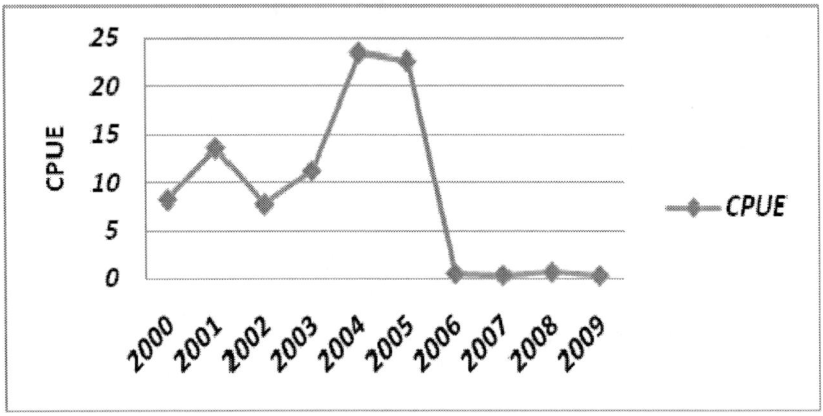

Figure 5. Annual evolution of Catch per Unit of Effort (CPUE) of mackerel in sahel Tunisian.

The relationship between the CPUE and fishing effort is linear: CPUE = -0.0044*f+15,139 with a coefficient of determination R^2 = 0.64 (Figure 6). Thus, we chose the global model of Schaeffer of the form U= U∞ -1/b*f.

2. State of Exploitation of Mackerels

The results of the global models applied to the data of production and effort in each region of the study area taken separately and overall show two production runs; a first with under exploitation between 2000 and 2005 and a second period of overexploitation from 2006 to 2009 (Figure 7). The equation of the total model is: $Ye = -0.0044*f^2+15{,}139f$ with a Maximum Sustainable Yield MSY = 12500 T/sea days for an optimum effort about 1700 sea days.

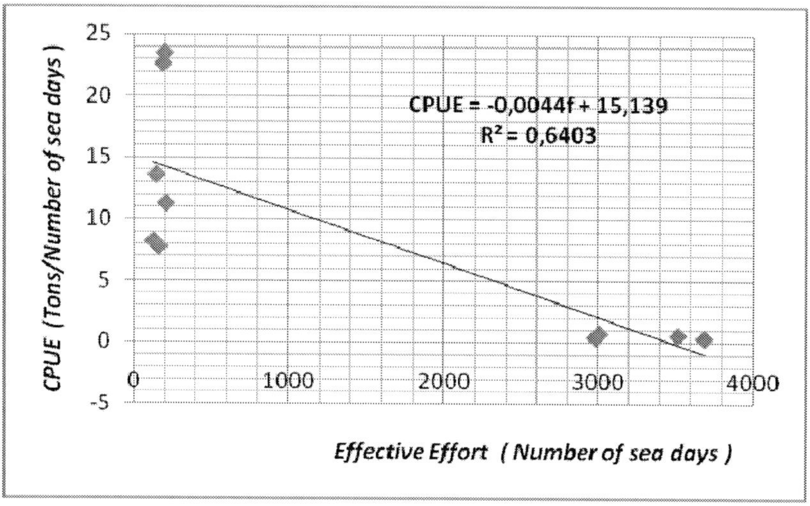

Figure 6. Relationship between CPUE and Effort.

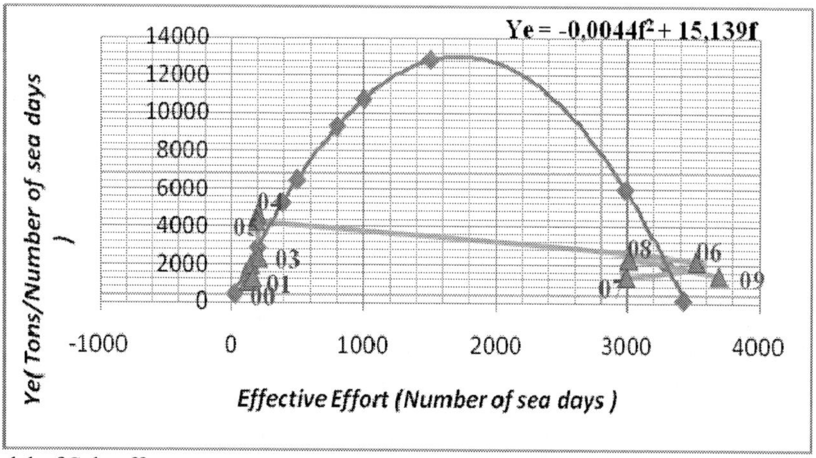

Model of Scheaffer.

Figure 7. Result of the total model.

Discussion and Conclusion

The mackerel is a fish with high commercial value in Tunisia. It is abundant on the Tunisian coasts and more particularly in the south of the country. In the area of the Sahel the mackerel accounts for 13% of the national production of mackerel in 2009. The production of this species during this last decade knew fluctuations and a tendency to a reduction. From 2000 to 2005 an increase in the production is noted. This is, partly, the result of the application of the presidential plan for the development of the small pelagic fishing activity. This encouragement which started in 2002 by the improvement of the boats and the work conditions of these fishing vessels especially in 2005 (Figure 8) contributes to an over fishing state of the mackerel stocks from the 2006. Concurrently to this over fishing, an effect of the temperature and of precipitations on the abundance of this species was shown by Belhoula (2011). Thus, sea surface temperature has a positive effect on abundance and the precipitation a negative role.

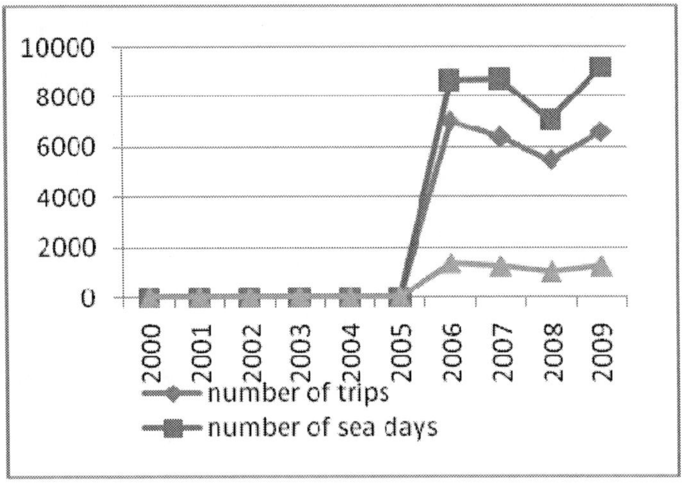

Figure 8. Evolution of effort and number of boats (senneurs) in the sahel of Tunisia.

Acknowledgments

The authors thank the head office for fishing and aquiculture for the accessibility to the data.

References

Belhoula F., 2011: Etat d'exploitation de quelques poissons pélagiques (*Sardina pilchardus, Sardinella aurita, Scomber sp.* Et *Engraulis encrasiculus*) dans le sahel tunisien et étude de l'effet de quelques paramètres climatiques dans la fluctuation de leurs abondances. Mémoire de mastère en Aquaculture et Biotechnologie Marine de l'ISBM. 95 p.

Gaâmour A., Ben Abdallah L., Khemir S. et Mili S., 2004: Etude de la biologie et de l'exploitation des petits pélagiques en Tunisie. Report of the MedSudMed Expert consultation on Small Pelagic Fishes: Stock Identification and Oceanographic Processes Influencing their Abundance and Distribution, Salammbô, Tunisia, 1-3 October 2003. MedSudMed Technical Documents. N°5. GCP/RER/010/ITA/MSM-TD-05. *Mazara del Vallo*: 48-66.

Hattour A., Ben Abdallah L. et Guennegan Y., 2004: Abondance relative et estimation de la biomasse des petits pélagiques des eaux tunisiennes. *Bull.* INSTM Salammbô, 31:5-16.

Laurec A. et Le Guen J.C., 1981: Dynamiques des populations marines exploitées. Tome I: *Concepts et modèles*, 117 p.

INDEX

C

D

E

H

I

N

O

P

Q

R

S

T

U

V

W

Y

Z